Praise for

Millionaire SUCCESS Habits

"In this book there are amazing recipes to get the life you want faster, easier, and with less stress. Read it and live rich!"

— **David Bach**, nine-time *New York Times* best-selling author and financial expert

"In this incredibly inspiring book, Dean Graziosi gives us the key to greater happiness, wealth, and freedom. A must-read."

— **Brendon Burchard**, # 1 *New York Times* best-selling author and world's leading high-performance coach

"Dean is a compassionate, experienced guide who wants you to win. This book is packed with heart, energy, and hard-won wisdom that will transform your life. A must-read for anyone who wants to take control of their life."

— **Marie Forleo**, entrepreneur, author, philanthropist, and founder of MarieTV and B-School, inspiring tens of millions to create a business and life they love

"Dean Graziosi has the unique ability to take what others make so complicated and boil it down to a recipe for success that anyone can follow."

— **Larry King**, award-winning television and radio host

Millionaire

SUCCESS

Habits

Also by Dean Graziosi

30 Days to Real Estate Cash

Be a Real Estate Millionaire

Totally Fulfilled

Millionaire

SUCCESS

Habits

*The Gateway to
Wealth & Prosperity*

DEAN GRAZIOSI

Hardcover ISBN: 978-1-4019-5687-5
e-book ISBN: 978-1-4019-5708-7

Printed in the United States of America

I'd like to dedicate this book to my dear friends Tony Robbins, Joe Polish, and Dan Sullivan, the three people who have had a massive influence on my life, my success, and my abundance.

I cannot even begin to express how grateful I am for those three men who came into my life exactly when they were needed. But I also want to dedicate this book to all the men and women throughout the years who had the will and selflessness to share their life-changing wisdom, through books and talks, with those eager for a new path.

I did my best to soak in all that I heard, read, and observed, and in turn, what I learned seeped into my thoughts and my words. The exercises, the stories, the recipes, and the success habits you'll find in these pages I've learned through decades of my own trial and error, failures and successes. But they have been greatly enriched by all the others who have walked the path before me, and for that I'm grateful.

This dedication, then, is my way of recognizing all the people who have made such a big difference in my life. I'm hoping that in the same way, I will serve you, and this book will make an equally big difference in your life.

CONTENTS

INTRODUCTION

When I decided to sit down and write a book exposing the raw, unfiltered habits that took me from generations of hardworking yet struggling family members to more success than I ever imagined possible for one man to achieve, I hoped it would make an impact on those who read it. But I have to be honest—I never imagined this book would become one of the best-selling books in the world and go viral. As I write this quick little update at the start of the book to let you know about two new chapters I've added, this book has well over 300,000 copies shipped and growing fast. Don't just dabble with this book. Don't just read the first few chapters and put it off until another day. Devour this book and put the lessons in to play in your life. And I almost forgot, the book got even better with two never-before-seen chapters on productivity and how to out-hustle and outperform everyone around you. This is your time. Make it real!

In the spring of 1944, a boy who we'll call J.P. was born to immigrant parents in a rough neighborhood in the heart of Los Angeles. Before J.P. was two years old, his parents divorced, his mother struggled financially, and by the time he was nine years old, J.P. was out on the streets looking for a way to help his mom make ends meet. Newspapers, flowerpots, Christmas cards—you name it, he most likely tried to sell it. When his mother could no longer take care of J.P. and his brother, the boys were placed in a foster home.

As a teenager with no parental guidance, J.P. fell in with the wrong crowd, joined a local gang, and struggled to pass his classes as a student at John Marshall High School in Los Angeles.

One day in 11th grade, J.P.'s high school teacher caught him and his friend Michelle goofing off and passing notes in class. He made them stand in front of the class while he proclaimed, "See these two? Don't hang around them because they're not going to amount to anything. They'll absolutely never make it in any business."

J.P. may have not realized it at the time, but moments like that create our life habits—successful ones, yes, but also bad ones that can hold us back from reaching our full potential. J.P. could have said to himself, "I'll never amount to anything." Instead he said, "The hell with that guy. I'll prove him wrong."

J.P. developed his first success habit on one of his first jobs. He told me, "I've worked all my life, starting from nine years old. I had things like paper routes at eleven years old that I continued throughout high school. I even worked for a while at the local dry cleaner sweeping the floors and doing odd jobs for an owner that was so tight with money that he squeaked when he walked! I was working as hard as I possibly could for a mere $1.25 per hour. Then one day after school he called me over and said, 'Last night I looked behind the cabinets, and there was no dust! Then I picked up a rug, no dust! You clean this place as if I'm watching you every minute!' I said, 'You hired me to clean and my job is to do the best I can.' He was so pleased he gave me a raise to a $1.50 an hour. For him to do that, it was like I won an Academy Award. And to be honest, I learned an important lesson from this period of my life. Successful people, whether they're working for somebody else or working for themselves, do whatever they do to the best of their ability—as if the boss is watching them every minute of every day. I learned that in everything you do, always do your best."

Some may believe that this makes you a foolish yes-man. I believe that doing your best is one of the success habits you should develop. The benefits are numerous, varied, and significant. In this instance, his habit helped J.P. complete a mundane task in the present (and complete it well), which led him to getting future tasks that he loved.

Before continuing with J.P.'s story, I'd like to tell you a little about success habits and how this book will help you to make them your own.

I am going to show you a path and process that will allow you to adopt success habits so they stick. You don't have to flip your world upside down or try to force "new habits" overnight that disrupt your life and cause you to go back to where you started. Rather, you can make barely noticeable, small shifts in your daily routines by nudging out those things that don't serve you and replacing them with habits that create a path to wealth and abundance. It doesn't matter if you are an entrepreneur, a business owner, an executive, an investor, an employee, or a young person just starting your first job. The habits, principles, recipes, and exercises in the coming chapters will give you a competitive edge, catapulting you to that next level.

So while this book's main focus is on financial success, the methods I'll share can also propel you to new levels of fulfillment in other areas of your life, including family, parenting, friendships, relationships, spirituality, health, physical fitness, love, passion, intimacy, and more. No matter what anyone has told you in the past, you are entitled to and can possess fulfillment, joy, and abundance in all areas of your life.

I'll help you develop these habits through a variety of methods. I'll share amazing stories of hugely successful people I know and how they learned and applied the behaviors and routines that allowed them to become high achievers and earners. I'll provide exercises that will help you develop and practice new habits. And I'll offer some stories from my own life that I hope will inspire and instruct.

More about all this a bit later. Now let's return to our friend, who when we last saw him was sweeping floors with great effort and skill.

J.P. graduated from high school, but he didn't go to college. Instead he joined the U.S. Navy and served two years on the aircraft carrier USS *Hornet*. After the navy, J.P. held various low-paying jobs, including working as a janitor, at a gas station, and as an insurance salesman. He worked briefly for Redken Laboratories but was fired after a disagreement with his boss. He even took a job as a low-paid door-to-door encyclopedia salesman.

Looking back on that time, J.P. says he learned another important, lifelong success habit. "I would knock on fifty doors, and all fifty would be closed in my face. So I had to learn how to be just as enthusiastic on door number fifty-one or one hundred fifty-one as I was on the first door." He learned to overcome rejection, communicate with people by listening to them, and persuade others to take action. This was not a dream job, but he was building some of the key success habits that would allow him to achieve breakthroughs later in life. He didn't realize it, but his habits helped him persevere. At the time, the average door-to-door encyclopedia salesman working for straight commission lasted only three days. J.P. lasted three and a half years.

Despite his work ethic, J.P. still became homeless as a young adult. "When I was homeless the first time, it was in my early twenties. My wife just couldn't handle being a mother anymore, so she left our two-and-a-half-year-old son in my arms and took off with all the money we had. I soon learned that she hadn't paid rent for three months, so with no money and being three months past due on rent, we were evicted. I was in between jobs, so my son and I were on the streets with no money coming in and attempting to live in an old car I owned at the time. I remember saying to my son, 'We're going to make this together.' I went around to vacant lots and picked up Coke bottles and 7UP bottles, because in those days you got two cents for a little one and five cents for a big one. When you're broke and you can't pay the bills, those are some of the most difficult times as a man and as a father. But what I learned was that when you're really down and out, and you're at the very bottom, all you can do is look up."

As difficult as J.P.'s circumstances were, he possessed an advantage that many others in much better circumstances lack: He had a vision for his life! He was determined to start his own company, and after selling encyclopedias door-to-door for those three years, he knew he didn't want to work for someone else. He could make it on his own.

But there was a major obstacle: J.P. only had $700 to his name. Everyone told him he couldn't start his company because he needed more money, more schooling, more experience, more smarts, a different economy, and countless other things that he lacked. Sound familiar? Well, after listening to all that advice, he did what most successful people do: He listened first and foremost to himself and started the company anyway. J.P. developed a success habit of believing in himself and ignoring the naysayers. "That was extremely difficult for me. I mean, how do you start a company, balance your bills, not get paid, and still go out door-to-door selling your products every day? It was extremely difficult. We should have gone bankrupt every single day for the first two years of the company, but two years later, we were finally able to pay our bills on time. Not only pay them, but pay them off. I remember saying, 'Hey, we made it. We've got $2,000 left over! We made it. We're successful!'"

Eventually J.P. was able to use his persuasion and communication skills to grow his company by leaps and bounds. J.P. even improved his listening skills and developed a key habit of being able to read his customers on the deepest level. "I think what I'm really skilled at is having the ability to listen. And not just listen, but to listen to everything people are saying instead of thinking about what I'm going to say next. That took a while, but I think I eventually got pretty good at that."

Through persistence and developing positive success habits—listening to understand, having vision, always doing his best no matter what, ignoring the naysayers, and staying positive in the face of rejection—J.P. built his company into an international success.

Perhaps you've heard the old saying, "It's not where you start, it's where you finish." J.P. is living proof of this adage. He started with nothing and rose to become one of the wealthiest people in the world. In 2015, Forbes magazine listed him as number 234 on the Forbes 400 list of richest Americans (with a net worth of $2.8 billion). J.P.'s full name is John Paul DeJoria. He's the founder of the Paul Mitchell line of hair products, Patrón tequila, and a dozen other successful businesses.

DeJoria often advises young entrepreneurs to develop positive habits, believe in their gut instincts, and take risks. He says, "You can't just let other people get you down. I mean, what the heck do they know? I was told, 'No, you can never enter the beauty industry' dozens of times. Everyone would tell me that 'there's too much competition and that I have no money.' I was even laughed at when I started Patrón. People said, 'Tequila? At $37 per bottle? Are you kidding? I can buy tequila for four bucks!' So go with your own gut feeling and always do something good for someone else."

Though I love all of John Paul DeJoria's story, I relish that early admonition of his high school teacher who told John Paul and his friend Michelle Gilliam they'd never amount to anything. Well, to say that they proved this teacher wrong is a gross understatement. John Paul is a billionaire who's changing lives all over the world, and Michelle Gilliam is better known today as Michelle Phillips, a founding member of the 1960s folk-rock band The Mamas & The Papas, which sold 40 million records. Michelle tracked down that teacher for John Paul's 50th birthday, and when the teacher learned of his former students' success, all he could say was, "Well, shit."

SUCCESS HABITS WILL PUT YOU ON A DIFFERENT PATH

You know, hearing a story like John Paul's can be inspirational. It could be that Rocky story or that Rudy story or the story of the underdog who climbs his way up and makes it happen. But as inspiring as John Paul's story is, in a way, it could also make you second-guess your own abilities. You might think, "I'm not what John Paul is—I can't do what he did! Maybe I don't have the energy he does or the nerve he does." If this is your perception, then realize that at this moment that it doesn't matter where you've come from. It only matters where you are and where you want to go.

But you've got to make the commitment to go there! You could be doing a thousand other things other than reading this book. In many cases, you could be doing busywork that dulls your senses and makes you carry on that status quo life that is less than you deserve.

Humans are busier now than they've ever been in the history of time. I love technology, but all the advancements to make our lives easier have really just allowed us to go faster. Let's face it: What it has really done is made everyone flat-out busier. With text messages and e-mails buzzing in our pockets, our constant availability for phone calls, and hot new apps and social media on our phones, we are more distracted, more unfocused, and more enmeshed in sweating the small stuff than ever before! Many of us feel like we're sprinting every day but really not getting anywhere. Well, what if I told you it's true: you are going faster than ever before, but you may be on a treadmill and not a ladder. Fast is only good when you have the right path. Otherwise all you do is get lost quicker. When you have the right success habits, you get to go fast in the right direction because you know the destination in advance. I promise to share these habits in a way that will allow you to digest them and use them with ease. It will soon become apparent how you can quiet all the other "noises" in your life and expose the clear path to your next level. Let me tell you why this time will be different.

Like John Paul, you'll see a growing number of small shifts you can make now that will have a massive impact down the road. When I was in special reading in seventh grade, I was mocked by my own teacher, Ms. Thompson, just as John Paul was by his teacher. Often, she told me I was stupid, but unbeknownst to me, I had dyslexia and had trouble wrapping my mind around reading and spelling basics. I just couldn't figure it out. But there is, of course, a silver lining to those struggles, and even a silver lining to Ms. Thompson's misguided actions. In fact, there were a lot of silver linings that came from that situation, but one specifically that will benefit you.

A unique ability emerged from my not being able to read and comprehend like other kids. Because of this "handicap," I became a visual and audible learner who knows how to create easy-to-follow recipes for success. And following a recipe is much faster than trying to figure something out from scratch or through trial and error.

RECIPES SAVE TIME

Having the right recipes can get you to success quickly. If you wanted to recreate for your friends and family the tongue-tantalizing taste of the spaghetti and meatballs from your favorite Italian restaurant, there are many ways to go about it. You could go to Italy and study Italian cooking for months. You could go to the Culinary Institute of America in Hyde Park, New York, and study for years to get a degree in Italian cooking. You could try recipe after recipe searching for the secret sauce.

Or maybe you could wait until a Sunday when the chef worked a 12-hour shift, and when you see him walking wearily to his car, approach him and say, "Hey, Chef, I love your spaghetti and meatballs. I'm not in your business and I'll never be a competitor. I just want to make your spaghetti and meatballs for my family, and truthfully, I don't want to waste any time. Could I give you one hundred dollars for the recipe?"

You can then go home and make spaghetti and meatballs that taste just as incredible as the chef makes them! And you can do it that very same day because now you have the recipe.

This book will give you a different type of recipe. That's what I do: create recipes that get people the results they want—fast. There are probably a million options that exist to help people achieve success. You've probably read personal development books, or maybe even gone to a motivational or inspirational event. But for some reason, maybe it didn't stick at the level you wanted it to; that's why you're reading this book. And I don't take that lightly. Not in the slightest.

Here is my promise to you: I have recipes that will help you make tiny shifts in your habits that will in turn make you unrecognizable to yourself down the road. We only need tiny shifts in our millionaire success habits today to be completely different in the near future and for years to come. When I decided to write this book, I reflected back on my own life and figured out the habits that have gotten me to where I am today. And that's what you will get in this book.

SMALL SHIFTS YIELD BIG RESULTS

This book isn't just based on my personal journey to success. It's filled with universal principles that will work for anyone. I went on a quest to discover the habits used by billionaires, top athletes, business leaders, and some of the world's thought leaders—people whom I know through my work. Many of these individuals started at the bottom, in much harder times than we can imagine today. And when I extracted their strategies, and viewed them within the context of my own personal strategies, I identified the tiny shifts that have made the difference in our lives—and will make the biggest impact in your life. That's what this book is going to deliver. It's going to show you how to replace old habits with new ones that will help you make the leap to the next level of success.

I'm grateful you picked up this book and have come even this far; please don't stop now. Most people buy a book because of the title and let it sit on a shelf, hoping that by some magical power the knowledge and action steps will transfer into their brain. I know that you're busy and that it takes time and will to read a book. But I urge you to make the time and find the will to keep reading. I promise I will do everything in my power to keep it compelling and exciting, but also to deliver the tactical strategies to throw away the habits that are not currently serving you and replace them with those that can grow your life, wealth, and joy exponentially. Believe me, I know you may feel like there's no extra time for you to implement these habits. I know you're not sitting around reading this book right now with five extra hours in your day. But as you'll see throughout this book, it's like removing a battery and putting in a new one. I've already shared this, but it's worth repeating: You don't have to add time to your day to learn new habits; you just have to replace the old habits. To do so, you need to recognize the counterproductive routines you've fallen into. Once you acknowledge them, you will see how realistic it is to be able to switch them out.

There are a million different paths to success. But with all of those options, I have learned that the fastest path involves one option above all others. When success habits become your new routine, your life can change dramatically.

You've picked up this book for a reason. Maybe you're a baby boomer who has been in a job for 30 or 40 years because it was the responsible thing to do, and it's finally time to reinvent yourself. Maybe years ago someone told you, "Stop being a dreamer and do what's right. Do what's secure and safe." And what you are doing has dampened your enthusiasm for work and life, especially when you know you were meant for so much more.

Or maybe the world has made you insecure and you're staying in a job that has you living day-to-day just hoping something will change. Maybe you have your own business and it's not doing so great or it's time to take it to the next level. Or maybe your back is against the wall and money is tight, so you need a new path.

It really doesn't matter who you are or what your situation is. Whether you're a college student unsure if the world still has the opportunities that your parents had, or you're someone ready to tap into your full potential and start something new, this book can help you take control of your life. It's time to stop being the thermometer of life and start being the thermostat. Stop hoping a "break" will magically come. You can create your own break, and do it so much faster than you could ever imagine.

But before we get into the "how" of it, I want to share with you the "why now."

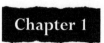

Chapter 1

THE TIME IS RIGHT TO CHANGE YOUR HABITS

"Here's the thing: when it comes to confidence and taking coura-geous action, so much of that is going to have to come from what you believe you should do, through being able to hear and distin-guish your heart's call, how your intuition's speaking to you, that small voice inside that says, 'You know what? Pick up the phone and make that call,' or 'This is the next action to take.'"

— Marie Forleo, interview with Dean Graziosi

This is a volatile, even crazy, time in American history. From the influence of divisive politicians whom people feel they can't trust, to the negativity toward entrepreneurs who work hard and make a lot of money, societal norms are changing. As I noted earlier, most people will tell you that they feel they are working harder and faster to get things done, but to little effect; they strive to move up the ladder of success, yet for some reason it just isn't happening.

Do you feel like you're not getting the results you desire or deserve? Well, besides technology affecting this outcome, another factor exists that you may not even be aware of. The good news is that you're not crazy for feeling like all your effort is for naught. It's not your fault. Let's see what's really to blame.

PRODUCTIVITY VS. INCOME

In doing my research for this book, one statistic on productivity grabbed my attention the most.

If you look at the graph below, you will see that for many years productivity and wages were going up unilaterally on a steep 45-degree angle. However, as 1973 rolled around, things changed. Wages went flat, but productivity remained on the same incline. And what does that massive gap between wages and productivity suggest? It means we are getting more done as a society yet income hasn't reflected this output. So when you feel like you're working harder and faster and using today's technologies to accomplish more, you are. However, wages are simply not keeping up.

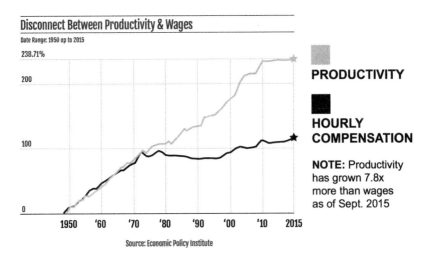

Disconnect Between Productivity & Wages
Date Range: 1950 up to 2015

PRODUCTIVITY

HOURLY COMPENSATION

NOTE: Productivity has grown 7.8x more than wages as of Sept. 2015

Source: Economic Policy Institute

2

That's why you feel busier than ever and squeezed financially. The unfortunate fact is that the gap continues to widen. We can ignore it and blame others, or we can create the habits that multiply the income and success in our own homes.

The middle class is taking a serious hit. Some even say we are going toward a two-class society. Now, I know that politicians and those pushing their agendas have harped on this point, but I'm "localizing" the conversation—I'm talking about how it affects the economy in your house and within your family.

I'm not bashing the wealthy. Heck, in this book I am giving you the habits to become wealthy or increase the wealth you already have. But the statistics don't lie. If you are not prepared and armed with the right tools, the shift that is happening in America could greatly affect you. And when I saw the graph below, I knew I had to share it. Up until 1981, all classes of income were rising at about the same rate. However, in about 1981 a split started to happen. The 1 percent broke away from the crowd, and since then the top 1 percent of earners' income has gone up 138 percent, while the bottom 90 percent of earners' income has only gone up 15 percent.

Here is an alarming look at the actual graph. But give me a minute to go through the so-called facts and then let me explain how they impact you.

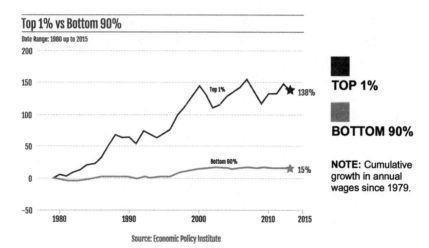

Top 1% vs Bottom 90%

Date Range: 1980 up to 2015

TOP 1%

BOTTOM 90%

NOTE: Cumulative growth in annual wages since 1979.

Source: Economic Policy Institute

3

From one perspective, the gap is getting wider and wider; it seems as though we are evolving into a two-tiered society. The middle class is getting squeezed out, and it's obvious from this graph that this is not just a theory. This is real life. And it's why you may be feeling the effects I talked about earlier.

As scared as that graph makes you feel, imagine this: What if that income gap you saw on the graph did not matter to you? What if you knew there were ways to become financially bullet-proof and for you to create the "class" you desire in your life, in your home, and with your family?

NEW MEASUREMENT OF SUCCESS

You see, I have to believe statistics. And if they are alarming to you, great! More reason to continue reading and take action in your life. But what is even more alarming is what the term "middle class" means these days.

If you and your spouse make $120,000 a year combined, that means you are in the middle class. But should we cheer? What if one of you is working two jobs and the other has to put in extra time during the weekends? Sure, you might have a nice car, a beautiful house, vacations, and some other cool stuff. But maybe the kids are in day care and you rarely get to spend time with them. Maybe you and your spouse haven't had quality time together in a while because you are just too busy. Maybe you and your spouse are, in fact, less engaged with each other because when you do talk it's in between e-mails and text messages. Maybe you have your own business and feel overwhelmed every day. These are just a few scenarios of many. But my point is simple: Is this truly the middle class you want to strive for?

It's time to redefine the middle class. More specifically, we need to start talking about the unfulfilled middle and the em-powered middle. We need the same type of redefinition for the upper and lower classes.

It doesn't really matter if you believe the middle class is disappearing. If you are doing okay financially but have a horrible quality of life, or if you are not living up to your full potential, this is not what life is meant to be about. Having money and no life sucks, and having no money and wishing you could create a life sucks. And I am going to continue to tell you throughout this book that with the right habits, it doesn't matter where the economy is, what's happening to the class system in this country, or who the president is. What matters is that you dance to your own beat. Remember, you want to become the thermostat, not the thermometer. In that way, you are in control of your personal economy and lifestyle. You can shape both to fit your requirements in a way that is meaningful and fulfilling. And yes, this goal is more than just a possibility when you believe in and have the right habits.

MONEY IS NOT EVIL

In my years of traveling and meeting thousands of my students firsthand, I've discovered that many of them have a limiting belief that money is somehow bad. This idea may have arisen from many sources—an antimaterialistic parent, a political ideology, or a religious doctrine. So before we get any further, let's address this concept and make sure we have some clarity around it.

Getting wealthy may not cure every problem, but it sure can cure a lot of them. When you secure the economy in your household, then you can go out to dinner more, get someone to pick up your dry cleaning, hire someone to clean your house, pay off debt, buy a new house, take vacations, and give to charity. You can also allow your spouse to retire, enabling another person to fill his or her job and gain the income you no longer need.

So whether you want to help change the economy in the world, or you're simply curious about what the next level of life would look like for you and your family, I believe this is the greatest time in history for you to gain what you desire. Let's face it, capitalism is getting a bad name; entrepreneurs are sometimes seen as greedy and amoral rather than as crucial to our economic system. It sounds crazy to those of us who believe in this system, but it's a belief that has taken hold in certain segments of society.

But here's the real truth: money earned ethically allows you to do incredible things for the world.

Just about every single billionaire and supersuccessful multimillionaire I know made their money to secure a great life—and then they had a massive impact on the world. Most billionaires employ thousands of people. They also help family members and parents retire and support their kids as they move on in their lives. They help build churches, deliver water to places that don't have it, and create charities and help fund them, often without asking for any public recognition. Because, like I wrote, money earned ethically can have incredible byproducts—benefits for friends, family, and the world.

If you're reading this book, you have a desire for more in life. Go make yourself wealthy, become secure, and watch how much good you can do for the world.

Here is something else to think about. Society seems to be looking down on capitalism, entrepreneurship, and making money. Simultaneously, a lack of money causes more stress in people's lives than any other one thing in this world. Experts say most divorces are caused by money problems, and that most people on anti-anxiety pills admit that it's because of financial worries.

Most people who don't feel connected to their children or spouse claim it's because of a lack of money, time, or having a job they hate. Have you ever worried about money? Of course you have. "Do I have enough? Am I enough?" Those questions can rattle anyone's cage. Here's what one of my mentors taught me: "If you can cut a check for a problem, you don't have that problem." Repeat it like a mantra. If you can cut a check for the problem, you don't have that problem. If you have bills that you're stressed over, you cut a check, and that problem goes away. Worried about your kids' college education? Cut a check, that problem goes away. Worried about your parents getting old and not having enough for retirement? Cut a check and let your parents retire, like I did. Are you worried about your future? Cut a check, that problem goes away. Is your business not doing as well as it could? Cut a check, that problem goes away.

Don't tell me, "Money can't solve issues." When you get money out of the way, you're allowed to be your best self. Think of it this way: If I was sitting next to you right now and squeezed your throat, the only thing you would think about is oxygen. But prior to that, I'm guessing taking your next breath of air wasn't occupying your mind. You just go about every day knowing it's there. The reason people are stressed about money is because they're being squeezed by the amount coming in contrasted with how much they need to live the life they desire.

When worrying about money comes off your plate, you have the opportunity to be your best self. By shifting certain habits in your life, you will allow abundance and prosperity to flow to you in ways that might seem impossible at this moment. No magic money machine is in this book. There's no button you're going to push so your mailbox will be filled with checks. But what you're going to get are simple recipes ideally suited to the complex times in which we live. They cut through all the confusion of modern life and provide a straight line between where you are now and where you want to be.

Have you ever wondered how two people could be brought up in similar environments, work in the same field, have similar jobs, and yet one of them is making twice as much as the other? Or why one person may excel at his job but then leave and do his own thing, while the other person says, "Oh, but the economy is bad, and the President and Congress and my boss is holding me back." Two people, two completely different life results. The reason? The person who took his or her life to the next level had different daily habits than the one who sits back and simply wishes and hopes for more.

Throughout this book you're going to see these habits in action and be excited about each and every one of them. And like I said earlier, it doesn't matter where you're coming from. It only matters where you want to go.

DON'T LET GO OF THE WHEEL

I want to end this chapter with a story I've been sharing for years. Imagine a farmer gets up every single day, and he puts his grain on the back of the tractor. He puts the tractor in gear, he drives out a mile into the pasture to feed the cows, and they all come running. He dumps the feed and goes back to the barn.

If he gets up every single day for 10, 15, 20 years and starts the tractor, puts the feed on, puts it in gear, and goes out to the same field, what will eventually happen? He'll build ruts on the path to the cows. Eventually, he could just get up, throw the grain on the back, start the tractor, put it in gear, and let go of the wheel. That tractor will take him right out to that same spot he's been going to for years.

Apply this story to your life and ask: Have I let go of the wheel? Do I have ruts that keep me doing the same thing every day? It doesn't necessarily mean your entire life is in a rut, but that you might unconsciously do the same things daily expecting a different result. Do you have habits that make every day the same while you simultaneously hope an outside factor will change it? Maybe you're waiting for a shift in the economy, a person to intervene on your behalf, or fate to present you with the winning lottery ticket? Have you become the thermometer instead of the thermostat?

I'm not judging. It happens to us all. Most people have let go of the wheel. But it doesn't have to stay that way. So here's what's important about that farmer's story: To change that farmer's direction, to change his destination, he doesn't have to make a dramatic 180-degree turn. It's not like a New Year's resolution where you feel the need to change everything about yourself.

You don't have to wake up tomorrow morning and start an entirely new routine—do yoga and then meditate and then practice gratitude for an hour. Yes, all those things are worthwhile, but all you have to do tomorrow is put yourself in the position of that farmer and turn that wheel a quarter of an inch. Just a tiny shift.

If he got up tomorrow and turned that wheel a quarter of an inch, by the time he got out a mile in the field, he wouldn't even be able to see his old feeding grounds because he would be so far away. Those ruts would be no more, because he'd be carving a new path, a quarter inch at a time.

I know that there are other things you could be doing besides reading this book—watching television, going to a sports event, doing chores. But those things are always going to be there. Would you rather change a light bulb or your life? Getting rich isn't about a magic pill that puts money in your bank account for doing nothing. It's not about hitting the lotto. It's not about waiting for someone to do something for you. It's about changing your habits and your thoughts. And you can start today.

As John Paul DeJoria says, "The difference between successful people and unsuccessful people is that successful people do the things the unsuccessful people don't want to do." I would add that successful people have a core set of habits that propel them. The average person confuses success with luck. But luck has nothing to do with it. Millionaire success habits do.

Now let's look at where you are in your life and where you want to go.

Chapter 2

THE FOUNDATION FOR ALL SUCCESS

"One of the challenges we have in modern life is that there are so many options to do so many great things. There are so many things throughout our lives vying for our attention, that if we don't manage modern life, it will manage us. Part of managing it is just making the choice that this is what I feel, this is important to me, and then really focusing on your gut."

— Joe Polish, interview with Dean Graziosi

Where the heck are you going? In your life, that is. Many people struggle with this seemingly obvious question. Want to see the evidence of this struggle? During the week, ask five random people what they don't want out of life. I can all but guarantee they'll have sizeable lists. It will be as if they metaphorically lick their fingers, clear their throats as if about to make some life-altering announcement, grab their figurative list, and begin to enumerate the items on it:

- I don't want to stay at the same income level and job I have now.
- I don't want my spouse to nag me about money and time spent at home.

- I don't want to keep driving this same crappy car for another year.

The "I don't wants" always flow out easily. So easily, that sometimes they seem like they have been rehearsed! It's as if people are constantly thinking about them. And why is that? Because they are.

So after you ask these people what they don't want out of life, and they're ticking off their fifth or sixth item, stop them abruptly, pause for a second, and say, "Okay, I understand what you don't want out of life. Now let me ask you this, what *do* you want out of life?" This is where things get interesting. After you ask this question, you'll see puzzlement followed by a creased brow. They're starting to think about what you asked. Their reactions will be the polar opposite of the reactions they had when you asked what they don't want out of life. Many people will respond, "Well, that's a good question" or "I'll have to think about that one."

It's like they're saying, "I'm in a fast car, I'm driving 100 miles per hour, and I know for sure I don't want to go to Florida, Texas, or Arizona. But I'm not sure where I actually do want to go." What happens then? You end up nowhere! You end up out of gas and unable to reach your destination because you only know where you don't want to go. Sounds pretty simple right? Maybe you're saying, "Oh boy, Dean, is that the grand wisdom you have for me?" Actually, it's a huge part of it. But you have to wrap your head around what the wisdom really is. Once you understand it, you'll see why this may be the biggest reason you are holding yourself back from breaking through to the next level.

So, let me ask you a question: Do you know anyone who fits this description? Someone who has an easier time expressing what they don't want out of life than expressing what they do want? Maybe a friend, a relative, or a spouse who goes through life this way? Maybe even someone a little closer to you, that someone you see when you look in the mirror after rolling out of bed each morning? You see, what's crazy about today's society is that everybody is racing around with "Ferrari brains" but no one has her GPS on!

And here's the unfortunate truth for a society like this: It doesn't matter how fast you can go, it doesn't matter how much passion you have, and it doesn't matter how much energy you put into something. If you don't have a vision and clarity on the destination you want to reach, you'll simply never get there. The reason I call it a Ferrari brain is because you can buy the most expensive Ferrari in the world and drive as fast as you possibly can, but if don't know where you're going, you'll get nowhere quickly. Would you rather drive a Ferrari off a cliff at 200 miles per hour or drive a Prius to the promised land?

In the next section, I'm going to share one of the most important millionaire success habits of them all. It's a habit that I have shared with my students for the past 20-plus years and a habit I will share until I can't share anymore! Look, I hope you read this entire book from cover to cover. Getting through this chapter alone will put you ahead of 98 percent of the world—the same 98 percent that is out there running on a treadmill wondering why they aren't getting where they want to go, or driving in a Ferrari with no GPS and wondering why they just drove into a lake.

Here are things I hear far too often: "I need more hours in a day, Dean. I wish I could clone myself or find good help. I never have enough time to do my own business or take my business to the next level, or get a promotion, or make more money." Most people think they need 36 hours in a day, when in reality they are just lacking a crystal-clear vision of what they want out of their own personal lives. Did Bill Gates or Mark Zuckerberg have 36 hours in a day on their path to success?

If you feel overwhelmed daily because of a lack of time, distractions, or your own procrastination, I would bet you a shiny nickel that you don't accurately know where you want to go in life. Believe me, it's the first question I ask all my students, and most scratch their heads as they consider it. When you have no idea about your direction, you tend to spend your time doing things that are preventing you from making more money, receiving promotions, seeing your family more, or even just enjoying life at an optimal level. And while you're doing these things that are in no way serving your future, you're forced to say no to doing the things that could further your business, your income, and your happiness.

On the flip side, when you have a clear vision for your life, you'll stop wasting time on the things not serving your dreams, goals, or aspirations. Your actions will have purpose and your hours will be spent achieving those goals. Your procrastination will cease because you'll know with 100 percent certainty what you cannot put off anything until tomorrow. So let's get your vision dialed in using the habits I've learned over time—habits I've acquired through my own trial and error, as well as those that I've borrowed from other supersuccessful people. Once you develop a vision for yourself, things will become so clear, it will be as if you got a new pair of glasses and realized your old prescription was outdated.

We all know that setting goals is an extremely important part of success. I believe that Benjamin Franklin was one of the first people ever who documented his goals and knew where he wanted to go in life. But what we are about to go through together in this chapter transcends the typical "goal-setting" process. Sometimes setting goals is hard when so much around you is noisy, busy, and even scary. But together we are first going to get honest about where you are in life right now. Then I am going to give you a secret tool that will allow you to look into the future to discover your path. After that, we will anchor where you want to go with your true "why." Then the only thing left is learning how to do it. Fortunately, this entire book is designed to give you the tools, techniques, and, of course, the habits to accomplish the "how."

WHERE ARE YOU? DON'T LIE

Before I ask you to take stock of your life at this moment, let me make a request: be honest. Here, and throughout the book, I'm going to be asking you some tough questions. Don't try to answer what you think I want to hear or what makes you feel good. This is what most people do without thinking, and though I understand the reflex, I'd like you to think about the importance of being truthful. It is only once we are honest with ourselves that we can move onward and upward to our dreams, aspirations, and desires. So with that thought in mind, let's start with where you are in your life right this second. What does that mean exactly? What I don't mean is for you to answer literally—that you're reading this on your couch or on vacation or in the bathroom. I'm not talking about where you are physically. What I mean is: What situation or situations are you currently experiencing in your life? Why are you reading this book?

Maybe you're struggling with the feeling of having untapped potential or you fear you're living just an "okay life" rather than the life of your dreams. Maybe you're trying to find something that can secure your finances because your back is against the wall and your mortgage and student loans are kicking your backside. Maybe you just want to start something new to help change your life for the better. If you can relate to any of these situations, great.

Maybe you're just getting out of college, or going through college, and you are confused about your future. If so, congratulations for being at this place in your life! Maybe you think it's time to reinvent yourself completely. Maybe you're just sick of listening to someone giving you orders at the same mundane job you've had for a decade. If so, congratulations! Maybe you're a business owner who is ready for more profits, ready for that next level, or ready to get the secrets that can catapult you to the next level. If so, I congratulate you for being here as well.

I suggested these examples to help you think about your own situation, as well as to reassure you that wherever you're at in your life, you're not alone. So dig deep and just be honest with yourself. Sometimes we pretend that everything is okay. We forget what really matters. You must try to break down that everything-is-okay mind-set and write down what truly is in your heart.

In fact, stop reading right now and take a yellow pad, or your phone, or your computer, and make a note of, "Where am I in life?" You can go beyond just your finances and write down where you are in the different areas of your life that matter most: love, intimacy, health, your career, and your family. Go ahead and break out these areas on a piece of paper and, next to each one, describe where you are. Don't write other people's perceptions of you. Instead, when you look in the mirror and you're dead honest with yourself, where are you? Before we can create your ideal destination, we need to know your starting point.

GET CLEAR ON WHERE YOU WANT TO GO

Here's a story that will help you think about where you want to end up—versus the place you don't. A dear friend took a church group of 18 boys on an adventure trip to Durango, Colorado, where they planned to go white-water rafting. When they arrived, the guide informed them that the rapids were higher and stronger than they had been in many years. Rapids range on a scale from 1 to 5, and most of the ones they were going to experience were 4's. Anxious about their safety, the guide made them do practice drills many times during the first mile of the adventure. The guide kept hammering into their heads one idea: the "positive point." He said, "Boys, when I point, I will always be pointing to where we want to go. I will never point at the downed tree we could get caught on or the jagged rock that could puncture the raft. If I pointed to what we didn't want to hit, that's where all your focus would go, and I assure you we would run right into it. Don't worry if we get even inches from the rocks, you just focus on the positive point and use all your energy and attention to get us there." With this positive point to guide them, their minds focused on the solution (steering into a clearing) rather than the obstacle (crashing into the rocks). The chances of them actually getting in trouble decreased substantially.

And yes, it's easier said than done, but once you begin focusing on what you do want rather than on what you don't want, it becomes a success habit that can completely change the outcome of so many things in your life.

When this chapter's lesson becomes a part of you, you may look at the jagged rocks for a second when something goes wrong, but then you'll immediately look for that clearing, the "positive point." And the more you practice this, the more likely you'll look only at the clearing when life puts you in a spin. For years I've taught this truth: When you focus on the outcome rather than the obstacle, your life will never be the same.

How do you think John Paul DeJoria and the richest men and women in the world became so successful? By having a clear vision of where they wanted to go and then taking action toward it. Most of us want more out of life, but we aren't specific enough with our intentions, so we don't know how to get there. That's why you may be sidetracked by phone calls and e-mails. It's why you may feel disorganized, stressed, or overwhelmed. It's why you may have the feeling that America is just not the same as it used to be and there is no opportunity for you to go to that next level—completely false beliefs. There's more opportunity now than ever before! This might be one of the greatest times in history to get ahead of the curve. However, first and foremost, you must have your destination locked in and create the map you need to get to that next level of life. Once you find a truly crystal-clear vision, things that once bugged you or slowed you down no longer have any power to stop you from achieving your goal.

LOOK BACK FROM THE FUTURE

We know that goal-setting is arguably the most important step to success. But let's be honest here: Sometimes setting goals the traditional way by just looking forward a year, two years, or even five years is hard. We lead crazy, busy lives, and we can become so bogged down in the details of things that we can't look up and see the future clearly. With your business, your family, your work, and so many other things moving so fast, it's difficult to focus on the road ahead. You spend so much time just managing what you can see—what is within your reach—that looking into the future may be difficult.

So here's how to see past the daily grind. Dan Sullivan, one of my mentors, taught me the following activity, and it was an immediate game-changer for me and for thousands of people I've shared it with.

Imagine it's one year from today and when looking back over the past year, you realize that it was the best year of your life. What does that look like to you? What would have had to happen for you to wake up every morning on fire, free of dissatisfaction, and convinced you weren't wasting your potential? As I'm writing this paragraph, I'm looking back at my future year and getting goose bumps because of what I'm envisioning. I want you to experience that same sense of excitement. Think about what the best year of your life would look like and get emotional, get engaged, get engulfed, and visualize specific details about what made it so amazing.

More specifically, ask yourself the following questions when you look back at this year:

- How much money are you making? How much money do you have saved away for your family's security? Who are you taking care of financially?
- Where do you work every day? Do you have a home office or are you driving to a new location?
- Are you taking your existing company to the next level? Are you starting your own company? Are you evolving through the ranks at your job? Do you have a better relationship with your boss? Better yet, are you the boss?

- How does your spouse or your partner look at you in the morning or after a long day?
- How do your relationships with your kids or family members look now?
- What exactly does your life look like when it's a year in the future and you look back and it was the best year ever?

Feel those feelings with no restrictions and nothing holding you back from these raw emotions. Don't say, "Well, I could be in shape, but I'm too busy to work out" or "I could start my own company, but I have to stick with this job just to pay the rent." That's looking into the future with current obligations holding you back like an anchor.

If you have not done so already, I encourage you to stop and write down your answers fast and continuously. Get specific about each area. As you write, just let it flow.

You see, when you know where you are right at this moment, you possess a true starting point. Then, when you take the time to look back in order to create where you want to go over the next year, you've done more than most people who are stuck in place do—they ignore this simple habit and practice. You know who doesn't ignore it? Successful people! When you know where you want to go, you'll start having a filter that will allow you to say no to certain friends, say no to certain obligations, say no to certain opportunities, and say no to certain e-mails. You will know deep down that those things are not contributing to your vision. Once you know where you want to go, you can start taking action steps toward the best year of your life, which will evolve into the best 10 years of your life, and ultimately, into the best rest of your life.

By doing this exercise, you'll stop feeling overwhelmed. You'll find more time, and your stress will melt away. All the successful people I've ever been blessed to meet or become good friends with know where they're going in life and what their ultimate goals are. They have an inner vision that they live by, and it's time for you to get yours or take yours to another level. Once you know where you are and where you want to go, you'll also find it easier to acquire other success habits.

IDENTIFY YOUR "WHY"

Let's move on to the next key component—the piece that makes your vision become your reality. This is the step you must complete to make it real: understand your "why." Here are critical "why" questions you should answer:

- Why do you want to take your income from where it is to a "next level"?
- Why do you want to start your own business?
- Why do you want your company to evolve, or to quit your job, or to rise up through the ranks at your current job?
- Why do you want your parents or your spouse to retire?
- Why do you want to lose weight, have more intimacy in your life, have more passion in your actions, have more joy on a daily basis, and live a life with more smiles than frowns?

I bet when you think of having all of these things you say to yourself, "Hell yeah!" But why do you really want them? I know for a fact that the reasons you want them are deeper than you think, and I'm going to show you how to dig those reasons out. And when you do, be prepared to be unstoppable. Maybe you'll shed a few tears as well; I know I did.

The issue with most people is that they simply don't go deep enough into their hearts and souls to find out the truth about why they want what they want. It's unfortunate that our brains can so powerfully obscure what's in our hearts and souls. When you ask people what their "why" is—and I have asked thousands of my students—most will say, "I want more money to have financial freedom," or "I want more money to eliminate debt," or even things like, "I want to lose weight so I look good." And yes, these are all good answers, but they're not sufficiently deep ones. Without a depth of purpose, you can't push through your most challenging times. If the struggles of life are pouring down on you like a rainstorm, is "I want a new house" a strong enough motivation that you'll ignore the storm to get what you want? Is "I want abs" a strong enough "why" to get you to the gym after a long day at work? I doubt it! But when you can attach a much deeper meaning to "why," it all changes.

Let me stress how important this is. Throughout this book I promise to deliver success habits that will wow you and have you eager to put them into play in your life. But if you don't have these fundamental habits to start, then nothing else I share with you will matter. So get ready to be honest with yourself on even a deeper level than before, because together we are going to dig out your true purpose.

The question we usually don't ask ourselves is, "What is the purpose behind our actions?" Which is crazy, because it's a question we should be asking ourselves daily. When we can uncover our true "why," our driving purpose in life, and translate that into actions, we obtain the momentum we need to push forward, faster than ever.

WHY IS YOUR "WHY" SO IMPORTANT?

Even if you could teach a group of people how to sell $20 bills for 10 bucks, some of them would let what's between their ears stop them from succeeding. Even with something so simple, they could still talk themselves out of success and not even realize that they are self-sabotaging. Because so often, fear is the brake on our momentum, slowing us down so much that we eventually come to a complete stop. And it's for that reason that I've always been obsessed with discovering the tools, strategies, and recipes that lead to the habits that can help you demolish any obstacles. This way you don't find yourself on the cusp of greatness and give up and turn around when you are just an inch away from a breakthrough. If you loved the life you are in 100 percent, you'd go back to where you were and continue living the life you love. But you aren't one of those people. You realized, or are realizing now, that you can access all the potential you have—and that you don't have to live like others do or live how others tell you to live. You don't want to look back in 5, 10, or 25 years and realize that you lived the same mundane day, over and over again, for most of your life. You don't want to miss out on invaluable years that you'll never get back.

As you read this book, I hope you get inspired. But if you just get motivated and excited for a week and then fall back into old habits, then I didn't do my job. Rather, I want these success habits to be like behavioral superglue. I want these lessons to stick with you so long that this could be the last book you ever have to read about success. It is my mission for you to implement these habits and look back in a couple of years and realize that the old you, the you of today, is unrecognizable because you're using each and every ounce of your full potential. That's all we're supposed to do in this world and in this life: reach for our full potential each and every day. You're not supposed to be me or Bill Gates or Peyton Manning or Oprah or anybody else. You're simply supposed to be the best you possible.

Okay, I'm done with the pep talk! Now it's time for you to do my favorite exercise in the world and find your true "why," the thing that can get you through even the toughest of days and bring even more bright light into the good days.

LET'S GO SEVEN LEVELS DEEP

About eight years ago I hired a consultant named Joe Stump to help me get my students and my readers more engaged in what I do and what I teach. Joe was incredible at what he does and it wasn't cheap to hire him, but I knew it was well worth it for my students and my clients. So I was going to pay him a big fat check to help me out, but at the last minute he said, "Why don't I consult with you on your questions and your goals in the morning and then you consult with me in the afternoon?" I was totally on board with that and ready to absorb newfound knowledge and wisdom from Joe. I remember the meeting like it was yesterday. Joe Stump; my good buddy, Joe Polish, who had made the introduction; a few team members; and I were sitting at an outside table at my old house in Scottsdale, Arizona. I loved this outdoor space! It had big, hand-carved wood chairs that were so high that the backs on them were two feet over my head. They had soft, yellow cushions and they surrounded a beautiful, large, and long Tuscan table. It was a 75-degree Phoenix afternoon, and the perfect sort of day for an outdoor meeting. These may seem like mundane details, but there's a reason they remain so vivid in my memory; my life would never be the same after this meeting.

As we sat around the table, Joe Stump said to me, "Why do you want me here, Dean? What's the main reason?"

I responded, "Because I know I provide proven strategies for success and wealth to people, but I can't always get them to take action. I not only want them to get my books and trainings, but I want them to use the information, get engaged, and then stick to it, so more of them can see the results of their actions. I've even been doing a weekly wisdom [check it out at www.weekly-wisdom.com] for my students for many years now to help them on their journey to success. I do all I can to try to get them engaged, but so many of my students are sucked back into their old routines. They seem to hope something changes, rather than making something change. I just need them to stay in the game long enough to make those little shifts and stay passionate about their goals. And once they get a glimpse, I know there will be no turning back for them."

He looked at me and said, "Wow, Dean, that was powerful. Have you ever done the seven levels deep exercise?"

I said, "I don't know what that is."

"It's the most profound thing that I've ever done, and it can massively transform the lives of the people you teach and make them stay engaged and motivated longer than ever before. It will actually keep them engaged for life."

I was like, "Okay, amazing! Give it to me—let me have it!"

Then Joe said, "Sorry, Dean, but no. I want to put you through the full experience first."

"Joe, come on, man. I want to get there quick. I'm a fast learner. I want this seven levels deep thing, and I want to give it to my students and my readers ASAP."

Then, even more persistently, he said, "Nope, the only way you're going to get it is if you go through it."

I finally gave in and said, "Fine."

Now, as you read the next few paragraphs, I want you to picture yourself doing this exercise with someone else. Whether with a spouse, a colleague, or a friend, imagine doing this exercise together.

As you'll see, when Joe asked a question, the answer I gave him would be the basis for the next question, and we would repeat this seven more times. For example, if he asked, "Why do you want me here," and I answered, "I want to learn how to help my students," he would then ask, "Why do you want to help your students?"

This exercise is called "seven levels deep," because you move progressively deeper into answers by asking "why" questions seven times. I'm not sure why seven is the magical number that gets you where you need to go, but it is always the right number.

Joe sat down in front of me with a piece of paper—he was right in my face. He said, "I asked you why you wanted me here earlier, and you basically said because you want to get your clients, your readers, and your customers more engaged so you can help change their lives for the better, even more than you have. I think that's a great answer, Dean. Very noble! Now let me ask you this: *Why* is it important to you to get more of your students engaged, to understand more, to overcome obstacles, to take action, and to see that next level of life?"

I remember thinking about it for a second before answering, "Because so many people get stuck in the routine of mediocrity, and I know I'm giving them good strategies, but not all are using them. I don't want to be the sales or infomercial guy who just sold them a book. I want to be the person who opened their eyes to a new way of life by using what I've discovered. And at the end of the day, I want to create a legacy that my family can be proud of."

Joe responded, "That's great stuff. Now, I first asked you why you hired me. You then said it was to help your students get more engaged. Then when asked why that was important, you basically said you want to leave a legacy for your family. Both are great reasons and great answers. So, Dean, why is it important for you to create a legacy?"

Again, I thought for a moment before saying, "Because, in this business, a lot of people write crap and teach crap, and I want to set a new standard. I want to set a standard so high that others in the industry will either step up or step out. And, don't get me wrong, I love the great people in this industry. Some of my dearest friends and teachers like Tony Robbins, Wayne Dyer, Eckhart Tolle, Brendon Burchard, David Bach, and many others have had a huge positive impact on my life and millions of others through this type of industry. I wouldn't be the man I am without those and other incredible influences. But we all know there's also a ton of crap out there. And I want those people to either raise their standards or get out." As I was sharing this, I wasn't even sure where the answers were coming from, but I was digging deeper and deeper into my "why."

Then he said to me, "Dean, that's wonderful. I asked you why you hired me, and you said to get deeper and to help your students more. I asked you why that was important, and you said you want to create a legacy that you and your family can be proud of. Then I asked you why that was important, and you said you want to have the standards raised in this industry. All those are great answers."

What I didn't realize at that time was that while yes, these were all good and true answers, they came from my head. And as he asked me the same question a couple more times, I continued to give him answers from my head. They were all well thought out, but I wasn't even close to the real "why."

When there were three levels left to go, he said, "Why is that important?" to my previous and now forgotten answer.

What came out of my mouth next shocked me. I said, "I never want to go backward," and for some reason I got emotional. With hindsight, I realized the most important thing that happens when you ask yourself "why" seven times is that you switch from grabbing the answers from your head to pulling the answers from your heart and soul. My heart was speaking and I could feel it. I remember that I started sitting differently and speaking with a different tone, because physically, my body started to feel different. I was working hard to stop the tears from streaming out of my eyes because my staff was watching. Then Joe, whom I had just met for the first time, was staring directly into my eyes, only a foot away. He asked, "Why is it important that you don't want to go backward?"

And here's what I meant, and here's what my heart was trying to express: I know what it's like to be broke and grow up with no money. I know what it's like to wear hand-me-downs. I know what it's like not having food in the refrigerator. I know what it's like to be basically homeless as a kid, because I experienced it with my dad. When I was 11 years old, I moved in with my dad and we literally lived and slept in a small bathroom inside a house my dad was trying to fix up. There was no heat anywhere, and the bathroom was the smallest room to keep warm, so that's where we slept. And growing up in upstate New York, we had some brutal winters. We had an electric heater and took the doorknob out of the bathroom door and put the cord through the hole. We plugged in the electric heater and dragged in a small mattress and slept on that together. I'd get a ride to school in a car that had no heat and with doors held closed by rope. I remember making my dad drop me off down the street so no one would see just how poor I was. I was in a steady state of feeling insecure and feeling inadequate and that was a place to which I never wanted to return.

This is my story, and I'm not suggesting that you and others haven't had it worse. But I remember my mom struggling before I helped her retire. I remember my dad always struggling before I helped him retire. I remember what it felt like not to be able to help other people or even myself. And I know for a fact that I don't ever want to go backward to where I was as a kid.

After I explained all of this, Joe could see that I was getting emotional. And at that time I was thinking to myself, "Well, I found my why!" But there were two more questions left for me to answer. Joe looked at me and asked, "Dean, why don't you want to go backward?"

At that point, I couldn't hold the tears back; they were streaming down my face. The first things that came to my heart were my children. I said, "I think I know it. I think I know my why. I want to give my kids the choices and the options that I never had when I was a kid."

I want my daughter and my son to be able to choose where they want to go in life and have the ability to become their best selves. I want them to live without the worry over money choking them. I want them to know that they're financially secure, so if they want to be teachers, or astronauts, or be in rock bands, or teach yoga, or anything else, they can. I want them to have the freedom I never felt like I had growing up. I'm not saying I want to raise two entitled brats. I work very hard to make sure that never happens. I'm talking about giving them choices to be who they want to be, not spoiling them so much they don't have to make any choices at all. And the more I thought about it, the more emotional I got. I said to Joe, "I know my why! It's my children."

But then he said, "I bet you started working really hard before you had children, didn't you, Dean?" He was right, and I had one more "why" left to answer.

"Dean," he said, "thank you for sharing this, but I have to ask you: Why is it important that your children have choices?" And my true "why" emerged like a miracle; it just flew out of my mouth.

I said, "Because I want to be in control."

Before that moment, I'd never thought or talked about wanting to be in control. And I'd never felt that surge of passion run through me to my core. I realized at that very moment what my whole life was about. I finally realized why I wanted to go to the next level, why I got into business, why I started cutting firewood and fixing wrecked cars when I was a teenager, why I knocked on a million doors and did my first real estate deal before I was 20. It all made sense now. It was all because I wanted to be in control. Not a control freak, just in control.

You see, my parents were married nine times between them. In fact, as I write this book, my dad is engaged to a great lady, and it will soon be an even 10. Also, growing up I moved a lot. I moved 20 times by the time I was 19 years old. Over the years of my childhood, I would have new stepbrothers, stepsisters, and step-grandparents that I loved, and then I'd be uprooted and have to move without any say in the matter. I always felt totally out of control. We would find an apartment I loved, couldn't pay the rent, and would get evicted. I'd move into my grandma's house and love it, and then within the year I would have to move and go someplace else with a new dad or a new mom and with new siblings that in some cases hated me for intruding. I would move to a new school, find new friends, and then we'd pick up and have to relocate again.

It was an epiphany, this seventh "why." I don't want anybody to tell me how to dress, where to live, or even how to raise my kids. I don't want anybody to tell me where I can eat, how I can function, what I can do with my time, or how much money I can make. I want to be in control so I can make the decisions that empower me, bring me joy, and make me feel alive! And at that very moment, I realized I didn't want anybody to take that away from me in any area of my life. I had finally found my true "why," and my mission had never seemed clearer.

WHAT'S YOUR DEEPER "WHY"?

What about you? Would you like to have total control of your life and make the choices you want? Of course you would, but that's my story and my "why." I don't know what yours is yet—and you probably don't either—but I assure you that you need to find it. When you have a tough day, when things don't go your way, when your new business fails, when things go wrong in your relationship, when your kids disappoint you, what pushes you to keep moving forward? Financial freedom? That's not deep enough. You need to find the root of your "why." Why are you reading this book? Why do you want to make more money? Why do you want wealth to come into your life? There is a much deeper level of purpose that is driving you.

And when you find it, you discover the driving force that will never allow you to get off track. Listen, I feel blessed for the life, the security, and the income I have right now. But do you think I don't have tough days? I absolutely do! We all do, no matter our level of financial security. And at the end of the day, my "why" guides and pushes me through hard times. When I have a tough day or even think of quitting, I remember my "whys" and know there is no way I could possibly give up. Because I know I am never going backward, I know I'm giving my kids that security they deserve, and I know I'm always going to be in control of my life.

The seven levels deep exercise is the foundation to all success and possibly the most important millionaire success habit you can develop. This is an exercise you should do four times annually. And once you know your "why," you will use it in 100 different ways to motivate your actions—it will become one of your daily success habits.

ANCHORING THE PROCESS

At one point in my life, I was on stage speaking at an event every month, year after year. During that time, I did the seven levels deep exercise pretty much every time I was on stage. I would randomly pick someone out of the audience to come up and participate. I remember each and every person's story to this day, but there's one that comes to mind at this moment and touches my heart. This tall, awesome dude with dreadlocks who seemed nearly twice my size came up on stage, gave me a hug, and nearly lifted me off my feet!

So I sat him down and said, "Hey man, glad to have you up here," as I handed him the microphone. The audience was just sitting, staring, waiting for what was going to happen next. I asked him, "Why are you here? Why did you spend money to come to an event like this and learn how to take your life to the next level?"

I remember his first answer was typical. It was "financial freedom" or a version of that. I, of course, proceeded to ask him why financial freedom was important to him. And his second answer was really deep and freaking awesome: "Dean, in my neighborhood a lot of dads just aren't there. They're either in jail or they abandoned their kids. I'm working to create a way to give those kids a fatherly influence." Wow, could there be a better "why"? It was an amazing "why" and an amazing driving factor. I mean, how could he not be empowered and inspired. He was at that event to get juiced up, ready to obtain the tools to go faster and make more money to turn that dream into reality.

But from my experience I knew I could get deeper, so I asked him why that was important to him. He then gave another good answer. Then I asked him why again and again and all of his answers were great, but they were coming from his head. Then we got to the last couple of questions, and I watched as his whole body changed. His smile disappeared, his lips started to quiver, and his hands started to shake. This is when he began to speak truth from his heart. He looked at me dead in the eyes and said, "Dean, I can't believe I'm sharing this with a whole audience. But my mom died a few years ago, and when she died, I was a drug addict. I feel like I completely let her down as a son. She was a good mom who worked her butt off to raise a good boy, but when she died, she didn't see that. And after she passed, I quit doing drugs. I got my head on straight, and I am on this mission."

He then said, "I'm going to show my mother in heaven that she raised one awesome son who's going to make a positive impact on the world." The audience members were either in tears or at a loss for words or jumping up and clapping with wild enthusiasm. He officially found his "why"! And what a "why" that was! That's a purpose that will carry him through the toughest

The Foundation for All Success

days life could ever throw at him. This man has a true "why." Not only does he know where he is, and where he wants to go, he knows why he wants it.

When you attach a "why" to your actions, you get your emotions involved and you anchor your goals to your life to a point where they become a part of your soul, a part of your heart, and not just another well-intentioned thought. Imagine the conversation he has with himself when he has a tough day. It doesn't sound like, "I need to keep working because I want to be a good role model for people." And while yes, that is a good "why," it is not powerful enough to push him through the most challenging of days. What his conversation sounds like is, "I need to get myself into that office and work my tail off because I want to show my beautiful mother up in heaven the amazing son she raised down here on earth!" It's an emotionally potent idea, isn't it? Consider the effect that man's "why" has had on his success. And then think about how much your "why" will affect your life.

NOW IT'S YOUR TURN

I think it's crucial that you go through this process with someone else; though it can work if you do it on your own, it's much more effective when you have a partner. Because you're familiar with the exercise, you go first—lead them through the seven "whys." Then take your turn. Find a partner who will take the exercise seriously and is willing to write down what you share. Start the exercise by simply asking why you are reading a book like *Millionaire Success Habits*. The initial question gets the party started. Then proceed to ask the seven "why" questions in the sequence I've suggested, with the previous answer restated each time. Remember, you're going to have to ask or be asked the question seven times. It's not five, and it's not nine—it's seven times. I've been doing this for years now, and it works every single time. When I share the exercise with an audience, half the room is crying by the end because they realize with crystal clarity why they're sitting in the audience—what the deeper reasons are for attending my presentation. When you finish the exercise, you will realize why you're reading this book, why you desire more, and why you want to unlock your true potential.

To make this exercise easier to complete and to gain more clarity on how it works, go to www.thebetterlife.com right now and grab the "7 Levels" exercise sheet by clicking the "Book Resources" tab. Also, I have filled out and completed my own seven levels exercise sheet below to give you an even better snapshot of how this exercise will play out when you complete it! Note the natural evolution, especially the evolution from head-thinking to heart and soul sharing.

THE SEVEN LEVELS DEEP EXERCISE

Why did you write this book, Dean?	*To change a million lives by helping them see a better path and better habits to success.*
Why do you want to change a million lives?	*Because it feels amazing to serve and help others.*
Why does it feel amazing to serve and help others?	*It allows for an even more successful business based on solid principles and values.*
Why is it important for you to have a business based on principles and values?	*I want to leave a legacy my family will be proud of.*
Why is it important for you to leave a legacy for your family?	*I never want to go backward, and I hated being broke as a kid.*
Why do you never want to go backward?	*I want my kids to have choices as they grow up.*
Why is it important for your kids to have choices you never had?	*Because I want to be in control. I want to live life on my terms and be free to do as I choose.*

Now that you've reached this point, you possess one of the most important success habits needed to create true abundance and prosperity.

When you know where you are, where you want to go, and what you want (and why you want it), there is only one thing left: How do you get there? Well, great news! I've spent the last year of my life crafting the pieces of this book to be your "how," and deliver the road map to your next level of life.

As part of that "how," you should be aware that there is a hidden villain inside you, and it's working against your goals. This villain is made of the self-doubt and inner resistance that's been holding you back for your entire life. I'm going to show you how this villain was created by the outside world, how to identify it, and then how to ultimately kill it, allowing an inner hero to awaken. It will all make sense soon, so don't stop now.

Chapter 3

THE VILLAIN
WITHIN

"Who are the people that when we're around them we feel more alive?
Who are the people that make us feel more energized, more fulfilled,
and more confident? These are the people we must gravitate towards for
progression. But you see, the truth is that there are also toxic people in
our lives working against our progression. Imagine you're on a train, and
in your compartment is your family and your close friends. Suddenly you
look to your right and you find that a handful of toxic people, people
who are draining your motivation and your drive, have somehow found
themselves in your compartment. What can you do now? There is only
one thing you can do, and that is to politely let them off at the next
station. I believe the people in our lives who are negative, competitive,
jealous, et cetera, can really drain our energy and our confidence."

— Arianna Huffington, interview with Dean Graziosi

So who exactly is the villain within? Well, the villain within
can disguise itself as many different things. But no matter what
form it takes, we all have it somewhere inside. To most of us,
it's that self-doubt, that inner voice saying, "You can't do this"
or "What makes you think you deserve that?" And in so many
cases it holds you back from taking the proper actions to move

your life in a better direction. It's that inner resistance that in the past talked you out of pursuing the things that made your heart smile and helped you reach that next level of life.

I call it a villain because it's sneaky and up to no good. It hides in the back of your mind, and you don't even realize it exists. And the worst part about this inner villain is that, in most cases, external factors in your life that seemed innocuous created this villain. We'll address these factors soon. You may not realize it, but this villain has created a glass ceiling—an artificial limit on what you can achieve and who you can be. And what's even worse, once that villain is inside you, it is anchored down by multiple internal factors that prevent its escape. You may sometimes find yourself wondering why you're working faster, your life is going by quicker, and you're ultimately working harder than ever before, but you haven't found that next level of life. And the simple explanation is: You have a villain working against you and you don't even know it. The good news: We're going to expose it once and for all.

WHICH WOLF ARE YOU FEEDING?

I once heard a fable about a Navajo woman who told her grandson a story about how we all have two wolves that live inside us, constantly battling one another. It starts with the grandmother sitting her grandson down and explaining to him that, "One of the wolves is jealous, has envy in his soul, is malicious, and has a scarcity mind-set. To that wolf, everything in the world is wrong and unpleasant. He believes that people are mostly bad, things are no good, and the world is a cold place. As you can imagine, nothing good ever happens for that wolf because it is a negative, pessimistic animal, always seeing things as glass-half-empty." Then the woman says to her grandson, "But you also have a different, powerful wolf that lives inside you. This wolf has empathy, love, compassion, and positivity, and knows it can accomplish anything it puts its heart and soul into. This wolf sees the bright side of everything and constantly sees things glass-half-full. And grandson, this wolf, the powerful wolf, can take you to so many amazing places."

Then the grandson looks at his grandmother and says, "Well, which wolf wins the battle, Grandma?"

She replies, "The one you feed, grandson. The one you feed."

I love this story because it is applicable to all our lives. We all have the bad wolf, or the villain, as I call it, living inside us, but we also have this hero just waiting to be released. Here, I'll help you learn how to expose the villain hiding inside you, discover how it got there, and proceed to destroy it. Because in so many cases, once it's gone, you can't even begin to imagine how much more you will be able to accomplish in your professional and personal life.

THE VILLAIN IS A PARASITE

A few years back, a man went to a third-world country in South America to volunteer for a worthy cause, helping those in need. After his emotional journey, he arrived back in the States filled with gratitude and ready to kick his own life into high gear. But shortly after the trip he started feeling sluggish and a bit weak and sick. He was in his 50s, and he simply assumed the cause was aging, and it was something he just needed to start accepting. Over the next few weeks he stopped doing certain activities that he loved. He stopped playing with his recreational basketball team and being active in the community, and he started to try to process the new thoughts of an aging man.

What he didn't realize is that when he was in the jungles of South America helping out families in need, he was infected with a dangerous parasite. And from that moment on, this parasite had been living inside him, feeding off him. Every minute of every day it was robbing him of nutrients, sapping his energy, and diminishing his quality of life. He simply had no idea something was living inside him, holding him back from his full potential. However, he eventually went to the doctor, found out about the parasite, got the right medicine, and the parasite was gone for good. This man appreciated life once again. In fact, he appreciated it even more so after this experience. With a new perspective on life, he felt like he could accomplish anything!

Why do I tell you this story? Because the villain that I spoke of earlier in the chapter is, with all intents and purposes, a parasite that is living inside you. No, it's not robbing you of your nutrients or feeding off your body, but it's taking away from the quality of life you deserve! It's decreasing your confidence, your joy, your inspiration, and ultimately, your passion for life. So I'm going to show you how it was created and how to destroy it, plain and simple! This chapter will be like going to the doctor and getting medication to destroy the self-doubt and the pessimistic voice that has made you miss opportunities.

If we don't flush this villain from your system immediately, it will continue to do damage. And even worse, it will continue to erode your confidence. And we all know that reduced confidence hampers your ability to move in a better direction. When was the last time you made a great move, made a sale, had a great date, got a promotion, or started something new when your confidence was in the toilet? Probably never. Think about your best days, best sales, and best dates; they happened when your confidence was high and all things seemed possible! By identifying the toxicity living inside you, then flushing it, you will restore your confidence. And this is just the start.

As I explain to you how this villain was created and sustained, I'm also going to give you strategies that will show you how to kill it off, piece by piece. So let's start identifying it right now and allow you to discover its origins.

THE VILLAIN GROWS OUT OF YOUR PAST

Let's start with one of the external factors that feed this success-robbing parasite: watching, listening to, and reading the news. Think about it: We've grown up as a generation that gets nothing but negative news pounded into our minds. Every second of every day our brains are bombarded with the news of wars, scarcity, economic crisis, disasters, terrorist attacks, murders, sicknesses, and suffering.

Did you know that in the 1950s *Time* magazine covers were about 90 percent positive in tone and content? Then, through the years, *Time* magazine realized that the more negative their stories, the more copies they would sell. In fact, they realized that negative superlatives worked 30 percent better at snaring readers' attention than positive ones. And not just that, but the average click-through rate on headlines with negative superlatives is a staggering 63 percent higher than that of their positive counterparts. This emphasis on the negative isn't just an editorial decision. The negative content reflects the increasing number of anxiety-producing global events, such as the rise of terrorism, ecological disasters, and many other crises and calamities. All this contributes to our perception that things are getting worse.

Now is *Time* magazine the only one who has gone through this transformation and is delivering negative news? Of course not. *Time* magazine has to make a profit, as does every other news outlet in the world. If they decide to focus only on the positive, they won't generate the readership and revenue they require. And the media has developed a disaster reflex—whether it's a devastating hurricane or an urban riot, they provide saturation coverage, creating the impression that the end of the world is near. As a cynical television news producer once said, "If it bleeds, it leads."

As a result, the majority of the daily data we digest is completely negative. It's difficult to focus on positive thoughts and that next level of success when at every turn we are receiving information about a world that seems doomed. The news can affect you in such a negative way that, even if you are someone who has an "I'm going to be the thermostat of life" mentality, you can soon become the thermometer. The negativity is overpowering the positive-thinking part of our brains. According to research done by UCLA, the average human being has around 70,000 thoughts per day. And out of those thoughts 80 percent of them are negative, with the majority of those thoughts carrying over to the next day. Based on everything I've read and observed, digesting negative news is a leading cause of this frightening statistic.

And I understand that throughout history there have always been wars, economic hurdles, and natural disasters. But never before has all this information been so readily available. We get it from our apps, our phones, our social media accounts, and TV at an alarming rate. And it affects you, whether you like it or not. That's the thing about our subconscious: it takes in what it wants.

So what happens is that this barrage of negativity is strengthening your inner villain. It encourages thoughts like, "Why would you want to start your own business when the economy is just going to crash? Why do you think you deserve love when famous movie stars keep getting divorced? Why do you think you can get in shape when the world is more obese now than ever before?" When you consciously or subconsciously absorb even a portion of the negative news out there, it slowly chips away at your confidence and reinforces that you're staying exactly where you are, rather than motivating you to get where you want to go.

To kill off this aspect of the villain, do the following: Go on a 30-day news diet. I recommend a total separation, in which you don't watch the news, can't read about it, and can't ask your friends about it. Instead, use that time and energy to search within yourself, spend time bonding with the people you love, or work on the things we're discussing in this book to empower you. Spend that time working on the things that can allow you to gain confidence, instead of something that strips it away. I don't know how much time you'll recover with this news diet, but take the time you usually spend on the news and spend it on you instead. And remember, it's not just the time you lose by watching or reading the news, but it's the damaging aftereffects that cause the most harm. So commit to yourself right now to take a 30-day news challenge and write down a list of things you will be doing instead. Will you meditate, cook yourself some healthy meals, and hit the gym? Create the business plan for your new idea or expand your current one? Will you read the rest of this book without delay? Will you hang out with your kids, your spouse, or your parents? Whatever it is, my guess is that a sabbatical from the news, while engaging in alternate activities, will function like a cognitive "cleanse." It will allow you to escape the drag of negativity and move forward in a positive direction.

WORK ON STRENGTHS, NOT WEAKNESSES

Your inner villain also thrives when you focus your time and effort on things at which you're not good. No doubt, throughout your life you were taught to work on your weaknesses, to try to improve your skills and abilities in areas where you did not thrive.

Hands down, that may be the biggest lie we've ever been told. At the end of the day, all this does is rob you of your confidence. This belief may sound crazy when you first read it, since from a young age onward, you've probably been told, "You're not good at calculus, so go do more calculus. You're not good at history, go study more history." By focusing on your weaknesses, though, you end up feeling inferior subconsciously. Just as troubling, this focus encourages you to ignore your exceptional capabilities and strengths.

So though you may not agree with me yet, I hope you'll soon say, "The heck with my weaknesses. I'm going to get amazing at what I'm already good at!"

This misconception about improving weaknesses is practiced by many people, including educators, parents, managers, and other authority figures. It's a well-intentioned but misplaced idea that almost held me back from going after the life that I always dreamed of. I was in serious danger of living a complacent life I loathed.

According to society's rules, I wasn't supposed to become a success. I barely got out of high school, I was in special education until 10th grade, I had no money, I didn't have a mentor, I didn't know anybody rich, and I sure as heck wasn't wise enough to read books on success like you are today. And one of the things that almost sentenced me to a life of self-doubt and mediocrity was being told to work on my weaknesses.

About 10 years ago I wrote my first book, entitled *Totally Fulfilled*. When I first decided to write it, the only reason I did so was because I wanted to share my passion for helping others. As you may have figured out, I write books exactly the way I talk. A lot of times they're not perfect as far as grammar and structure, and I tend to digress, but they deliver the message and lessons I want to share fast and compellingly. I've learned that I have the ability to deliver simple yet effective strategies, sparking people to action so they can transform or even transcend their circumstances. But no, I definitely am not an English major.

As I sat down to write my first book, all these thoughts about my lack of writing skills started to fill my mind. I began to think things like, "You barely graduated high school, there is no way you can really write a book." Or I would tell myself, "Your ADD won't allow you to focus that long; it's impossible." But what made me move forward was my conviction that I had a message to deliver to the world. So I wrote my first book. Not without some difficulties and episodes of self-doubt, but I got through it. When I was done, I knew it would need an editor to go through it and clean up some of the mess that I was sure I had created through my lack of formal grammar and writing skills. So I found someone I was told was one of the best editors in the country, and I took a plane to meet her. We had a nice meeting, and I explained my desires and my passions and the fact that I knew the manuscript needed some cleaning up. I left her with this task, and I couldn't have been more excited to get the manuscript back and get it published. However, two days later I got a call from her, and I remember to this day what she said: "Dean, this isn't a book. This is a two-hundred-page conversation. You don't need an editor; you need a complete rewrite."

I was devastated. I remember hanging up the phone and allowing disempowering thoughts from the past to flow back into my mind like some sort of dam had just broken. And the reason they came back so fast was because like many of you reading this, I had been taught to work on my weaknesses for most of my life. My subconscious tried to make me believe I was incompetent for thinking I could ignore my weaknesses. I immediately started thinking back to criticisms my teachers directed at me in school, and I reflected on them in such a negative way that I started saying to myself, "I should have better grammar, better spelling, understand how to punctuate, and do all the other things that good writers do! Who are you, Dean, to think you could write a book?" My negative, defeatist thoughts ran away with my mind, and my confidence was temporarily destroyed; my momentum disappeared. The villain grew stronger and stronger as I spent about 24 hours beating myself up for not taking the time to work on my weaknesses before I wrote the book.

Luckily for me, about 48 hours later my thoughts shifted, and I remember thinking, "Stop it! Look at the stories you're telling yourself! Are you kidding me? I may not be a trained writer, but I have a powerful message, and I need to share it with the world. I know my message can change people's lives. Who cares that I'm not perfect at grammar and my book sounds like a two-hundred-page conversation?" I called the editor back the next day and said, "I respect your opinion, but I don't need your services anymore. You're fired." Okay, I'm not sure if I said the words, "You're fired," but I like to remember it that way.

I soon found someone else to edit the book, and I sat them down and said, "Do me a favor: just make this readable, but leave my words as intact as you can. Don't rewrite my personality or my message—just edit the spelling and grammar. I don't want to try to sound like someone else because this book is me. This is who I am. People can take me or leave me, but I'm going to be me."

It was the first book I ever published and it became a *New York Times* bestseller in weeks. I'm truly honored and blessed to be able to write that, but at the end of the day, who cares about the *New York Times* bestseller status? Let's be honest. What I'm proudest of is that the message in that book changed many people's lives. What could be a better victory than that?

But what if I hadn't written it? What if, after my first editor called my book embarrassing, I said to myself, "Man, I have no business being an author! I should've worked on my weaknesses, but I didn't." My life as I know it today would be completely different! You surely would not be reading my sixth book! There are so many "what ifs" that pop into my head, but luckily I'll never know how many of them would have come to pass because I didn't give in to working on my weaknesses. I let myself focus on the lives I was going to change with my message.

What opportunities have you passed up through the years because you questioned yourself based solely on flaws you think you have or others told you that you have? As you think about that question, also think about this truth: Working on your strengths will help you overcome anything that you consider a weakness.

EVERYONE IS GOOD AT SOMETHING

A dear friend of mine, Ned Hallowell, is one of America's leading doctors and an expert on the topic of ADD. Ned is someone you may have seen on *Dr. Phil* or on *The Oprah Winfrey Show* numerous times. Oprah, in fact, calls him the world's number one ADD doctor. He's Harvard trained and a Harvard professor as well. One day I was having lunch with Ned, and because I grew up assuming I had a form of ADD, I asked, "Ned, what exactly is ADD?" He described it in simple terms, translating his vast store of knowledge into language I could understand.

He said, "What people don't realize is that ADD is a blessing. Having it is like having a Ferrari engine, but unfortunately, you have bicycle brakes. You have all this gas and the fastest engine, but you just don't know how to slow down. I just teach kids and adults how to control the brakes. And when I do, they go faster than anybody else."

I then asked, "How do you have so much success curing kids, curing adults, and in many cases, taking them off medication?"

He said, "Let me give you an example. When a kid has ADD, and he is sitting in class trying to read a book, and his foot is tapping on the ground and his focus is drifting, the truth is he probably really doesn't want to read that book. To anyone with ADD, trying to read a book of little to no interest is harder than it is for other kids. And most times the teacher who wants what's best for the student thinks to herself, 'Johnny is going to sit in that chair and not get up until that book is finished. I'm going to teach him how to sit still and read like the rest of the kids.' And when the teacher makes him sit in that chair to the point where he can't handle it anymore, Johnny finally gets up and runs around the classroom or walks into the hall or just gets up and does anything but read that book. Now, not only does he have ADD, he also has ADHD. It's unfortunately a self-fulfilling diagnosis.

"What I do is I go and find out what Johnny is good at. Whether it's art, baseball, math, science, or whatever it is. Everyone is good at something, if not multiple things, so we dig for it and find it. We get his teachers, friends, and his parents involved, and together we help Johnny take what he's good at and help him become great at it. When he becomes great at that one thing, his confidence goes through the roof, and it trickles down to all areas of his life. All of a sudden you fast-forward a couple of months and Johnny is in that same classroom reading the book because he wants to."

Can you relate to this in any way? Have you been holding on to a weakness? Have you been letting it somehow define you, diminish your true value, or make you feel inferior? If so, can you see how it fuels this inner success-robbing villain? And can you see why it has to stop today?

I went through school struggling like the hypothetical kid in Dr. Hallowell's example. No one in my early years of school saw all the things I could do well and the talents I had. They only saw what I couldn't do and what I was bad at. I was shy and insecure, and truly felt stupid regularly because of it. Yet what they didn't realize at the time, and I'm not sure I did either, was that I possessed an amazing capacity for visual and audible learning. I could watch somebody drive a bulldozer for 15 minutes and jump on and drive it like a pro. I could watch people on stage and be able to emulate them with ease. Through these two senses, I was able to absorb knowledge and skills that took other people years to acquire. I was able to start things fast and get them accomplished fast, but I was told to work on my weaknesses so many times growing up that it almost crippled my learning ability and career.

Many adults inadvertently strip kids of their confidence and their abilities because of this insistence on addressing weaknesses. The truth is that when we're taught to work on the things we suck at, it makes us struggle constantly and it diminishes our belief in ourselves.

There is only one way for us to say, "heck no," to working on our weaknesses and to make sure this doesn't cripple our success like it does for millions of people around the world. And that's to do the complete opposite of what most people suggest when it comes to weaknesses and instead say, "Forget about it!"

GET AMAZING AT WHAT YOU'RE ALREADY GOOD AT

You're good at something. Heck, I bet you are good, if not great, at a lot of things. Take a moment right now, stop reading, and write down a list of what you do well. (You can find this "Get Amazing" form at www.thebetterlife.com under the "Book Resources" tab.) Are you good at communicating? Are you good at selling? Are you good at just being honest? Are you good at being a friend? Are you good at being a listener? Are you good at organization and structure? Are you good at developing systems or programming computers? Because here's what I know: You possess gifts, your unique abilities. There's no real explanation as to why you're good at some things—you just are. And your success depends on making it a habit to focus on improving what you're already good at to the point of greatness.

Because when we are told to work on the things that we naturally don't do well, we focus on this little 10 percent bucket of things we suck at and ignore the other 90 percent. And out of that 90 percent there is undoubtedly something at which you excel. Remember the story of the two wolves? About how the wolf that you feed is the wolf that wins? If you put energy and effort into the things you stink at, it's inevitable you'll lose your confidence and your momentum toward success. If you put energy and focus into the things that you're good at and become great at them, you can eventually pay for someone else to do the things you are not good at. This one strategy will help improve more than just your bank account. It will improve every area of your life.

So create your "good at" list and then, next to each entry, write down how you can improve those skills and enhance those abilities to become great at them. As you do this exercise, don't even think about your weaknesses. You're soon going to realize that if you can spend all of your focus, energy, time, and effort on the things you're good at, you can overcome all the other things at which you're not so talented. Becoming exceptionally good at one key skill is far more valuable than struggling for years and years to become average at the things that you find difficult. If you want financial success, if you want to build real wealth, make it a habit to focus on the things you do well.

To cement this thought process and success habit into your life, here's a story I think you'll appreciate. A few years back I was doing a small round-table mastermind, and there was a great guy in the group named Tom. I taught Tom real estate investing skills to help him diversify his portfolio and create long-term wealth. He was in his 60s, recently retired, and at the time of this session, he had done four real estate deals. From memory, Tom told me he had averaged roughly $15,000 profit on each deal, which is absolutely great! Tom was one of a dozen people at the table, and I remember going around the room and asking each person, "What's holding you back from that next level? What's the biggest obstacle in your way of going faster and doing more?" And then I asked these questions of Tom.

He answered, "Dean, I have to tell you, I'm so unorganized and sloppy, you have no idea. I can clean my car, and a week later it's a disaster. My home office has invoices and papers and clutter all over the place. I'm just so sloppy! Here's what I'm going to do. I'm not doing another real estate deal until I go to OfficeMax and get a filing cabinet and a filing system. I'm going to label everything, and I'm going to create a system to be organized."

When he finished, I asked, "Are you done, Tom?"

He said, "Yep, that's it."

Then I responded with this: "Let me just be frank with you, Tom. It's too late—you're going to be sloppy and disorganized 'til the day you die, and who cares?" He was shocked that I had dismissed his admitted weakness. He sat in motionless silence. I think the others may have thought I was being rude. But after a few moments passed so slowly they seemed like hours, I watched a thousand pounds and 60 years fall from Tom's shoulders. For a second I thought he was going to break down and cry. I said, "Tom, not that long ago you had never done real estate in your life. You had a completely different job, and now you've done four deals. You're amazing at finding a deal other people can't, getting it rehabbed, and getting it sold for a profit. Go spend all your time getting even better at that. Who cares that you're not that organized? What if you did one extra deal a year and then paid somebody part-time to organize for you? You'd never have to worry about being disorganized ever again."

Tom remained silent, the hamster wheel spinning in his head. I think he most likely was reminiscing about a teacher, a parent, or maybe a spouse saying, "You're sloppy. You better learn to get organized!" He had all those years of bad advice sitting there, and then I watched them just melt away as he shifted his focus from weakness to strength.

And you can do exactly the same thing. What weaknesses are holding you back? What have people told you that you need to work on? What false beliefs do you have about yourself because of a so-called weakness? For the next level of success in your life, answer these questions, make going from good to great your success habit, and plunge a dagger through the inner villain's heart (not a fatal blow, perhaps, but one that does the villain some serious damage).

THE COST OF BAD ADVICE

So what is the costliest advice in the entire world? Yes, of course: bad advice. Let me ask you this: Have you ever had an invention, a thought, an idea, or a creation that you thought could change the world and make you money? Then you told a family member, or a friend, or even a loved one, and they gave you every reason why they thought it wouldn't work.

Maybe they said things along the lines of, "Inventions take money and you don't have enough. It's probably been thought of already. You'll have to get a patent and you don't have time for that. Oh, you want to get it on TV? Well, it's too much money to be on TV; it will never work." And maybe their advice swayed you enough to make you ignore your idea. Then, some years later, you see your original concept changing the world and making someone else wealthy. Well, what robbed you of that experience? What robbed your life of that invention or opportunity being yours and those experiences being yours? Nothing more than bad advice. You see, we so often get advice from our single friends telling us what to do about our relationships. We get pounded with advice from our broke friends on how we should make money. This is truly why bad advice is the most costly advice in the world—because we are learning from the wrong people. Would you learn how to sing opera from Jimmy Hendrix or how to throw a football from LeBron James? Of course not, because they are not the right people to listen to in those specific instances!

At the end of the day, bad advice feeds that inner villain and just as troubling, encourages us to "play it safe." By safe I mean it stops us from taking the actions and calculated risks that can help us evolve to the level of life we desire. And this dream-stealing advice comes at us nonstop. What's even worse is that friends and family wrap it with a bow of love.

It's Mom and Dad thinking they're protecting you from failing. It's your spouse afraid that change may negatively impact your relationship. It's a coworker who thinks you might get ahead of him, or a boss who's afraid of your power. It's a friend who was burned by a relationship so badly that she wants to protect you from that same pain. It's a relative who experienced bankruptcy and wants to save you from starting your own business and falling as hard as he did. In some cases, people may sabotage you maliciously, but most people genuinely feel they are protecting you or saving you when, in fact, they are feeding the villain, creating doubt, lowering your confidence, and keeping you at status quo.

So we must make it a habit to be consciously aware of the bad advice that is flowing at us 24 hours a day, 7 days a week, and create a filter that doesn't allow it to get in. When someone is spewing their bad advice to us, we can force a smile, but we need to shove that advice into our inner trash can immediately. I have no doubt that bad advice has created pain in your life or cost you dearly, as it has me. So don't worry—you are not alone. But it's time to stop that negative flow and become bulletproof to it in the future!

Here's a cautionary tale about bad advice, albeit one that is also humorous. A handful of years ago, during a book tour, I found myself having a conversation with a group of students about why they had not yet reached the level of success they desired.

As each person shared his or her thoughts, I started to spot the similarities in their stories. It wasn't lack of knowledge, experience, or money that was holding them back. Rather, each and every one of them had a basket of bad advice delivered by someone, and it had robbed them of the courage to take action. They'd heard it from husbands and wives, parents and coworkers, and it had killed their momentum.

So after I left this group of people, I jumped on a plane and flew back to my office in Phoenix, Arizona. As soon as I landed I called my team and said, "Guys, go ahead and set up the studio.

I want to film an infomercial for my new book, and I don't want to wait because I'm fired up right now."

I have to admit, I was aggravated that all these people were robbing my students of their next level of freedom with often well-intentioned but destructive suggestions. So I got to my studio, threw on a sports jacket and a tie (still wearing my gym shorts and sneakers, which were hidden by the desk I sat behind), and we started filming. From there, I proceeded to do my first ever direct-to-camera infomercial, which means no host, no announcers, no fancy graphics, just me talking to the camera for half an hour and offering my book to viewers a few times throughout the show.

But I did the show with pure passion, no notes, and no script. I wanted nothing more than to serve and help people. And what was on my mind? The bad advice that was robbing my students of their confidence, happiness, and ability to go to that next level. So as I was recording the show, I found myself saying something I hadn't planned to say, but it just emerged in the moment! I looked at the camera and said, "I really want you all to listen. You can't ever take advice from people who have failed at what you want to accomplish. You may think you can learn from their mistakes, but in most cases you simply can't! They only know how to do it wrong, and they'll put the wrong spin on any advice they give you. For example, my parents have been married nine times between them. I love them dearly, and they're both in amazing relationships right now, but as I was growing up, marriage wasn't something either one of them was great at. If I want advice on relationships and marriage, I'm going to find a couple who's been married for 30 or 50 years—who has intimacy, passion, and love for each other. Not from someone who's been in and out of relationships their whole life." And I meant what I said because it was the truth. And I want to stress again, I love my parents dearly, and I'm not trying to make light of the many hard times they must have experienced, but the truth is that taking advice from them about marriage would be like asking Bernie Madoff for a lesson on ethics.

But here's the kicker! After I filmed the show, I completely forgot my spur of the moment reference to my parents. The show ended up being the most successful infomercial I'd ever filmed, and it aired on national TV day after day after day for over a year. And about three months after it aired, my mom called me. I picked up the phone, and all she said was, "Really?"

I said, "What's up, Mom?"

"Really?" she said again. "You had to tell the whole country that your mom was married five times? Most of our family doesn't even know that!" She made the remark with a chuckle in her voice—she saw the humor in the situation, fortunately.

And of course I apologized and then explained to her that I had been in the moment and not reading a script. But during our phone conversation, we discussed the bad advice she had gotten in her life and how costly it was to her. And even better, two days later I bought my mom a new car as an apology.

Take the time to filter all the advice that comes your way and see if the person sharing it is qualified. If you want advice on how to play tennis, get advice from someone who is a pro, or who knows how to train pros, not from your great-aunt Edna who has never played but watches tennis matches on television religiously.

At www.thebetterlife.com, under the "Book Resources" tab, you can get your bad advice cheat sheet. On it you can write down all the bad advice that you've gotten over the years, the ill-conceived warnings and instructions, and the ones that have cost you the most. Write down what they cost you. When you see these formal descriptions of bad advice you've received, you'll understand that you no longer can allow someone's unqualified advice to steer the direction of your life. Create this new habit of ignoring bad advice and getting good advice from qualified people. Diminish your internal villain and gain a new level of confidence.

DOING WHAT THEY DO

As children we're taught to stand in line and do what everybody else does. We're taught to get good grades, follow the crowds, do what's popular at the time, go to high school, get into a college, then find a job, start a 401(k), save our money, and hopefully retire with enough to get us to death without running out. We're taught to paint inside the lines because when we step outside the lines, everybody looks at us funny.

Given this conventional path, let me ask you a question: In high school or college did you have a passion or a dream of what you wanted your life to look like? If you're like most people, you graduated and threw your cap in the air and thought the world was going to be yours.

Here is the craziest part about this scenario: In so many cases, if you followed your passions and they didn't align with friends', society's, or your parents' vision for you, then people would put their arm around you and say, "Hey, isn't it time to grow up? Isn't it time to get responsible?" We've somehow created this world where we think being responsible is doing what everybody else does, and we force ourselves into something that makes everybody else happy but doesn't feed our soul.

Parents and friends don't mean to hurt you; they think they are protecting you. No doubt, they have a lot of influence and can cause you to do what's conventional or expected. When you give up on your dream and settle for less, these influential individuals will express their pride in your grown-up attitude.

Really? I'm forsaking my dreams and becoming an unhappy conformist and you're happy for me! As crazy as it sounds, it happens every day, and maybe it has happened to you. I don't mean this disrespectfully in any way. But so many of you took a job years ago as just a "temporary" thing. And now you're just coasting through life stuck in your routine. And if that were satisfactory, you wouldn't be seeking more. That's okay, though, because no matter what your story was, you're reading this book right now. You're here at this moment for a reason, and hopefully, this sparks something in you regardless of your situation. You know what you like and what you don't like. You know what makes you light up and what dims your light. So it's time to stop following the crowd and follow your own heart.

When you follow the same path everybody else is on, you get where everybody else has been. I'm giving you permission to forget all the guidelines, forget all the rules that other people have put on you, and forget what society has told you is right or wrong. Be yourself and do what makes you happy. I'm not telling you to go out tomorrow and quit whatever it is that you do. What I am saying is, start realizing your true worth and know that you can evolve in the direction you choose.

What made America great were forward-thinking, visionary entrepreneurs that didn't conform. They thought outside the box. And what's going to keep this country or any country thriving is people just like you, willing to follow their hearts, tap into their full potential, and make a difference. You have the courage to find your own way. Successful people live by a different set of rules and success habits and they don't conform or accept mediocrity.

So what changes would you make today, if you didn't care what anybody else thought? If you actually listened to your heart, your dreams, and your desires, what direction would your feet be heading? Think through what makes your heart smile and write it down. To make a change in any area of your life, you must start with a first step. Saying it out loud or writing it down can be that step, right here, right now. Confidence builds and doubt dies when your heart is aligned with your actions.

Because starting to change is difficult, here's an exercise designed to provide you with some momentum. Draw a vertical line down the center of a piece of paper. On the left side write, "Things I am no longer willing to accept in my life." On the right side, write, "Things that are now musts in my life." Let the answers to those two questions flow from your heart, from your soul—don't try to answer based on how you think you should respond. Dig deep and answer with complete honesty. When done, circle the top two or three items on each side. In most cases, you'll notice the contrast. You'll be struck by the gap between what is unacceptable and what is necessary. To bridge the gap, you'll be motivated to change—motivated from your heart as well as your brain.

AN OUTER REFLECTION OF THE INNER YOU

There are literally thousands of external inputs that we are exposed to every single day that impact us. Whether they feed the inner villain or empower us, they come at us nonstop. From a teacher's instructions to a parent's advice to a news report, the barrage of messages is constant and unrelenting. It doesn't matter where your inner villain derives its energy, the impact can last a lifetime; you lose so much confidence that you stay right where you are, or life gets even worse. So pay attention to the external factors you need to protect yourself from, or adjust the way you receive them, because eventually they start running you. I'm talking about not just the decisions you make, but also the ways you walk, talk, and sit. Let me explain through a story how the inputs from the outside world can affect us physically.

Imagine you're at a café with outdoor seating and across the courtyard there are two people sitting at different tables. One is an unsmiling man with poor posture. The server comes by, and says, "Can I help you with anything?" He mumbles in a barely audible voice, "No, thanks."

What kind of person would you assume he is? How do you think he does at work? Is he the boss or a low-level employee? What kind of father do you think that person is? What kind of lover? How much passion for life does he have? How much joy? Does he like his job? Does he make a lot of money, or is he struggling to get by? Just based on that quick snapshot description I gave you, you'd probably conclude that the guy slumped over at the café is struggling in life. His posture, gestures, and appearance are giving off the vibe of complacency at best and depression at worst.

So, let's look at the other person sitting a few tables away. This guy is sitting up straight, and he's smiling. When the server approaches, carrying his lunch, this guy says, "Oh, that looks good, thank you." He notices the waitress's name tag and says, "Thank you, Jessica." What would you assume about this guy? Think about his enthusiasm on display. I'm not talking cheesy salesman-type charm, but secure and confident friendliness. More than that, he seems comfortable in his own skin. How do you think he does at work? Is he the boss or a low-level employee? What kind of father do you think that person is? How much passion for life does he have? How much joy? Does he like what he does for a living? Does he make a lot of money, or is he struggling to get by?

I'm sure you sense the difference between these two men. That's because your subconscious is much more powerful than your conscious mind, and it's constantly working in the background. Your subconscious is like a hard drive into which you feed data throughout your life. When you have a gut feeling, that is your subconscious speaking to you. In the case of these two men at the café, your gut is saying, "I can identify these two men in half a second. I've been pulling in this data for years about people, and that first guy is probably depressed, or lazy, or beat down, and he's probably not getting much done in his life. The other guy, however, is most likely a go-getter, full of high energy—enthusiastic and a winner." This isn't "judging a book by its cover." This is just listening to your subconscious.

So given your intuitive, subconscious judgment, how important do you think your outer appearance is to your success and happiness? Extremely! Did the inner villain get to the first man so badly that it's now showing from the inside out, or has the outside appearance reflected back to him so much that it's actually feeding his self-doubt? It's a chicken-or-egg question; it really doesn't matter. What matters is the effect, and that effect is bad. Is that person you see with his shoulders down, a frown on his face, and his eyes staring at his shoes the person who's looking back at you in the mirror? If so, you've got a villain inside trying to convince you that you're not worthy. You've turned that villain's accusation into a self-fulfilling prophecy by the way you carry yourself.

Spend the next few days observing yourself and other people. Pay attention to how you carry yourself and how others carry themselves. You will see all postures and styles, but your subconscious will clue you in to what you like and what repels you.

The point of this exercise isn't to be someone you're not. You may observe someone with swagger—who's strutting around like the king of the roost—but that may be so far from who you are, it would be silly to try to be that type. What I am talking about is taking the time to check how you're presenting yourself to the world. Check your physicality numerous times during the day and try to smile, stand, talk, and gesture in a manner that represents the best you.

If God walked into the room you were sitting in right now and said, "Pull up a chair and tell me something going on in your life," how would you sit? Would your shoulders be straight? Would your eyes be half shut or wide open? Would you be attentively listening or just waiting to talk? Create a role model in your mind (God is good, but anyone will do) and pretend they are always watching. Not only will these physical traits become a habit, they will create a by-product so much bigger than you think.

What do you think a smile is worth? Did you know there have been numerous studies done about the power of a smile? This absolutely blew my mind! Some day when you have time, try Googling "effects of a smile." I recently learned that when you smile, your brain says, "I thought we were stressed, but maybe we're not, because we're smiling." Stress literally goes down immediately when you show the pearly whites. Your subconscious is so powerful that it's able to tell your brain, "Hey, everybody, we're smiling! We must be happy!"

The science and the studies prove that if you smile more, you'll live longer, and it will actually lower your blood pressure. You'll make more and better friends, and it will actually improve your marriage. A doctor took a collection of high school photos and studied the people with the biggest smiles in the yearbooks compared to the people who took yearbook pictures with a serious look on their face. They then studied them 30 years later because they wanted to find out who was happier, who made more money, who had better relationships, and who lived longer. The people who smiled in the yearbook blew away by far the people who didn't smile in every category! Insane, right?

If a simple smile can do all that, what would life be like if you also stood up straight, held your head high and your shoulders back, and talked with energy and enthusiasm? What if you were a positive presence for the people you like to be around? Even if you're just faking it at first, soon you will become that person that people want to hang out with because you radiate positivity. When you become that person with a better outer appearance, you attract similar people into your life and you repel the people who could bring you down. Yes, this is a success habit that can allow you to attract abundance into your life, but it will also lift you up when you see yourself in a picture or the mirror. Don't take this success habit lightly. Don't let the outside factors we have discussed feed the villain and affect you physically. You are a bright light; don't let anything dim it.

CHOOSE YOUR WORDS

Have you ever thought about what people say to you or what you say to them? Have you ever considered how these utterances affect people's lives? Words can feed the inner villain or they can starve it. In this section I want to make you aware of their impact in a variety of ways. Without knowing it, we start attaching certain emotions to certain words in ways that alter our daily lives as the years pass by.

We know that if someone calls us stupid, lazy, ugly, fat, or hopeless, it can really hurt. But what's even worse is when we attach an emotion to each and every one of those words. As humans, we feel sadness, loneliness, anger, and many other emotions based on the words we hear. And let's face it, those emotion-packed words can stay with us for years. But do they have to? Remember the childhood saying "Sticks and stones may break my bones, but words can never hurt me"? Yeah we've all heard it, but it can be hard to live by. As I write this, my kids are seven and nine. The number one thing I try to teach them is that other people's words and actions can't affect you unless you let them. I've said this a lot throughout the book, but it's a question I'd have you ask yourself during every chapter and every day: Do you want to be a thermostat or thermometer? Do you want to suffer from hurtful words and allow them to create negative physical changes (tears, stress-induced illness, etc.), or do you want to decide to live in a more beautiful state where you don't care what other people say or do, because you create your own joy and passion?

You can absolutely choose to disempower the words that cause negative emotions. The words said a month ago, a year ago, or maybe 20 years ago—if they still bother you, then you are the one responsible for providing them with the power to hurt. You can take away the capacity of words to hurt you. Why not do so now?

Keep the concept of the inner villain in mind to motivate yourself. The more we allow those negative, emotion-laden words to hurt us, the more we give strength to the inner villain. As a result, our confidence goes down, self-doubt increases, and we start having a negative perception of the world. We can easily go from an abundance mind-set to a scarcity mind-set in an instant.

If you get sucked into a scarcity mind-set, it doesn't mean that you're a horribly negative person. But it does mean your state of mind was compromised. And when you're in a bad state, it's hard to be your best self.

Try this Tony Robbins exercise to take the power away from words that may have a strong negative effect on you. To get his audience to see the association people give a group of letters stringed together, Tony will say "bum" and tell the audience that is what his British friends say; that for them it's the same as when we say "butt." He pauses, then asks, "What if I said *ass*? Does that make anyone feel different or offend anyone?" He will also do that same word evolution with other private parts like penis or vagina. You can use your imagination to see the direction he takes those words. When he gets to the more colorful word that describes the same body part, you see people in the audience cringe or smile widely. Tony asks, "What's the difference? All the words I said mean exactly the same thing. You just associated a different meaning to them."

He is so right, and the audience immediately gets it. Tony uses what some people may think of as foul language, but I love this example because it conveys how people give certain words power they don't deserve. It's only the negative context that gives words their power. You gave them the power they possess, and you can take that power away.

Try writing some words that have tremendous power in your life. For instance: "sloppy work" or "I'm disappointed" or "do it again." It can be any word or group of words. Your assignment is to think about why these words have so much power in your life, and then recognize that you've given them the power to create crippling anxiety and other negative emotions. Recognize that they are just words and that they're no more powerful than you allow them to be.

Now let's switch from the negative effect of words spoken to us to the power of the words we use daily. Think about what happens when you say to someone, "I'm so stressed and overwhelmed." Once you start using these words it triggers the spoken emotions. Even if you weren't stressed, now you are, because you are telling your subconscious that you are. Everyone has a trigger word or 10 or 20!

Think about when you get a phone call that doesn't go well, and afterward you say, "I'm pissed!" What happens after that? You walk around pissed off! You say, "I can't handle this," and pretty soon you've locked in those emotions and you're stuck with them all day. Each of us has different words that are strong triggers that lock in negative emotions in our life. What are yours? Right now is a perfect time to stop reading and write down what trigger words you sometimes say that put you in a negative state. (You can find an easy "Trigger Words" cheat sheet at www.thebetterlife.com under

"Book Resources.") I know for me, when I say to myself, "I'm overwhelmed!" it starts to intensify the feeling. I've learned to change those words and their meanings in time, and I'll share my easy-to-implement technique.

Before I share it, though, consider the subtle ways in which our bodies reflect our words. I have a friend who, when asked how he is doing, his shoulders slump immediately and he always says, "I'm doing okay." His body mirrors his words—he looks okay but certainly not good or great. I have another friend who always says, "I'm so damn busy," but he says it even on weekends when he isn't busy at all, and immediately I can see him tense up. Contrast their physical reactions to Joel Weldon. Joel is someone I met in recent years, and every time I see him and ask how he is doing, he always says, "Fantastic!" Joel is in his mid-70s, and I watch him perk up every time he says, "Fantastic!" It makes him look vital, engaged, and intensely alive! His eyes light up, and he looks 25 again! He programmed himself to feel good when he says those words, and consciously or not, he is becoming fantastic as soon as he says it. "Fantastic" is Joel's trigger word, and while trigger words are a good thing, having the right trigger words is a must!

So write your trigger words. And as you write them, describe the emotions each word brings out in you. If your trigger word is "stressed," it could cause all sorts of different feelings besides a sense of being overwhelmed; you might also experience fear, loneliness, self-pity, and so on.

Here is the cool part about bringing those words out in the open. You can flip them. Earlier we talked about our appearance—shoulders back, big smile, and eyebrows up. Doing those things alone can make a big difference in your life. Your days will be better with just those minor physical adjustments. But what if you also took all those negative trigger words out of your vocabulary? What if, instead of saying, "I'm overwhelmed," you say, "I'm busy because I'm blessed with opportunities." Make it a success habit to catch yourself and the negative word or statements before you say them. Take a moment and use a new word that doesn't spark those negative feelings.

And if you slip like we all do, then just readjust and restate. For instance, if you find yourself saying, "I'm overwhelmed today," you can stop yourself and say, "Wait! Nope, let me rephrase that: I'm blessed with opportunity, and I'm learning a ton." Replace the negative triggers with positive words that won't strengthen that inner villain, but rather engage and enlarge your inner hero!

WHO'S IN YOUR INNER CIRCLE?

Who are the people who surround you? Who do you spend the most time with? Who is in your inner circle? You probably know where this is going, but go there with me. We all know how impactful the people closest to us are. Some rob us of confidence while others empower us, right? And you may think, *I know I have negative friends, but I don't let it bother me.* I'd have to disagree there. Every industry mogul, life transformer, and world-changer I've ever met has said pretty much the same thing about their inner circles: "With whom you surround yourself is who you become."

If you have three negative friends and three positive friends, your outlook will end up somewhere in the middle. If all your friends are coasting through life and barely scraping by financially, then it's going to be hard for you to break out of your financial rut on your own. If you have a spouse who is negative every single day while you're trying to be positive, you will both land somewhere in the middle. Now, I'm not saying go get a divorce. Please don't take that the wrong way. Maybe you could read this book to your partner or share its lessons with the people closest to you. Keep reading for another way to deal with this situation.

You see, there are two types of people in this world and in your life. There are battery chargers, and there are battery drainers. I got this concept from my good friend, Joe Polish. We were having lunch one day, and he said to me, "Just so you know, Dean, if you're around somebody and within a few minutes you just start to feel amazing and you're not sure why, it's because that person is a battery charger. The more time you spend with that person, the more energy you have, the more you think you can accomplish in life, and more and more you start to pick up on their positive success habits. In contrast, you can be around someone else for a few minutes and feel drained. That person is a battery drainer that is sucking away your positive energy! And soon enough you're picking up their bad habits and negative attitudes and adding them to your own life."

Before talking with Joe, I had my own definition of the people I should surround myself with, but Joe's labels of charger and drainer were perfect, and I adopted them.

When it comes to strangers and first encounters, create the habit of identifying quickly if they're chargers or drainers. For example, ask someone, "How's your day going?" You'll be able to tell a lot from their response. If they say, "It's great, fantastic, or good," that is a quick sign they are a battery charger who you want to strike up a conversation with and get to know. Pay attention to how they act, the habits they have, and even their work ethic. On the other hand, if a person responds, "Having another rough day, man. I can't wait for this week to be over," you may want to just nod and walk the other way. Your energy is too valuable to have it drained away by someone else.

Keep that in mind when someone asks you the same question: "Hey, Dean, how are you doing?" Why not make it a habit like Joel did, and learn to say, "Fantastic!" or "Never been better," or something close to that? It's truly a subtle but powerful success habit.

This law of human nature is very simple: If you want financial success, you must surround yourself with financially successful people. If you want to be an entrepreneur and start your own company, socialize with other entrepreneurs and other people who have started their own companies. Want to be in better shape? You get the idea.

How do you develop your inner circle? You must make it a habit to expand your social circle and deliberately include successful, career-oriented people and business owners. Maybe you are saying, "I don't have any successful friends." That is the case more often than not, so start one step at a time. Read a lot of books about success or listen to podcasts and audiobooks while you work out. Go where successful people are likely to be, like meet-up groups and masterminds. You can start with the success habits 30-day challenge at www.thebetterlife.com.

I mentioned this earlier: you don't have to push negative people out of your life. They will, however, in many cases, drop by the wayside as you evolve. Because once you start changing your physical demeanor and you start changing the words that come out of your mouth, those people may be inspired to follow your example; or they may self-select and drop out of your social circle all on their own.

And yes, I know that in certain cases you have someone very close to you that is negative, and you can't push him away or you don't want him to fade away. Unfortunately, you can't teach someone to be positive or point out their negativity—you can't just talk people out of their bad habits. Instead, you need to model the way you hope they will begin to act. You can brighten the room so much that they can't dim your glow and instead, they are motivated to get brighter with you. You have the strength to change the select few people that you want to take with you on this journey to becoming your best self. Be a light in their lives and even the most negative people can change for the better.

As simple as some of the preceding success habits may seem, their impact is undeniable. Success isn't luck, and it isn't magic; it's a series of habits that those who have thwarted their inner villain know to be true. The fact is, they work.

And remember, as is true with anything new and significant, there's a lot to remember and integrate into your life. With that being said, remember what I shared earlier: It's not about adding more things to your already busy life, but replacing things slowly and subtly. What you're doing is taking out the negative habits—like watching negative news reports—and replacing them with habits that serve you better and help propel you forward with no extra time needed. You just have to switch out a few bad habits with these new empowering success habits. Same amount of time, totally different results.

Speaking of time, I am grateful that you are spending this time with me. I know how busy life can get and that you have a lot of choices. And for you to come this far, I know that you are someone who is serious about wanting more and not just someone who wants overnight riches by luck or a shortcut. If you can find the time to read this, you can find the time to start incorporating these success habits into your life. If this book helps light the fuse to rocket your life to that next level, then I'm doing my job. No one is holding your hand or making you read this. You have the desire and interest to know what the next level of life is for you, and your actions will carry you there. I urge you to finish the entire book. You deserve all the advantages you can get your hands on, and I have many more great ones on the way.

Next, we are going to get to the critical success habit of understanding your "story." Now that you understand the villain within and what gives it power—your physical appearance, the words you use, or the people you surround yourself with—you can put all those negative thoughts and habits into a bucket and shake them up. What comes out is the story you tell yourself. Your story is your internal narrative, and it can be the heaviest anchor in your life, holding you back from experiencing the joy of using your full potential—or it can drive you to achieve massive success, wealth, and abundance.

Chapter 4

THE POWER OF YOUR STORY

"If we didn't have the struggles that we have had, the challenges, and the pushes, we would never develop our character. Our character is coming from those times when we didn't believe we could do it, but we did it anyway, and we fought our way through. In that struggle, we developed our character and our strength."

— Brendon Burchard, interview with Dean Graziosi

Each and every one of us has a story—or many stories—that has shaped our lives. At its core, your story is where you live, emotionally, mentally, and sometimes even physically. Your story can either be the wind behind your sails or the anchor that is weighing you down.

Our inner villain tells us the stories that hold us back. If you'll recall the ways in which that villain sabotages us, you'll understand that he does so by telling us those stories again and again—stories that we believe are fact, even when they're nothing of the sort. What we need to do is figure out what stories we should be telling ourselves—the ones aligned with the new vision we have for our lives, the ones that enable us to leave our old story in the past.

The habit of aligning your story with your vision takes a little work. But aren't your wealth, happiness, and future success worth a little effort now for a better tomorrow? Of course they are. So get engaged, roll up your sleeves, and let's do the work together. In this chapter we're going to uncover the story or stories that you tell yourself and how even the seemingly harmless ones may be holding you back and limiting your full potential. And our first step is to understand why you tell yourself and other people certain stories. Once you gain this understanding, you'll learn how to switch that story from a limiting, disempowering one that's robbing you of your confidence to one that can take you to the moon and beyond.

GENA'S STORY

One of my students, Gena, is an amazing lady who eventually became a dear friend. When I met Gena, she had a very specific story she told herself about who she was at that point in her life and who she believed she could be at some point in the future. But before telling her "story," let me give you some background about who Gena used to be.

She was a stay-at-home mom, and an amazing one at that. While her husband worked hard outside the house at his job, Gena ran the household and managed the family with great diligence: organizing, scheduling, taking care of her husband, Nick, giving piano lessons to make some extra money when she could, and basically being supermom. And Gena enjoyed this role immensely. In the back of her mind, she sometimes thought that she had deferred her dreams and goals in order to make sure her family was solid and secure. We all question our choices at times. But for all intents and purposes, Gena was happy with her chosen role. What would eventually make her unhappy, though, was the inner villain who used this lifestyle choice to create a story in Gena's mind that would become debilitating and cause her to question everything.

A big shift occurred when, one by one, Gena's kids started going off to college and finding their independence. One daughter married a great guy, and Gena was blissfully happy over this event, as well as her other children's accomplishments. Simultaneously, however, her inner villain created a much different story and a negative emotional state. And when her husband, Nick, came to her and said, "We need to make some extra money to handle the escalating costs of college and our daughters' weddings," Gena's old "story" gained power. This old story went something like this:

At 60 years old I have done what I was put on this earth to do and was the best wife and mother I could be. I supported my family at every turn. But now that job has come to an end. Now I'm old, lonely, and with nothing of significance to do anymore. As my friends say, this is the time in life to wind down, to cherish the past, and to spend less so we can make it through until the end. I have no special skills, so hopefully I can make some extra money teaching more piano lessons, or maybe by being a greeter at the local department store. This is a youth-based society and there is no way an older woman like me could do anything of significance. Well, at least I did a great job as a mom.

This story isn't that bad, is it? Actually, it's worse than bad—it's horrific! This story made her feel depressed, that she had no worth, and that her best days were behind her.

Even though it was fiction, she told it to herself so often that it started to become her reality. She said it so many times subconsciously that she actually believed it as fact—a common reaction. The emotions that result from the stories we tell ourselves every day create the life we are going to live.

It's impossible to boil down what I want to convey into one statement, but if anything comes close, this is it: Your emotions, your thoughts, and your "story" are your life. It is who we are at any moment, and we project those three things into everything we do. In Gena's life, she was projecting, "I'm an old lady now, and I just can't do much. Maybe this is the down part of my life, and I'll just settle in." And that was the life she was living until I helped create a pattern disruption. She started reading one of my books, and, slowly but surely, she exposed her story as a lie.

When Gena learned about her internal villain and how it shaped the story she heard in her head, she was motivated to defeat the villain. She treated this villain as an actual foe rather than just a symbol of her stagnation. The more she learned about the villain and how it functions, the more motivated she was to stop its harmful storytelling. Gena recognized that if she changed her story, she could change her present and her future.

And that's exactly what she did! Gena began telling herself a brand-new story, one that totally transformed her life, her family, and the future in front of her.

I am a strong, young 63-year-old who has discovered the next phase of my life. I'm vibrant, beautiful. There is nothing anyone at any age can do that I can't do. Age doesn't limit us; it empowers us to use the wisdom we have gathered to be and act smarter and faster. Nothing can stop me from the joy, happiness, wealth, and abundance that I desire. God gave me so many amazing gifts, and I intend to use them all.

Wow. A little different from the woman thinking her best days were behind her and it was time to curl up, get old, and fade away. Gena's new story launched her on a new path, and here is what she has accomplished in the five years since she changed her story and her habits:

- Started her own business that's making more than enough for her perfect life—and her husband doesn't need to work anymore
- Traveled to over 25 cities in America and multiple other countries
- Spoke to a variety of audiences about her transformation
- Co-authored a book about her experiences
- Bought a dream home overlooking the bay in Seattle
- Paid for all her kids' college educations
- Used her profits to pay for incredible family vacations

- Lost weight
- Got in the best shape of her life
- Convinced her son to quit his energy-draining job in corporate America and work in her new business
- Loves to drink great wine, eat wonderful food, and cherish her relationship with God on a new level
- Crossed off almost everything on her bucket list
- Smiles more than any other person I know
- Inspired her children as they watched her go for what she wanted and achieved it (Gena noted that this may have been her greatest accomplishment.)

Okay, think about this for just a moment. Gena's new reality didn't emerge because of some change in the outside world. She didn't hit the lotto or inherit money; she didn't get lucky and run into someone at a party who gave her a great job. What changed were her habits and eventually her story. She became the thermostat of her life rather than the thermometer. If you're not motivated to change your story by how Gena changed hers, then you're really dug deep into your old story.

And no, Gena wasn't broke or living in desperation or despair when she finally realized her story was holding her back. She was just living a life that was status quo, and she was being held back from her full "next level" potential. When she discovered that she didn't need anything from the outside world to achieve more, she started rewriting her story. It was only then that she achieved her dream of unshakeable peace and inner happiness. And the money was great, but it was only the icing on the cake.

Now you may be thinking, well maybe this worked for Gena, but what if I'm not as smart or as strong as Gena is? Well, if Gena were the only one who had ever experienced such a dramatic change, then maybe you should still have doubts. Gena isn't the exception but the rule, at least in my experience. I've worked with all types of students—a wide range of IQs, backgrounds, personalities, abilities—and they've all been able to do what Gena did. It actually doesn't matter where you are in your life right now. It doesn't matter if you already have a great job and family, or if you have wealth with no fulfillment, or you have fulfillment with no wealth. Regardless, there is a story you must stop telling yourself, or a story you must adjust, because it is preventing you from leading an optimal life in the areas that matter to you the most: Change your story, change your life.

I could stop at this point, leaving you inspired by Gena to change your story. But it might inspire you for a day or two and then your old story will drift back into place. You need to anchor this awareness and this change so it sticks with you for life. Together we will make this happen. I'm going to give you the tools to make that shift, to change that story you've been living with, to change your mental state, to develop millionaire success habits, and to build the confidence to go to another level in your finances and in all areas of your life. Now it's time to uncover any stories that could be holding you back.

UNCOVERING YOUR STORY

To flesh out the stories and flush out the self-limiting beliefs in your life, we must move some of them to the forefront of your mind. To do this, think about in which area of your life you want to experience the biggest breakthrough. Since you are reading this book, the odds are that making more money, starting or expanding your own business, or finding work you love represent breakthrough areas for you. So stop for a moment and ask yourself why these things you desire have not happened yet. Make sure you don't filter your responses; don't make excuses, offer rationalizations, or go into denial. Be honest and write the reasons you haven't achieved the breakthroughs you desire.

To facilitate this exercise, think about which of the following factors might be stopping you from breaking through:

- The economy
- Lack of time
- Your boss
- Your employees
- Your unsupportive spouse
- Your education
- Your lack of capital
- Your health
- Your relationships

Many other possibilities exist; I list these just to get you started thinking about what stands in the way of your dreams.

Focus on what comes to mind immediately when you think of why you haven't reached the point in life that you desire? What is the story you have in your head? In most cases, when you want growth in any of these areas but can't seem to find it, it means there is a story standing between you and your next level, kind of like a wall that you can break down (but only once you realize it is actually there).

Now think about the stories that popped into your head and complete the "Negative Story" exercise sheet at www.thebetter-life.com under the "Book Resources" tab. Can you see now how the factors from the previous chapter—the internal villain, the lack of a deeper why—fuel these limiting stories and make them real as heck in your subconscious? Consider, too, how your story became a part of you. Maybe the negative news reports you received daily supported your negative story? Maybe hearing that you need to work on your weaknesses helped create your story? Or maybe friends' bad advice anchored your negative story until it became your truth and your belief?

Did some stories come to mind? If they did, write them down.

If not, stop reading for a moment and think of what you are holding back. Perhaps you're resisting this exercise, telling yourself, "Well, I don't have a story; this is reality." If that's what you think, good; write down what you consider to be your reality. Remember Gena's "before" story or use the previous bulleted list to spark yours.

Now let's dig a little deeper and find the limiting beliefs that crafted this deeply imbedded story. Just so you know, these stories may have been with you for many years—they may stretch back to early childhood. The crazy part is that in most cases, the stories that disempower us have been instilled in us by the people we've encountered along life's journey. These stories create the excuses our subconscious gives us for not living up to our full potential. By the end of this chapter, I want you to be able to dig out from under your limiting beliefs and stories and throw them away for good. So let me share a scenario here that hopefully can help you dig deeper and achieve this objective.

If your grandparents went through the Great Depression, they most likely have extremely conservative beliefs about saving money. They might say and believe things like, "You have to play it safe. You have to get a job regardless if you like it or if it aligns with the person you are. Taking a risk can be devastating." And here's the thing: People went through hell during the Depression. Many in that generation couldn't even put food on the table for their families. At that period in history there wasn't much margin for error—the focus was on survival. A huge part of the population took any job they could find; if they hadn't saved every penny, they could have lost everything.

If that was the experience of your grandparents, they probably raised your parents with a frugal, cautious mind-set. They may have instilled their "Depression era" beliefs in your parents, and they trickled down to you. Those beliefs may be holding you back and you don't even realize it. Maybe you want to branch out on your own, expand your business, or take a new job, but fear has you locked in place and you don't even know why. In this case, I know why! It's a generational limiting belief or story that was handed down to you from your parents and their parents before them. You are living with the ideals of someone from the Great Depression even though you are not living in that period. It is simply an invisible fight, or as I've called it, the villain within that is causing you to be stagnant.

These beliefs can limit all areas of your life—from the religion you follow, to the political party you gravitate toward, to the type of person you choose in a relationship. Your limiting beliefs are sneaky and guide so much of what you do and who you become. Wouldn't you call it crazy if someone suggested that someone else was controlling your mind? Well, in many ways this is exactly what is happening in your life.

So focus on the beliefs and stories that are limiting you in different ways. When you consider doing something new or challenging like starting a business or trying to make more money or get in decent physical shape, what do you say out loud or to yourself? Write down the beliefs or stories that come to mind and what you want to improve. Don't worry if they repeat what you wrote earlier in the chapter; they should be similar. This is all about extracting the beliefs that currently guide your life.

Next, write where these beliefs came from. If you're like many people, you'll examine your stories and beliefs and say, "Wow, that's my dad's belief, that's my college professor's belief, or that's my ex-spouse's belief." Even though they may have come from these people, if they live inside you for long enough, they will become your reality as well. So we need to identify them and see how artificial they are in most cases. You must see that they are not your beliefs but rather beliefs handed to you by others.

So now that you have identified them, I want to guide you on a path to not only prove your story isn't true, but also show you how to reverse it and make a new, limitless, empowering story that powers you toward all different types of life success.

HOW HAS IT AFFECTED YOUR LIFE?

It's possible that you don't realize just how negative the impact of your story has been. Take a moment and assess its impact by answering the following questions:

- Has it diminished or possibly destroyed your confidence and lowered your self-esteem?
- Has it made you angry or vengeful?
- Has it left you living with doubt, confusion, or maybe even going to therapy?
- Has it cost you your health, your career, your peace of mind, a relationship, or your joy?
- Has it stopped you from finding the real relationship you deserve or from fixing the relationship you're in?
- Has it prevented you from being the parent you want to be?
- Has it made you fearful of trying to start your own business or create more wealth with your ideas?

Chances are that you answered yes to one or more of these questions. If so, assess and write the cost—what specifically have you been denied, what loss have you suffered, and what problems have developed because of the story you tell yourself? Don't worry about writing complete sentences. Just get it all down on paper so you have something tangible to look at. I want you to come face-to-face with the pain or the missed opportunities a bad story or a negative belief can bring and therefore build even more resentment toward it and more urgency to change it. But let's go even further.

Look to the future and think about what these stories will continue to cost you if you don't change them. On your journey to where you want to go in life, how might these stories get in your way? Think about your life in 5 years, 10 years, or maybe even 20 years; what did you miss out on again because of these stories and beliefs? Close your eyes and imagine missing out on a great opportunity at some point in the future. Let yourself experience the pain of that missed opportunity. Are you really going to give these stories so much power? Recognize what they have cost you and what they will continue to cost you.

When I think back and imagine what my life would have been like if I hadn't changed the stories I told myself, I know that all the success, love, and abundance I have had would not have happened. I never would have started my own career, touched the lives of millions of people, traveled the world, and so much more. Even scarier, I may not have ended up the father I am today to Breana and Brody!

Clinging to one bad story or one bad belief can have a ripple effect in so many areas of your life. So let's get to flipping it to an empowering, limitless story!

PROVE IT'S NOT TRUE

To get rid of your old story for good, find proof that it is a load of garbage! A part of my old story was that since I was in special reading and never got good grades, I wasn't smart enough to go to college, and if I didn't have a college degree, I would never amount to anything. I told myself that I could never start my own business, and that you need money and smarts to make money. I surely don't miss those crappy stories I used to tell myself, but I know what it's like to have them.

Let me ask you this: Was the story I told myself true or was it just plain garbage? Do you know any millionaires or financially successful people who didn't go to college? Of course you do! Two good friends whom I've spent lots of time with are Tony Robbins and the billionaire Richard Branson. Neither of them started out with money or went to college; I don't think Richard made it past the second grade. And here are a few other massively successful people who lack college degrees; maybe you have heard of a few of them: Bill Gates, Michael Dell, Abraham Lincoln, Andrew Carnegie, Andrew Jackson, Benjamin Franklin, Coco Chanel, Henry Ford, James Cameron, John D. Rockefeller

Sr., Walt Disney—the list goes on and on. I researched the topic many years ago and found out that the story I was telling myself was total nonsense. And then I proved to myself that the story was wrong and a lie.

Maybe you can tell by my writing style that I don't always express myself with the best grammar and that I haven't read as many of the great books as I should have. When I was younger, I convinced myself that I had no chance of doing anything in life that required reading or writing skills. I couldn't conceive of writing a book, let alone multiple *New York Times* bestsellers.

Am I an exception to the rule? Or are there other people who have written *New York Times* bestsellers who aren't good at grammar or reading? Of course there are! So clearly, my old story was completely false. With a little research, I was able to figure out that the story didn't hold water.

Have other people with no money and horrible childhoods gone on to do great things, be great dads, enjoy rewarding relationships, have amazing friends, and be massively successful financially? Yes! The chances are that the old story you've been dragging around is wrong; you just need to prove that it is a bunch of crap. It's nonsense to think you are the only one with certain issues holding you back. Get the proof that those limiting stories and beliefs are nothing more than fiction.

HAVE A CONVERSATION WITH GOD

Here is an exercise that will elicit true disgust for your old stories. Pretend that you're having a conversation with God, the universe, or whomever you believe your creator is. Imagine God saying to you, "Why are you not living up to your full potential that I wanted for you? I put you in this amazing world and gave you limitless possibilities in your life. What's stopping you from being your best you?" Sit in silence and contemplate that question. Then imagine yourself responding to God with the story you may have uncovered recently, or, should I say, the excuse: "I'm not living up to my full potential because my dad was rough on me when I was little," or "The economy shifted," or "My spouse doesn't support me." Could you really say anything like this to your maker with a straight face?

Now imagine offering these excuses and rationalizations to someone who endured unthinkable cruelty or tragedy like a war, or a concentration camp, or cancer. Maybe you've endured an equally tragic life, but the odds are, your story is more typical than tragic; you endured your parents' divorce, or you've had a lot of expenses, or you always felt shy and had low self-esteem. I'm not discounting your difficulties, only asking you to think about them relative to going through the worst that life can throw at you. And even if you've experienced the worst, I have seen people endure epic struggles and still pull through to achieve the seemingly impossible. And most of them overcame their dark past because they refused to let the tragedy and hardship define them. They created a different story for their lives. So when you tell God about how you never have achieved your career goals because your parents were highly critical of you, doesn't it make you resent this story? Aren't you sufficiently angry at the story that you're motivated to change it? Well, I surely hope so.

SAY IT OUT LOUD

Because of the process we have gone through so far in this chapter and how we have framed "your story," another way to rid yourself of your old story is to simply say it out loud and listen to how silly it sounds. Say it several times, over and over, and listen to yourself articulating it repeatedly. Say out loud, "I don't have a good life because [fill in the blank with your reason]." Here's what I say: "I can't reach my goals because I'm dyslexic and can't read well." Yes, I'm embarrassed by my story, but that's the point. I know your story may have been traumatizing in the past, but when you say it out loud as an adult you start to hear how misguided it sounds. Again, your life might be worse than anything I can imagine, and I'm not in any way trying to minimize your experiences. But no matter what it was, no matter how bad it was, you need to get disgusted enough with the old limiting story to take the steps that help you replace it with a new story.

LOOK FOR THE GOOD IN EVERY STORY

Now let's start the process of flipping that limiting story to an empowering, limitless one. When you change parts of the story, your narrative begins to improve. Let me share my own experience of how this is so. I was deemed "stupid" in school, and it certainly hurt a lot, causing me pain and setbacks for years. Or so I thought.

As I've noted, I suffered from dyslexia and struggled to read because of it. Back then, teachers and other kids called me stupid because of my reading problems (I didn't attend a politically correct school). But without realizing it, not being able to read like the other kids taught me how to be good visually and aurally; I figured out how to learn by watching and listening. These are skills many of the other kids probably never developed, and if they did, it took them a lot longer than it did me. This is why I can stand up on stage for hours and speak without a teleprompter or a script. My childhood dyslexia taught me to be able to communicate in a really simple, straightforward way. Even if the content is really complicated, when I teach it, it comes out easy to understand because that's the way I think. And I know that's one of the reasons my message resonates with millions of people from all different walks of life.

So what is something good that came out of your story? What is something that you once thought was an obstacle in your life, but in fact created skills that have made you who you are today? Maybe you were cheated on in a relationship and at the time it seemed like the end of the world, but now you are with the best partner possible because you've learned what kind of love you deserve. Maybe you got fired from a job once and it made you feel like you weren't good enough, but it was that event that allowed you to spend more time on yourself and get in the best shape of your life mentally and physically.

Find the good that can come from your story and start changing it into an empowering story. Remember the words of Tony Robbins: "What if life happens for us, not to us." When he shared that with me, the last 10 percent of the old stories I was holding on to about my family disappeared. If that hadn't happened for me, I wouldn't be right here, right now. So those supposedly bad stories were just part of a bigger plan creating and forming my character. Look back at your story with this "find the good" perspective, and those old stories start losing their power fast.

TIME TO SHIFT YOUR STORY

Imagine you're in a house full of old memories from your life, and some are good memories, but others are those negative stories that remind you of bad things that happened in the past. Now imagine that the house is on fire, and you have a tiny suitcase in your hands and only a minute to save some of those memories. In order to reach that next level of success in life, you must choose to pack only the memories and the stories that serve you going forward. If it's a negative memory that weighs on your heart or mind, let it burn up in the fire. Only carry out with you those things that will help you make the best life possible. Remember, the past only lives inside you. You have to think of the past as research and development. It is there to learn from and develop your better self. If the past haunts you, holds you back, or doesn't serve your grander future, then let that memory burn up in the fire.

In *The Power of Now*, Eckhart Tolle says that yesterday is the past, and we can't change it. Tomorrow is a movie in our head that's not even filmed yet. And we only have this moment! So why carry all that heaviness of the past when you can let it go forever?

It's time to adjust your story. Now that you're aware of what the old story has cost you, why it's not even true (though it feels like it is), how it is fueled by small outside factors, and most of all how you should be disgusted by it, you should be primed to remake it. For example, I took my "I'll never be successful because of my rough childhood," and flipped it 180 degrees to my new story: "I'm empowered because my childhood circumstances taught me to communicate better, to be a visual learner, and I learned to fail a lot when I was a kid, so failure doesn't bug me! When I combine the ability to learn fast, not fear failure, and be tenacious, my life is limitless!" That new story is empowering and my new truth.

You can find your new, better story, just as I did. Remember, no matter what your old circumstances were, you have the ability to leave them behind. If you were cheated on, your partner stole your money, or your parents didn't love you, throw those stories away and develop a better version of your story in their place.

WRITE YOUR NEW STORY

As you craft this new story, do the opposite of what we did earlier and find proof that your new story is true. Search the Internet to get proof, ask successful friends, seek out a mentor, or talk to one of my trained coaches. Do whatever it takes to find proof that what you are now saying is possible. If, for example, you say, "My adversity made me strong, bulletproof, and I can handle anything that comes my way," do a search for strong women of the past and see the adversities they went through. Look up Rosa Parks or Mother Teresa or Helen Keller. Most successful people went through hell once or many times in their lives. Find their stories and use them as leverage to create your own. The proof is everywhere, so go find it.

Write it, revise it, but get it crafted. When you think you've perfected it, then e-mail it to your phone and copy and paste it in the notes app so you can read it every day. Start repeating it to yourself like it's a mantra and try to memorize it. And when the old story pops back into your mind, be consciously aware of your thoughts. If you wake up in the middle of the night and find that you're telling yourself that old crappy story again, say to yourself, "Whoa, whoa, whoa, I threw that out. That's a horrible story! It's nonsense." And replace it with the new one.

SAY YOUR NEW STORY OUT LOUD

In fact, once you have the new story or stories, then it's time to anchor it in your subconscious. Remember, you may have been thinking those old limiting thoughts for 10, 20, maybe 30 years, or more. Just as it takes more than one session at the gym to get in shape, so, too, do you have to embed your new story into your life many times. Through my 30-day challenge, or on your own, say the story out loud for the next 30 days, every night before you go to bed. Make it the last thing you think about as you're nodding off, and make sure it is the first thing you think about when you wake up in the morning. Try to make this a daily ritual for at least the next month.

Also, find someone in your life that you can tell your new story to who would appreciate it—someone who will smile and encourage you rather than pooh-pooh it and call you a dreamer. Tell this person how you've evolved and share the process of exchanging old story for new with this individual.

Ask someone to be your accountability friend, a partner or coach who can help guide you or at least keep you on track. If you have somebody who can mentor you and guide you, grab hold of him or her and don't let go.

I'm willing to commit dollars to make sure two of these folks are in my life at all times. I go four times a year to meet with Dan Sullivan at Strategic Coach, and he's my accountability coach, delivering the wisdom that helps me be a better educator, a better businessman, and a better person. I also am a member of Joe Polish's Genius Network mastermind in Phoenix; Joe assists me in sharpening my marketing skills and allows me to be immersed in better thinking and positive focus.

I pay $25,000 a year to each of these guys because they keep me accountable to my own goals. I'm a teacher, and changing people's lives is my obsession, but I want to be held accountable for my own growth as well. A coach is someone who can really help you do that. If you have someone in your life who can be your mentor, please allow him or her to guide you. Either way, make sure to take my fun and engaging 30-day challenge at www.thebetterlife.com. You can also call my office at 866-505-4200, and we'll see if one of my certified success coaches can assist you on your journey to becoming your best you.

COMPARE YOUR TWO STORIES

Lastly, after you've written your new story, compare it to the old story. See how radically different the outcome of your life will be by not only changing one story or one belief but by changing all the stories that do not serve your higher purpose or your true "why." You've spent so many years with the old story that it may take some time to erase it from your consciousness. And that's okay. So don't be impatient, but stay persistent! Remember to make a commitment to repeating it every night and every morning. It may require 10 minutes each day, but meditate on it and try to feel that new story.

You can learn so much about yourself and your future success by changing the stories of the past and killing the villain within. More importantly, once you kill the villain within and change your story, you've started down the path to unleashing the hero that lives inside you and finally attaining the wealth and happiness you deserve.

Chapter 5

AWAKEN THE
INNER HERO

"There's no way in hell you're going to have a lasting success on a large scale without confidence, because without confidence you're not going to take massive action. Massive action, learning from what doesn't work, changing your approach until you get to where you want is really what makes someone succeed long term in any context."

— Tony Robbins, interview with Dean Graziosi

Hero: noun – a person who is admired or idealized for courage, outstanding achievements, or noble qualities

---

Inner: adjective – situated inside or farther in; internal (either mental or spiritual)

Those two definitions are pretty clear, and each taken on its own can represent a lot of different things to a lot of different people. But when you combine the two, the words take on a new meaning. Inner hero represents your full potential, your best you, the one designed by God that made you special, limitless, and the one who needs to be in charge of your life. When you awaken your inner hero—and, yes, we all have one—you will open your world up to new opportunities and amazing levels of abundance and joy.

As I explain the best way to activate your inner hero, don't forget its opposite, the inner villain. As you have learned by now, the villain fights against your growth and does all it can to rob you of your confidence, trying to prevent you from developing and anchoring new success habits. If the villain doesn't work hard to be in control, it will have to bow out and let the inner hero take over. The villain doesn't want to lose its power over you. The way the villain works is by telling or, better yet, reminding you of an old, disempowering story and trying to sabotage your subconscious so you can't create a better story. Yet by the time this chapter is over, you will have the tools and the clarity to let the best you guide your thoughts, happiness, and abundance.

Recall the definitions: When the inner hero runs your life, you are filled with confidence and optimism, and are a solutions-focused person. When the villain is in charge, it's the polar opposite, robbing you of the courage, energy, and confidence to make the shifts toward the best you. This mind-set ends today. I've given you tools to know where the villain came from and how to eliminate it. Here, though, we're going to put a dagger in the heart of that villain once and for all and let the inner hero be in control.

This process isn't about turning you into something you're not—changing an introvert into an extrovert, for instance. It's about accomplishing something deeper, better, and more custom tailored to you, and only you, that can last a lifetime. Once the villain doesn't run your life, but your confident inner hero does, the possibilities are limitless and you will know what it is like to tap into the best you. Remember, I'm not offering you a magic pill for success; you're not going to read these words and instantaneously achieve wealth and abundance. Instead, as I've been emphasizing throughout this book, you'll learn how to make tiny shifts that can be implemented quickly and feel and see dramatic, positive effects in a short period of time. Working together, we can accomplish this. You are worth it, so keep reading, push forward, and stick with it. We've come this far, so don't stop now.

As we continue on this journey, and I continue to share new habits, thought processes, and exercises, keep your eye on your "why." It's easy to put exercises and behavioral tweaks off until another time. You have done that before, and typically it hasn't worked out. This isn't just about inspiring you and telling good stories—plenty of other books do that. Instead, it's about small actions that can add up to massive positive effects. No more roller coasters. It's time to move forward in a straight, sure line.

So to set the stage for this section, let's just say it like it is: Your state of mind and your level of confidence are critical factors in order for you to become a high achiever. Think about a time you were in a bad mood and then something good happened and it triggered a great feeling. Maybe you learned there was extra money in your bank account, your spouse did something special for you, or you got a promotion at work. Can you think of a moment or moments where you went from feeling down to feeling up in an instant? Of course you can, and that demonstrates that you possess the ability to change your state of mind and your confidence in an instant. You just need tools to be in control of this ability rather than to be at the mercy of outside factors.

Face it: Have you done anything amazing in your life when your confidence was in the toilet? No, with this state of mind, problems compound, opportunities are missed, and regrets are formed. On the other hand, when you had a day or a moment of high energy, confidence, or were in a great, positive mood, I bet you can think of incredible things you were able to accomplish, even if only for a brief time.

Yes, it's a great feeling when you are on an emotional high like that, to feel that burst and change of mood! But if the high soon goes away and is followed by a low, then your life is filled with peaks and valleys—peaks and valleys that are dictated by the outside world. Let's face it: This up-and-down emotional ride won't lead to the wealth, joy, happiness, love, or fulfillment you desire.

That's why I'm going to teach you how to change your state of mind and your level of confidence, no matter what's going on around you. With this ability, you can limit those valleys and eventually prevent them altogether because you will be in control of your emotions and thoughts rather than allowing circumstance to dictate what they are.

I'm going to show you how to tap into a higher level of confidence that lives inside you, to boost it, and have it on call when needed. Most people believe that they either have total confidence or none at all. But low points are not caused by you having zero confidence; they can happen when your confidence drops by as little as 5 percent. Even a small hit to your confidence can be deadly to your aspirations, goals, and dreams. So be prepared to learn how to keep your confidence at 100 percent, or at least ready to access its full potential instantly. This level of confidence simply does not leave any space for the villain to exist.

Your inner confidence is the hero inside you waiting to shine. I've seen my students fumble with tactical skills and wonder why they were stalled, or worse yet, overthink what to do to the point of paralysis. Why couldn't they build momentum and stay on a course that would free them to be who they aspired to be? Almost every student who didn't give up in the first few moments of transitioning learned that the problem was a lack of confidence. Once they went through this process, though, they obtained the ability to create confidence at levels they never thought were possible. And once they did, there was no stopping them.

Before we discuss how to tap into this resource and give you the ability to change your state of mind and raise your confidence when you need it, I want to give you the chance to visualize this internal power shift and the huge difference it can make in your life.

PROFILES IN COURAGE: TWO HEROES

Carol Stinson let the villain run her life, in no small part because she had grown up extremely poor in Philadelphia. Then she eventually moved to a not-so-pleasant area in New Jersey. She summarized her philosophy this way: "The poor stay poor. The rich get richer. They have advantages no one else does."

But it wasn't just her upbringing that allowed the villain to dominate her thoughts and her life. As an adult, she encountered one hardship after the next. Her husband lost his job during one of the toughest economic periods in American history, instilling even more negativity and supporting the villain's cause. She was raising five children of her own plus two grandchildren—the youngest was a special needs child. Some days all they could afford to eat was peanut butter, and their electricity was turned off because of nonpayment of bills. She told me she would wake up and immediately feel fear and panic, because in New Jersey, if your electric is shut off, CPS (child protective services) could take your children.

So you probably understand why Carol told me the following: "When you're from the wrong side of the tracks, this is what you believe is the lot in life you were dealt. You're supposed to live in poverty. You're supposed to live in scarcity. You have envy and disdain for those with money because you feel, somehow, if they're making money, they must be robbing it from us."

And of course it was really easy to assign blame: It's the economy, the president, rich people, smart people, and a hundred other scapegoats that encourage self-doubt and feelings of hopelessness. This happens when you resort to thinking, "This is what we have."

We create change when we desire to have more, and this desire is powerful and deep. But we can also create change when we hit rock bottom. Let's hope the second option is never the reason you have to make a shift, and you decide you want more.

Carol, for instance, was running out of time, money, and excuses. With her residence in foreclosure, no money, and the pantry empty, she did something completely out of the ordinary for her; she bought one of my books with her last few dollars. She went against her family, her husband, and even her own inner voice to do so.

And yes, I gave her strategies to make money. I gave her business ideas. But Carol told me that as she read, she kept saying to herself, "This can't be true; this isn't what I've believed for so long." But it started to make sense to her, and she realized that the negative stories she was telling herself were lies.

Based on reading about my personal journey, doing the exercises, and being inspired by the examples, she started changing her own thoughts, her success habits, and her story. Carol knew the villain had been in charge of her entire adult life and nothing good had come of it. She was brave enough to awaken her inner hero and allow that to be her new guiding force.

She realized that she didn't need a college degree, that she didn't have to come from the right side of the tracks. She didn't need money to go into business. She also realized how blessed she was to be raising seven children, have a great husband, and have opportunities in front of her. She saw that if she changed her habits, told herself new stories, and let the hero be in charge, everything could change. And boy, did it.

With these realizations, Carol no longer blamed the economy or fate or anything else for her struggles. Instead, she took control. And when she did so, everyone around her thought she was crazy.

She insisted she could be wealthy. She was sure she could do more. She thought she could take on the world. Well, guess what? When she started thinking that way, she drove the inner hero to be stronger and stronger.

Carol not only started her own company, she generated hundreds and hundreds of thousands of dollars and she got her family out of foreclosure. She bought a new house and a new car. She took her kids school-shopping in malls where they had never shopped before and on vacations that they had only dreamed about. She even changed the destiny of her family by putting her children through college.

Today, Carol Stinson looks 20 years younger than she did when I first met her. She is a strong, amazing, vibrant, highly respected businesswoman who's changed the destiny of her family forever, and not just financially. She's teaching them how to be different people by growing up with different habits, and letting the hero be in control of their lives. Tapping into their full potential and not leaving it up to chance. Not going to their deathbeds saying, "Wow, there could have been more."

No, there won't be any, "Could have been more" conversations for Carol. I have no doubt that spitfire, that amazing woman, will go to her deathbed knowing she was all she could be, and then some.

Think about the simple definition starting this chapter. Think about Carol's inner hero and its heroic qualities: confidence, courage, taking responsibility. And another success habit that Carol exemplified was that she simply stopped focusing on what was wrong and started the routine of focusing on solutions.

And that's where the villain and hero are so different. When people invest energy in blame, in figuring out why someone got a terrible disease, in obsessing about whose fault it is they didn't get the promotion or the raise, or why the partner stole their money, or why their first business didn't work, they allow the villain to be in charge. As big or small as the circumstance is, when you can accept that it simply "happened" and start looking forward to how you can create the best outcome possible, this is when everything changes. This is when you allow your hero to shine. Let me share another example so this truth will really sink in.

You may have heard of JJ Virgin, the creator of the Virgin Diet and multiple *New York Times* bestsellers, among many other great accomplishments. But what you might not know is that not that many years ago, a car hit her son Grant while he was walking home, and the driver fled the scene, leaving him for dead. In fact, Grant was still alive, but barely. He had 13 broken bones, and that wasn't the worst of it, because of the serious head trauma and likelihood of irreversible brain damage. The doctors didn't think he would survive but added that if he lived, he would probably not be able to walk, talk, or communicate coherently.

As of this writing, PBS is currently doing a documentary on JJ and Grant, and the journey they went through together after this tragic event. They asked to interview me for the documentary, and of course I said yes. I was unsure of what they wanted from me, but I was honored and delighted at the chance to support JJ and Grant or add value where I could. One of the questions they posed was, what did I think was the best way to get through a traumatic experience such as the one that had befallen JJ and her son?

What instantly came to mind and exited my mouth before I could even filter it was, "Focus on the best outcome, and try not to waste energy on why it happened and who is to blame." Now, that may seem naive, given the circumstances and the tragedy in this case. But is it? I went on to explain my thoughts, but as I did I realized that JJ acted in a way that focused on the best outcome. She, of course, went through the emotions we all would as a parent getting that call. But as quickly as she could, she got obsessed with Grant not only surviving, but also having the chance to live a normal life. She refused to accept what the doctors told her about Grant. When the doctors were not in alignment with her ideal outcome, she loaded Grant into a helicopter and against just about everyone's advice, took him to another hospital more aligned with that outcome and better able to deal with Grant's situation. She did what she had to, made cold calls, knocked on doors, was forceful when necessary, and got the best possible people to help Grant.

JJ found a vision, focused on solutions, and let the hero take over—and nothing got in her way.

When I was talking to the documentary interviewer about all this, she stopped me when I was almost done and said, "So the way you are answering, I'm guessing that you don't know that JJ didn't seek legal action against the hit-and-run driver; in fact, she never even spoke about her." I'd had no idea, but I wasn't shocked. It would have been so easy to place blame and expend energy on revenge. Others might have tried to get the driver prosecuted in the criminal courts, and if that didn't work, sue her for everything she had. JJ could have hated her and rightfully so, given what happened to her little boy.

Instead, she realized that revenge would do Grant no good and that we only have a certain amount of energy to put forth in the world. She knew in what direction her energy needed to go and focused on the solution with laser intensity. She let the inner hero be in control rather than the villain. Your inner hero can't stop things from going wrong. It can't prevent tragedies. But if you let it emerge, it can turn even the worst possible trauma you've gone through into a building block for a better life. It can help you generate energy from whatever challenge you face and use it to achieve the life you deserve.

This isn't about being glad if something goes wrong so you can learn from it. We don't want bad things in our lives, but the fact is they happen. So if they are going to happen, who do you want in charge? I think you are getting it: the hero focuses on solutions.

And I am happy to tell you that Grant didn't just live, but has thrived. Because of his fighting spirit and his mom's focus on the best possible outcome, Grant is working every day toward a bigger, better life for himself. JJ's latest book, *Miracle Mindset*, is about the journey she and Grant have been on and the lessons we can all learn from their experience.

So now that you have a better idea of what the inner hero looks like, we need to examine how you can develop the confidence to put that hero in control.

THE FOUR C'S OF CONFIDENCE

Let's take a look back to a time in your life when you lacked confidence and it cost you dearly. Have you ever wanted to ask a girl out on a date or talk to a guy you saw at a coffee shop and you let that person walk away without saying a word? Have you ever had an opportunity to tackle a tough project at work or the desire to start your own business but just couldn't move past the thought to the action? Or make it even simpler: Have you refused to walk into the gym because you thought you were too out of shape to be there? I've seen a lack of confidence destroy many people, and it usually happens when their confidence is just that 5 percent off that I noted previously. So when has a lack of confidence hurt you in the past? And how do you think your life could be different today had you been able to summon 100 percent confidence on the spot and do what you wanted to do?

A great man and dear friend by the name of Richard Rossi runs a remarkable company in Washington, D.C., creating empowering live events tailored to high-achieving high school students; they receive life-changing knowledge by attending. When I was talking to Richard about his events, I said, "You've been blessed to see so many successful high school kids come through your program. If you could identify one common trait they all have, what would it be?"

He said, "I don't even have to think about it. It's one word: confidence." He added, "It's not the smartest kids or the ones with the straight A's that become the superstars; it's the ones that have an incredible amount of confidence that go on to do amazing things in their lives."

Richard's words don't come from theory but real-life data, derived from experience and results. He's seen thousands of the most successful young adults in the country pass through his doors, and the word he used for success was simply "confidence."

But here is the million-dollar question: How do we make sure that confidence is always there for us when we need it? Think back to a time when your confidence surged because of something amazing that happened. Maybe you did something in your job, or at home, or in the gym that had you look in the mirror and subconsciously pound your chest and say, "Yeah, I did that!" In that moment you got a glimpse of what the power of an instant surge of confidence can do to your state of mind.

As you know by now, I didn't have much confidence as a child—I was the smallest kid in my class, I couldn't read very well, I couldn't sit still, and I got made fun of a lot. So as I got older, I had to learn to manufacture my own confidence. Through trial and error, as well with the assistance of some amazing people, I've learned how to build this bulletproof confidence from the ground up. You can do the same.

But first you have to understand the myth of confidence. Could some people have been born with it? Maybe in rare cases, but it's unlikely. In most cases, confidence is something that has to be learned. You're probably fooling yourself if you think of yourself as the "confident type" or the "not-confident type"—both are part of the myth. No matter what level of confidence you have, let me assure you there is more waiting to be accessed. Let's start building your confidence to the next level by using a great lesson that I was taught by a mentor of mine, Dan Sullivan, owner of Strategic Coach.

This is a four-step process that helps you discover what real confidence looks like and the ingredients needed to get there.

The first step, or I guess I should say the first C, is *courage*. All confidence, all change, and all new things start with courage. When somebody bungee jumps for the first time, it's not confidence that gets him to jump off the ledge, it's courage. Let's take a deeper look at this quality, since it will help us understand how confidence emerges from it.

Courage is walking through a door and not knowing what is on the other side. Courage makes you get off the bench, raise your hand, and get in the game rather than judging or envying others from the sidelines. Maybe you don't realize it yet, but you have already built the courage muscles in your life. Do you have children? You have to be extremely courageous to bring children into the world and take care of them. You didn't know (and perhaps still don't know) what the end result would be, but you jumped in and are learning as you go. Courage is something we all have inside us, even if it is hidden. So if you want the courage to do something, recall your seven levels deep and find your "why." This is where that core habit comes into play once again. Taking action is possible when true purpose is recognized. Think of all we have learned to this point: When you have vision and clarity, and don't let old stories hold you back, the ability to be courageous grows exponentially. So focus on where you want to go and your new story, pull your shoulders back, stick out your chest, and say, "This is my time!" Be courageous and go for it. It all begins with that first step.

Now the second C is *commitment.* You've already shown commitment by reading this book and engaging in the exercises I've recommended. You're committed to a personal transformation, since any significant change requires a commitment. If you want to lose weight, you have to commit to that; otherwise you'll fail. If you want to start a new job, you have to commit to that; otherwise you'll fail.

Or look at this second C, commitment, from the opposite perspective: Have you ever been successful in something to which you were not committed? Whether it was a relationship, a new business, or even a new diet? Heck no! If you want more wealth and that next level of life, then you're going to have to commit to it. That doesn't mean you have to devote every waking second to achievement of a single goal, but don't dabble; a shaky commitment means shaky confidence. So when you have the courage to take action, and the commitment to see it through to the end, you're halfway to confidence.

The third C is *capabilities.* What are you acquiring by reading these pages and developing success habits? Capabilities. Remember when we talked about where you are, being honest with yourself, figuring out where you want to go, and how you are going to get there? In most cases, you need to acquire specific capabilities to achieve your goals. If you want to be great at rock climbing, read a book by an expert rock climber or take a course or hire someone as a mentor. If you fail to take these actions and lack the knowledge to execute them properly, you will lose your courage to keep going and not commit to seeing it through. You will get frustrated and overwhelmed. So get a road map from the right person or source whenever possible. While this may seem like a no-brainer, don't you know people who get excited about something and think trial and error is the best approach? Then they hit a few roadblocks or challenges, feel defeated, and stop trying to reach their goals. With the right capabilities, on the other hand, you can spot the obstacles and know how to get around them; you can also access the path that will take you where you want to go faster and obtain the results you desire!

You see, once you have those first three C's and take action, you'll finally reach the fourth C, and that is *confidence*. Your confidence then starts to naturally grow. You just can't help it. Think about each C separately and how it has given you a shot of confidence at different points in your life. Have you ever been afraid of doing something new like dancing in front of people, zip lining, or public speaking? Maybe you were scared to death before taking action, right? You were probably obsessing over what could go wrong, but you finally just did what you had to do. That was courage. Then after the experience ended, how did you feel? Exactly, you felt amazing and that you could easily do it again!

How about commitment? You can dabble for years in a relationship or your business, then all of a sudden one day because of your kids, or because of your desire for more or some other motivator, you commit and your life takes off.

Consider capabilities. When you are in the dark about something, it seems so confusing. Have you ever tried to download and use a new app on your phone without any guidance? Have you ever wanted to learn a new language or learn an instrument and quickly grew frustrated when you weren't sure if you were moving forward in the right way? But once you acquired the capabilities—you read the instructions, saw an online video, hired a coach or teacher—the activity became second nature to you after some practice.

When you align the three prior C's to achieve one goal and one outcome, your confidence will skyrocket, hence the four C's to confidence. When the four C's are in place and your confidence rises, the hero inside you isn't being suppressed by negativity or bad stories. Your self-doubt and inner resistance fades away and the real you is in charge.

WHAT'S COOL ABOUT YOU?

No matter how strong you are, no matter how much you evolve, your confidence can still take a hit. And if you are going to reach your full potential, you must protect your confidence as if you are protecting millions of dollars in a vault. So when life knocks your confidence down, you need the tools to boost it back up fast. That's what we're going to spend time on right now.

Let me ask you this: What's cool about you? A crazy-sounding question? And perhaps a difficult one to answer? But don't diminish the value of asking yourself this question regardless of the level at which you perceive your life to be. The first time I did this exercise I was with Sean Stephenson, a three-foot-tall giant. Look him up if you don't know who he is. Sean is an incredible man who has accomplished more than most despite adversities most of us could never imagine. I was talking with Sean about an obstacle I was dealing with, and Sean said, "Let's write down what's cool about you."

I responded, "What? Dude, let's talk tactics to fix the problem at hand, not try and feed my ego." And boy, I was completely wrong there. Looking back now, I realize that he had noticed my confidence was down and was trying to boost it back up. So trust me. Let's do this exercise together. So go ahead and start thinking of the things that are cool about you.

One thing I know to be true is that when life gets stressful, we focus often on what we've failed at, or what we've not accomplished, or the mistakes we've made. We tend to forget all the things that we've done really well. So this is the time to ignore the failures and think of the wins.

When Sean first asked what was cool about me, I was scratching my head. He called me out because of my reaction. He knew I was focusing on what was going wrong at that time, and it took me a moment to think of what was cool about me. Like the great teacher he was, he started probing, suggesting examples of coolness to get me started, and slowly my answers emerged. I wrote down things like:

I put my kids first over work and accomplishments.

I was in special education classes and barely graduated high school, yet I'm a multiple New York Times best-selling author.

I can operate a bulldozer and a backhoe (I learned how when I used to build houses).

I was a mechanic when I was younger, and I can take apart an engine, fix a banged-up fender, and paint a car.

I donate money without anyone knowing.

I create simple messages that get people to take action in their lives.

I was the New England snowmobile grass drag champion in my 20s.

I still have my best friend from fifth grade.

I always try to show the people I love what they mean to me.

I can solve problems without conflict arising, even when someone wants to be confrontational.

I am good on camera after years of practice. I've met some of my heroes.

The list went on and on. Once I started really thinking about how I was cool, the items started to flow.

Now think about what you can put on your list. (Feel free to download the easy-to-follow "Cool About You" list on www.thebetterlife.com under the "Book Resources" tab.) Get creative and include unusual skills you may have, as well as accomplishments. Your list should include anything that you like about yourself that has a coolness factor. Maybe you're a great friend, or you have great fashion sense, or you're generous to the needy. Whatever these traits or achievements may be, write them down. What is cool about your job, your business, or how you treat your employees? What about the daughter or son you are to your parents, the parent you work so hard to be for your kids, or the partner you are in your relationship? Even though I don't know what's cool about you, I do know that with a little thought you will find plenty of items to list! And after you write them down, take a moment, be silent, and read what you wrote and let the list sink in. When I did this exercise, I remember thinking, "Wow, there are a lot of cool things about me. I have a lot of unique abilities and I've accomplished some ambitious goals." After completing the exercise with Sean, I remember my confidence grew immediately just by acknowledging my successes rather than my failures.

Just as I shared all the little pieces that created the villain within, now I am sharing the pieces that will replace that villain's voice and put the inner hero in control. When Sean first said do a "What's cool about me" exercise, I was like, "Waste of time." Doing it felt odd. I was wrong, though, and if you experienced the same negative thoughts for even a second, you were wrong too. Take the time and reflect: You are not only cool, you have already achieved so much more than you give yourself credit for.

A TALE OF TWO PICTURES

This next exercise may seem like a little work, but with effort comes results. And it's an exercise that will help you trigger an instant confidence boost any time you need it. (You can download the "Two Pics" blueprint at www.thebetterlife.com under the "Book Resources" tab.)

Start by finding an unflattering picture of yourself—it can be a digital image on your smartphone or an old photo that you've stored in a shoebox. It could be from a time in your life when you were overweight, just pulled an all-nighter, were broke, lost a job, or you just looked like crap on the day the photo was taken. This picture is going to represent the version of you that is letting the villain control your life. If it's a digital image, print it and also save it to your computer. Then I want you to create a list of the negative traits you associate with this version of yourself. For instance: I was fat; I was messing up at work; I'd just had my heart broken; I was really mad at my sister; I was focusing on all the things wrong in my life; I blamed others for my problems; and so on.

You see, these are the traits that have fueled your inner villain, allowed it to be in control, and absolutely demolished your confidence. Imagine how the person in that picture is letting the villain run his or her life and steal confidence. The villain is constantly saying, "We're not going to be able to pay the rent. Our career is not progressing. We're not financially successful. We'll never be rich. Why should we even get out of bed in the morning?" That's the definition of someone living with a scarcity mind-set and limited confidence.

Now attach negative emotions to that unflattering picture of yourself—were you angry, sad, depressed, embarrassed, ashamed, insecure, and so on. Then I want you to name that person. Maybe you name that person the nickname you hated as a kid or make one up that you would never like, but whatever it is, make it an unflattering name.

Next, take it one step further and create a complete avatar of that negative version of yourself. What are the limiting beliefs and habits of this version of you? What do you stand for in this form? What do you accept as a given in your life? Who wants to be around this person? Even if you've evolved since then, focus on the version of you that you observe in the photo—the outdated version of what you are. Describe that person in the picture, the one not reaching his or her full potential.

We are halfway done with this exercise. To complete it, find a picture of the happy you, the joyous you, the best you. It could be from a time where you felt great and you looked your best. It could be from a time when you were the shining hero or the top earner or just completely alive. Now describe in writing what attributes the hero version of you has. Is that person vibrant, powerful, energetic, wealthy, financially secure, a business owner, in control of his or her money, alive, passionate, enthusiastic, and strong? Does that person exercise regularly, eat right, and have an incredible relationship with his or her children? Does this version of you make a lot of money? Is he or she financially independent? Do others respect this person?

Then I want you to name your heroic persona. Maybe you borrow a term from the digital world and call yourself John 4.0

or Mary 5.0. Next, create another avatar, only this time the hero version. What are your new limitless beliefs and newly adapted millionaire habits? What does this version of you stand for? What do you accept in your life now? What will you absolutely not accept? Who wants to be around this heroic avatar? This version of you is officially the new version of you. Just explain you, living at your full potential, no boundaries, no judgment, totally in control. Who is the real you when the hero is in charge?

Realize this truth: The two versions of you aren't separate people. Each of us has the good wolf and the bad wolf living inside; the old you and the new you; the villain in control vs. the hero in charge. I bring up the wolf analogy for a reason; this is your chance to decide which one you feed, since that's the one who will take ownership of your life!

Next, put your two pictures side by side, along with the text descriptions of both underneath them. Use your phone to photograph these images so you have access to them anytime you want or need to see them. Memorize these two avatars, both visually and what they stand for. Don't just rely on the digital image. Place the two photos (or print out the one on your phone) on your refrigerator, in your drawer at work, or on your computer as your screen saver! Keep these images handy, because you're going to use them as your trigger whenever you need to require strength and whenever you need to summon your confidence.

In order for this to work, feel your avatar. You must become the new, heroic version of yourself. Whenever something is going wrong, and you find yourself getting into a negative state, and you're allowing that villain to creep in, look at these two pictures and say, "Do I want to be that old version of myself that lets life control me or do I want to be the new hero version of me?"

Can you start to feel who the inner hero is? The inner hero is the you that God meant you to be. You're crossing limitless boundaries and utilizing all the gifts you have to reach another level. The inner hero is simply you at full potential with nothing being suppressed anymore.

POWER PHRASE

Here's another habit to change your state of mind and build your confidence instantly. Tony Robbins taught this exercise to me along with many other great lessons over 15 years ago, and it transformed my life. I have adopted my own version of this specific practice since then, but it was a lifesaver when I learned it. Over a decade ago, I had everything go sideways at once, or so it seemed. I had an accountant steal a lot of money from me that literally compromised my ability to stay in business. My grandmother who raised me for much of my childhood and was my favorite person in the world was in a hospice, dying. My biggest stream of income at the time stopped overnight—and this is just the short list! I was telling myself horrible things and digging up old, limiting beliefs. I started thinking, "Maybe I'm not smart enough to run a business at this level. Maybe I got lucky and my time is up?" I was telling myself all these negative things, and it was destroying my confidence and feeding my inner villain.

But I changed my state of mind—and I changed it completely—and the one thing that sparked that change was Tony's incantation and what I termed my personal power phrase. I started saying to myself, "If I can get through this, I can get through anything. If I can get through this, I can get through anything. If I can get through this, I can get through anything!"

I said it repeatedly. I said it out loud as I would walk around the house or around the office. I said it walking to the gym in the morning and when I was on the treadmill. I said it louder and louder and with more conviction until my soul felt it. This simple little phrase empowered my life like I could have never imagined. It energized my cells, it got me into a state of mind where I felt I could handle anything. I stopped thinking about what could go wrong and focused on what could go right. It allowed me to kick the old villain to the curb when he was trying to move back into my life. No way was I letting that happen with my new power phrase! I felt the inner hero take over my soul!

I started using other power phrases to empower my life from that moment on and have never stopped! It's funny that Tony gave me this gift 15 years ago in one of his courses. At the time, I wrote in my journal: "Someday, I will thank Tony in person and he and I will do business together." Fast-forward 15 years, and I'm backstage getting ready to inspire 15,000 energized and amazing Chinese people in Shanghai. And guess who I was there with? Yes, Tony Robbins, who is now one of my dearest friends.

I was getting ready to follow Tony on stage, and about 10 minutes before I was scheduled to go on, I got incredibly nervous. I started to question myself and my abilities. I became anxious about letting Tony down, as well as the other 15,000 people who were there.

But guess what I used to turn this situation around? Nothing more than what Tony taught me 15 years earlier through his course. I started walking around backstage repeating a power phrase that I had used a few times before when I had to speak in public. I was literally walking around saying it over and over, and with more intensity each time: "I command my subconscious to use my God-given, unique ability to impact, empower, and transform the lives of the people who are here today!" I repeated it until my confidence grew and fear subsided, and then the inner hero kicked in. I got goose bumps up and down my arms and my face from the amazing experience. Then Tony said my name and called me onto the stage. After Tony gave me a huge bear hug, I was ready to light up that crowd. And that's exactly what I did!

Your power phrase can ignite your inner hero, and it doesn't kind of work—it works 100 percent when you use it this way.

What power phrases can you create to help you with whatever it is you want to overcome or accomplish? What can you say to yourself anytime you feel the villain emerging to make you feel small and weak? What phrase can you say to get the inner hero back in charge? Maybe it's something similar to one of the phrases I use: "Nothing can stop me; I've been through way worse!" Or it could be something like, "I'll never give up because my family deserves the best me!" Whatever it is, keep it active in your mind, ready to be implemented at a moment's notice.

Write your power phrases in a handy, accessible place right now. What could be your phrase as you're walking into an important meeting and you're a little nervous and need a confidence and strength boost? How about before speaking with a spouse about something critical in your relationship, or when talking with your kids about a difficult subject? Is there a phrase you can use before talking to employees or your employer about a tense topic?

Once you find the power phrases that fit you, pick one and say it out loud over and over again in a private setting—walking in the woods or around the house by yourself or when driving your car alone. Don't just say it, but feel each word. Do it until you feel the energy in your body change, your state of mind shift, and the hero take control. This is you living at your full potential, no boundaries, no judgment, totally in control. Don't be embarrassed; no one is watching.

Your state of mind and your confidence are vitally important to your next level of success, wealth, and joy. I've never met anyone who had limited confidence and still had massive success. On the contrary, all the billionaires, millionaires, happy, and successful people I've met not only had a vision of where they were going and an empowering story, but they also had the ability to manufacture confidence and change their state of mind on demand. That means they are letting their inner heroes run their lives rather than the scared, dream-stealing villains. Now you, too, possess the tools to create confidence when it's needed most.

This chapter was designed to put the final dagger in the villain's heart and allow the best part of you, your inner hero, to be in control. You now have the tools and knowledge to do that. Remember, this transformation doesn't happen by practicing once or twice, just like one or two killer workouts at the gym won't get you the body of an Adonis. The more you practice, the more these shifts in your life will become your new habits and routines. You will see that you can handle life in a totally different way and success will flow to the hero that's you.

To help make that happen, let's drill down to the "one thing" that could help you create the wealth, abundance, and self-reliance on the next level to which you aspire.

Chapter 6

ONE SHINING GOAL

"We can either focus on what's working in our lives or on what's not working. There's evidence for both in everybody's life. If we focus on what's not working, we're going to feel generally much less confident and optimistic. If we focus on what is working, that's just a great, great gift, and it's available to us right now."

— Arianna Huffington, interview with Dean Graziosi

Most of the millionaire success habits that can transform your income, your wealth, your happiness, and your life I learned through 25 years of being an entrepreneur, as well as from some of the most successful people on the planet. These habits will help you acquire wealth that is not just abundant with money, but abundant with all things this wonderful life has to offer.

In this chapter I want to go deeper into your next level of wealth opportunity, whether it involves pursuing a career, starting your own business, or inventing the next level of you. In this busy world, we can be overwhelmed by opportunities and choices and end up doing nothing other than standing still.

You are reading this because you want the next level of wealth, and I'm guessing you already have an idea of the direction you need to go to accomplish that goal. Maybe you've just been scared to take action. Or maybe you're trying to find exactly what that action could be. So in this chapter, I'll help you determine the exact route you should take for your personal abundance and wealth creation. Warren Buffett is quoted as saying, "The difference between successful people and really successful people is that really successful people say no to almost everything." So let's dig in and define what should be a yes in your life and what may be best left as a no.

At the same time, I'm going to help you avoid the mistake of saying no because of an "I can't do something" mind-set. There truly is nothing you can't do when you have the right habits and confidence in place. I also want to dedicate this chapter to one of my mentors, Dan Sullivan. His commitment to serve others and help them achieve their full potential through his incredible company, Strategic Coach, have given me the many amazing tools and exercises you are about to encounter. Dan has worked and trained top entrepreneurs from around the world for over 40 years and has made a significant impact on my life. Thanks for the guidance and the gifts, Dan. These tools are not only powerful, they have helped me tackle new projects and clear my thinking so I could create many successful enterprises.

YOUR MAGIC LIST

Right now I want to do an exercise that will help you accomplish two things. First, it will help you discover what you should not be doing. Second, it will open your eyes to the opportunity that truly is aligned with who you are and help bring you bigger checks. (You can grab this exercise and share it with friends and family at www.thebetterlife.com under the "Book Resources" tab.)

First, answer these questions: What do you love to do? What fires you up? What makes your heart come alive, puts a smile on your face, and raises your confidence? Do you love negotiating deals? Do you love helping people? Do you love solving complicated problems? Do you love math, science, art, or literature? Do you love taking risks? Do you love being adventurous? Do you love solving conflict? Do you love selling? Do you love marketing and advertising? Do you love inventing?

Take a moment and think about what it is you love to do. So many times in life we forget what we love because we get stuck in the mundane day-to-day, and we forget our passions. Make a list of five or six things that light you up. Next, think about what you're really good at. If you weren't in the room, and your best friends, coworkers, or employees were talking about you, what would they say you are good at?

Would they say that you can walk into a room when there's a problem and solve it? Would they say you're meticulous, someone who measures twice and cuts once? Would they say that you have the ability to try something new, and that while you're a risk-taker, you're an educated risk-taker? Maybe you're good at solving problems, creating ideas, developing ideas, or putting processes in place. I don't know what you're good at, but you do. Write down what comes to mind.

Next, we need to talk about money, and big money at that. What thing in your life, if you just took action on it, would bring you the biggest check? Is it advancing the career that you are in, starting your own business, or taking the business you are in to the next level? It could be getting a promotion at your current job. Maybe it's getting a loan or hiring a marketing expert to help create more sales in your business. Whatever it is, what one thing will cut you the biggest check in your life? Think it through and write down what it is.

Next, list your money goals. Earlier, you formalized your goals with the exercise that asked, "Where are you? Where do you want to go?" So where do you want to go with your finances? Take that earlier list and implement it here, making it specific to your income. Is there a certain amount of money you want to accumulate so you can retire earlier, help your parents, and protect your family? Where do you want to live; how much do you want to spend on a residence in a given area; and how much does your dream home cost? Do you want to work for yourself, and if so, what is your revenue target? Do you want to have more employees, and how much revenue do you need to make to afford them? Do you want to sell your company, and if so, for how much?

Then I want you to think about what actions you need to start taking today to move those goals forward. The action or step can be, and in many cases should be, small, but you must take a step in that direction to generate momentum. Like General Creighton Abrams Jr. explained, "How do you eat an elephant? One bite at a time." And how do you run a 100-mile race? One step at a time. How do you take your finances to that next level, start a new business, get a new career, obtain a promotion at work, or advance your company? With one step at a time, and that can start today. So what are the actions that you have to take? What e-mails do you have to send? What negative people do you have to start pushing out of your life? What people do you have to attract into your life? What do you have to say no to? Write it all down.

So far you have made a list of tasks that you love to do; skills or areas that you're good at; activities that will cut you the biggest check; your financial goals; and action steps you need to take to move toward these goals. Yes, this exercise can relate to any part of your life, but we're sticking with money right now.

Lastly, I want you to take a long, hard look at all the items on your list. Whatever is not on them most likely needs to go on your "make more money" what-not-to-do list. A not-to-do list is probably more crucial to your success than a to-do list. This powerful success habit will open up time and bring you clarity on a new level. So what should go on your not-to-do list because it fails to serve your future or help you become the best possible you?

To help you identify what should go on your not-to-do list, here are some common examples:

- Hanging out with friends a couple of days a week who are negative and bring you down
- Jumping online to pay a bill and ending up surfing the Web, reading gossip, watching negative news, and wasting hours of your life

- Procrastinating on your new business because you don't have the clarity of exactly what to do first

- Spending too much time on the couch, too much time at the gym (yes it's possible), or too much time bickering with people over pointless matters

- Mowing your lawn weekly (or some other time-consuming but mundane activity) when you could pay somebody to do it and use that time and energy to achieve your bigger goals

This is your laundry list of things eating up your time. It's a crucial list of things you cannot do if you want more wealth in your life. So get your not-to-do list written and memorized so you can spot when you start doing things that are not serving your higher self.

Once you have your not-to-do list crafted, here is an extra bonus step. Next to each item on the list, write one of five things:

Eliminate

Automate

Outsource

Delegate

Replace

For instance, look at the previous example answer #2: "Jumping online to pay a bill and ending up surfing the Web, reading gossip, watching negative news, and wasting hours of your life."

You might do the following: Automate all bill paying. Take the few hours and set up autopay or delegate someone in your family or possibly an employee to handle all bills, and check them once a month. For online surfing, you might write: Eliminate or replace with positive, uplifting messages that fuel my goals and my "why."

The wrong habits are much easier to change when you have a plan to bump out and replace what is not serving you with things that can empower you. This gives you the tool to figure out the best course of action to get rid of the not-to-do list items and replace them with empowering success habits.

I've met zero entrepreneurs who are billionaires or multimillionaires who hate what they do. They all do things that they love and stuff that they are good at, which fuels their passion. They all have figured out what can cut them the biggest checks. They have goals and they know where they are going. Lastly, every day they take action steps toward their goals and aspirations. The more you do that, the more you can realize what is on your not-to-do list, and you can start to eliminate the areas of your life that don't drive you forward in your business and don't drive you toward that next level of income.

I told you in the beginning of this book that I don't have a magic money machine. However, you might, and in most cases, you do! To activate that machine, cut out what you shouldn't be doing. I love the phrase, "I'd rather give a B-level opportunity to an A player than an A-level opportunity to a B or C player." You have the ability to be that A player. You have opportunity after opportunity at your feet to take your life, your wealth, your abundance to the next level. How? By focusing on staying away from your not-to-do list and gravitating toward your to-do list.

PUSHING PAST THE FEAR

Next levels are always scary. To go from kindergarten to 1st grade is scary. Going from 8th grade to high school is scary. Graduating 12th grade and making your way to college is scary. It's scary dating someone new, scary getting engaged, scary getting married, scary having kids, buying a first house, starting a new job, starting a new life, meeting new friends, or even just riding a bike when you're three. You get my point: Every change, every next level is scary!

But we have our biggest breakthroughs when we push through the scary changes, don't we? Our next level is always on the other side of an obstacle and always on the other side of a challenge. The people who are afraid to go through the challenge are the ones who stay stuck in their lives.

How many people do you know who were rising in their careers, whose incomes were increasing, and who were becoming happier, and then they hit a wall? Maybe they encountered an obstacle they couldn't get around or a challenge they didn't know how to meet. More likely, their fear of the obstacle or challenge stopped them in their tracks. What they didn't realize is that their next level of life was most likely right on the other side of whatever barrier caused them to become stuck in place!

SO LET'S DO THE D.O.S.

So how do you overcome the fear of starting your own business, advancing your career, getting a promotion, or taking your business to the next level? You have a couple of options. One way is the "D.O.S. Conversation"—it stands for Dangers, Opportunities, Strengths. This is one of those exercises I learned many years ago from Dan Sullivan and that's why this chapter is dedicated to him. I've altered this exercise from Dan's original concept so that it suits our purposes here. Here's how it works:

To do this exercise, you can go to www.thebetterlife.com and use the D.O.S. worksheet. However, if you just want to create your own worksheet, make three columns with one small line at the top for the D.O.S. headers. Then on the header line, write *Dangers* on the left, *Opportunities* in the middle, and *Strengths* on the right.

Across the very top of the page, write your financial goal. It could be something like: Starting an online training business that does $100,000 in profit year one. Whatever it is, it needs to be specifically yours.

Now I want you to think of all the dangers and all the fears that you have regarding the goal you set for yourself. Is the danger that you don't have money to start? Is it that there's too much competition? Is it that you feel maybe you're not smart enough? Do you worry that you may not have support from your family? Do you fear that if you focus on money, maybe you'll become a different person?

Whatever your dangers and fears are, list all of them right now and think about what stands in the way of reaching your goal. This will allow you to visualize the fears that are paralyzing you from taking action, the exact things that are holding you back from starting or expanding a business, or even simply making more money.

Next, go to the opportunities column and shift your mindset, thinking nothing but optimistic thoughts. What are the opportunities that you have by creating this business? What are the things that drive you and excite you about that goal that's written across the header? Is it a niche market where you know you could do great? Will it give you the security, the freedom, and the time with your family that you're looking for? Would it allow you to finally reinvent yourself, get out of the job you dislike, take your company to that next level, and finally make more income? Just thinking about these opportunities should excite you.

So you've found the dangers, you've found the opportunities, now I want to move on to your strengths. What are the strengths you possess that could help you achieve your goal? Borrow from the "What's cool about me?" section we did previously or create new ones that are just business related. Maybe you're a great manager of people or a great problem solver. Maybe you're an action taker and people look up to you for that? Perhaps you're skilled at acquiring knowledge and turning it into wisdom—as someone who sought out and is reading this book, this is a likely one of your strengths. Maybe you're a follow-through person and never procrastinate. Or maybe you're a quick learner—you read something, absorb the lesson, and can then put your knowledge into practice.

Now you have a crystal-clear list of your dangers, your opportunities, and your strengths. That's the power of this exercise. You get to see that yes, some dangers exist, but that's the price of growth, both here and in all areas of life. But I hope this exercise helps you see in one glance, on one piece of paper, that your opportunities and your strengths will usually outweigh the dangers. Stand with pride, say it out loud, and maybe even pound your chest and say, "No way am I going to let those hold me back from the opportunity to evolve my life and my finances!" Do you want those opportunities to die or even worse, that you miss your chance to pounce on them like you may have missed them in the past? Heck, no. You truly have so many options to live your true purpose. The opportunity to make more money, protect your family, and live the life you desire is now! *Carpe diem*: seize the moment.

THE U.A. (UNIQUE ABILITY) CIRCLE

Now that you have one specific goal in mind that can cut you the biggest check and take you to that next level of wealth and prosperity, we must find out how you can make the time to take action toward that goal as well as what specific areas of your life best serve that goal. And the way to do this is by creating your unique ability circle. Unique ability and much of what I share here is once again a wonderful brainchild of Dan Sullivan.

You can create your own U.A. Circle by following the directions below (or go to www.thebetterlife.com and download the "Unique Ability" sheet under the "Book Resources" tab). Take a piece of paper and draw a small circle in the center of the page. Then draw three more circles around it creating three rings. In the middle of the first circle, write the words, "unique ability." (I'll explain this in more detail soon.) In the next ring, write "excellent." In the next ring, write "good." Then in the last ring, write "stink."

So what do these circles represent? In the bull's-eye is your unique ability, which is the thing or things in this world that you are naturally amazing at, things that put you in a flow, make you the most money, and cause you to feel the best doing them. As you move outward on the circle, you start getting away from those things that can grow your life and income the fastest and end up focusing on things that keep you doing busywork; it's like running on a treadmill and getting nowhere.

To understand how this is so, let's take a deeper look at the unique ability section. Your unique ability is your financial sweet spot—it confers the capacity to make the most money you possibly can. When you're in your unique ability circle, you may be able to make $500 an hour, $1,000 an hour, or even $2,000 an hour. Whatever that number is, when you're doing the thing that you love, the thing you were put on this earth to do, that is when you will receive the biggest check.

I look at my time from a "return on investment" perspective, which is an incredible success habit to have. For example, I pay for different people to do different things for me that are not in my own unique ability circle. There's no reason I should mow my lawn when, not only can I pay someone else to do it and free my time up to work in my unique ability areas, but also I can help the economy, giving other people the chance to make money. While someone else is mowing my lawn and landscaping my yard, I can be working in my unique ability. I get a significant return on my investment and make multiples per hour what that costs me to have my grass mowed! The return on investment of your time when you focus on your unique ability can be huge.

Here's a quick story that will drive home this point. When I was younger and was investing in real estate for the first time, I decided to put energy, effort, and the little money I had into an old run-down mansion and convert it into nine small apartments. After this project was complete, it was time for upkeep and maintenance. It had a massive front lawn and mowing it took me many hours every Saturday. So one day I hired someone for $50 to do it for me. That same day my dad happened to stop by to say hi, and when he saw someone else mowing the lawn and found out I'd paid $50 for this service, he completely flipped his lid. He said, "I can't believe you, paying someone to do something you could do yourself! You are going to go broke! You are not too good to mow your own lawn."

Given that this was my father's "story" at the time, his response makes perfect sense. Being born during the Depression and raised amid lots of scarcity had fostered this way of think-ing. He didn't like borrowing money. He did everything he could himself and managed his affairs the old-school way, which un-fortunately hindered his opportunity to make great money. He is smart as heck and a hard worker, but that wasn't enough. His story kept him anchored to an income that never rose above $30,000 a year no matter how hard he worked. He was on a treadmill for many years. Luckily I got him off of it. He has changed in a massive way since then, but at that moment he was darn mad. He left so fast in his car that the tires spun gravel all over the yard as he peeled out, not even saying good-bye.

I was upset my dad was mad at me, but I realized how wrong he was. That lawn at that big old apartment complex used to take me a half a day to mow. At that period of my life, I was fixing wrecked cars and selling them, while also looking for and negotiating my next real estate deal, and in that same half day that I paid $50 for someone to mow the lawn I could fix or even sell a car or I could put together a real estate deal that would make me far more than $50. My time for that half day fixing and selling cars was worth $500 to $1,000, maybe even more. So when you can pay someone to do something that you are not good at, or pay for something to be done by someone else and create a return on investment on what you pay, then you can concentrate on the things that make you the most money.

I've carried this ideal with me for my whole life. Some peo-ple may look from the outside and say, "Well, Dean, you have money; you easily can hire people to do things." But I realize now, looking back, that I hired people to do the things I sucked at even when I didn't have much money at all. I knew from a young age that if I could hire a personal assistant to book my travel, to pick up my dry cleaning, to buy me groceries, and to get my house taken care of, then I could work in my unique ability zone and make the most money possible—this yielded the best return on investment. When I first hired an assistant, I finally found the time to work on the things I'm excellent at, the things that are in my unique ability circle. Eventually, this phi-losophy helped me focus on speaking on stage, writing books, educating others, doing bigger real estate deals, and meeting people to do deals with. In turn, these activities helped my businesses flourish.

This unique ability approach is especially relevant in today's world where you have interns and virtual assistants who will work for pennies on the dollar for the experience. In fact, I'll give you a list of companies that provide virtual assistants that are incredible and can do small projects for you; they will free you to work on the things that are in the inner ring of your unique ability circle.

Think about how you spend your time. What things can you say no to that are not in your unique ability circle that will then allow you to say yes to the things that make you feel the best and can make you the most money? Because I promise you, when you learn to say no to things that don't take your wealth to that next level, you will find yourself accomplishing your income goals faster than imagined.

So if you took the time (and I hope you did) to create the visual circle or went to our website and grabbed the worksheet, start filling it in. What do you think are your unique abilities? Then progress to the other rings: what you are excellent at, what you are good at, and what you stink at. You can also label the hourly rate you anticipate for each item you list.

As Dan Sullivan teaches, the U.A. Circle is designed to be peeled away like an onion. Each week, each month, and each year you're peeling away one layer at a time; and these outer layers are the things you shouldn't be doing. Eventually you'll end up at the core of the onion, which signifies the things you should be doing. This is the exercise that can allow you to have more hours in a day, make more money by working fewer hours, and align yourself with the things you were meant to be doing.

THE GAP

Now that you understand the value of working in your area of unique ability, you will see how much easier and smoother the ride can be when you are working in and on things that ignite passion and get bigger checks. In theory, you would never again fall into a funk or feel insecure. Oh, how I wish it were that easy! As much as I hope this was possible, the truth is we all fall into a funk at one point or another. We all have self-doubt and think we're not good enough. Most of us relapse, thinking that we're not living up to our full potential and that we can't do something.

And because I know this to be true, I want to go through an exercise that Dan calls the gap. The gap is the funk that we fall into and the funk that stops us dead in our tracks. And it's not about if it's going to happen. It's about when, and then how fast you can rebound when it does.

Did I ever fail? Absolutely! I failed a ton in my life, but the thing I did best was that I failed fast and I had a quick rebound rate. And there is a way that you can strategically get out of your funk quickly and back on track using a tactical process that will become a habit. Let's face it: We constantly chase an ideal or even more commonly, perfection. We are chasing the perfect finances, perfect body, perfect parent, perfect spouse—perfection in all aspects of ourselves. You know exactly what I'm talking about.

When you're hitting the gym and looking good, you stop and realize you're not spending enough time with your wife or husband and you criticize yourself for neglecting this person you love. Or your relationship is great in so many areas but you hate your job or you're not making enough money and you give yourself a hard time about this failing. Or you're making all the money in the world, but you're not the parent you always wished you could be and you beat yourself up over it. And why is this?

We all have major accomplishments in our lives. But when is the last time you celebrated one of them? When's the last time you did something that was a goal of yours and you stopped and let it sink in, congratulating yourself? When was the last time you said, "I'm going to do something in the next ninety days!" and you did it and you rewarded yourself? I bet you haven't done these things in a very long time.

In our culture and society, when we complete our goals, we immediately look to the next thing that we haven't accomplished. Maybe you got a promotion or started your own business in the last year. You should be celebrating, but instead you respond to this achievement by saying, "Yeah, but I neglected my kids. I need to work on my relationship with my kids more." Then you get a relationship going with your kids, and you look down and notice you're a bit overweight and you say, "Yeah, I'm closer with my kids, but look at my gut."

We start creating this imaginary perfect person in our minds, and we're always falling short of it—it immediately puts us in the gap. It's like we are all stuck chasing the sunset. No matter how fast you go west, you can never catch the sunset. The same holds true with trying to reach this imaginary perfect person state. We are chasing an impossible task and setting ourselves up for disappointment and depression.

I want you to think about it this way. When we compare ourselves against our imagined perfect selves, we will always come up short. When we compare ourselves to the perceptions we have of others, we lose confidence and we start to fall into a funk. We start saying things like, "I could never have a family as loving and perfect as my neighbor's." Or we say things like, "I may be making the money I want, but it's not as much as John or Mary is making." And in most cases we don't know what's happening in other people's lives and what they are dealing with behind closed doors, so who are we to use them as our role models when we don't know the facts? It's just a habit many people fall into, and it sets us up to feel less capable, successful, happy, wealthy, and wise than John or Mary.

So, whether the funk comes from comparing ourselves to the perfect us or someone else, here's how you get out of this comparative hole fast and effectively. First, look at where you are right now in life. What have you achieved? What have you accomplished? What have you done really well? And whenever you think you're sliding into this gap of not feeling good enough or that you haven't accomplished enough, the secret is looking back. Remember all you've done in your life to get you to where you are today. Look at all the crap that was thrown your way that you overcame and got through. Because you truly have accomplished so much amazingness in your life!

Understand how much you've evolved! Fill your soul with self-appreciation for what you've done. Even when thinking about your past mistakes, recognize that you got through them and you're still here standing tall. You didn't give up, and you surely didn't crawl into a hole and hide. You're still chugging away, you're still pushing, you're still persevering, and in my book that is pretty damn amazing!

If I were going to be in a room with thousands of people, I'd want you to be in that room. Why? Because you made the choice to read this book, which means that you want to move forward in your life. That says a lot about who you are, since most people wouldn't even make the effort. So when you're trying to chase the horizon and chase the perfect version of you, and you fall into a funk, stop, mentally turn around, and remind yourself of what an impressive person you are and of all the things you've done to get where you are today.

The quicker you can make it a habit to turn around and focus on how far you have come rather than comparing or berating yourself, the quicker you can make that funk disappear. When you get out of your funk quicker, you have the ability to rebound faster and get back on track, working on things that serve your true vision. Think about this: Do you know why the ideal person and that perfect version of yourself are there? It's not to judge your current state against them and beat yourself up over what you haven't accomplished! No, they're there for you to use as the source of your goals. If you're coaching your kid's Little League team and you look down and you see a little belly below, you don't beat yourself up and say, "Ugh, I am fat. I can't believe this. How lazy must I be?" No! You just take what you see and you use it as a new goal on your list! You don't judge yourself; you see something you know needs your attention and then apply actionable steps to it. You say to yourself, "I'm going to lose five pounds in the next two weeks by giving up sugar and dairy. Oh, and I'm also going to run on the treadmill three days a week." How much better is that than saying, "I'm fat and I failed"? The secret is to pull goals from the ideal version of you, but don't ever compare yourself to the ideal. Those are two completely different things.

We've covered a lot of ground in this chapter, but what I hope you hold on to most is the idea of one shining goal and how it can take you where you want to go financially. If you set that goal firmly in your mind—and if you identify what you should and should not do—then you'll reach the abundant life you've dreamed about. The exercises I've shared—the D.O.S Conversation, the U.A. Circle, and the gap—all will help you reach that one shining goal. It's like a beacon in the night. Its brilliant light helps steer you toward it.

Of course, that light alone isn't enough. You don't just need to know where you're going; you need additional elements to make your journey safe and fast. In the next chapter, I'll share with you two of these elements: attraction and persuasion.

Chapter 7

ATTRACTION
AND PERSUASION

"If you want confidence, you generate it. You pull it from within. You summon it. You make it happen. You put it into play. And the more that you do that over, over, over, and over again, the more you'll gain that skill. Then it becomes easier for you to do in lots of different contexts. No one's ever going to be completely confident in every context, and they shouldn't be, because otherwise you wouldn't learn."

— Brendon Burchard, interview with Dean Graziosi

THE MONEY COMPOUNDER

Let me ask you a question: How important are attraction and persuasion in the quest for more success and more wealth? To me, they are beyond crucial ingredients. If you don't have the ability to attract the right opportunities and people to you, and if you lack the ability to persuade others and yourself to take action, then you simply have a good idea that will never gain momentum. If you already know this to be true, then you are probably nodding your head and saying, "Heck yes, Dean. You are one hundred percent accurate on the importance." For those who don't, let me explain how this is true.

When I look back at my list of business achievements and success, attraction and persuasion are the two highest-level habits I have mastered that propelled me to a level of prosperity that seemed inconceivable when I was younger. I've been blessed to create massive momentum and revenue through these two skills alone.

I've seen over and over again where these two crucial pieces of wealth are discounted and sometimes ignored. Believe me, I've failed miserably in these areas in the past because I didn't realize how important they were. If you want, you can spend all your time experiencing the same failures I had in my past. But we both know you are smarter than that. You have this book in your hands and you can gain an advantage from me, benefiting from my many years of fine-tuning them.

And before I go deeper into attraction and persuasion habits, let me assure you that I'm not going to offer you some advertising gimmick that will allow you to sell "effortlessly." That's simply not what this book is about, and by now I know you realize this. These habits are about getting to the deep foundational pieces that allow you to become a next-level person and take your wealth to a higher level.

So let's define our terms. Let's just get to the point: attraction and persuasion are really just more elegant ways of saying marketing and sales. Let me give you two of the best definitions I've ever heard for each. "Marketing is attracting what you want into your life and repelling the things you don't want." These could be clients, prospective buyers, even relationships. And selling is "getting people emotionally invested to take the action you want them to take," whether you want them to buy something, say yes to your bid, agree to use your services, or consent to start a partnership or relationship. Add to that getting them to take action with something that can improve their lives, and you've truly hit a home run.

I believe those are great definitions. And that is how I plan on getting you to look at marketing and sales by the time you are done with this chapter.

The real issue, however, is that some people don't want to be labeled a marketer or a salesman.

Let me ask you this: Did Martin Luther King Jr. use marketing to get people to listen to him? Absolutely! And when they did listen to him, was he trying to sell his ideals? Heck, yes! What if we never received the message he delivered? What if he wasn't good at attraction and persuasion, and he didn't move our country in a better direction? What about Mother Teresa, Gandhi, Benjamin Franklin, and Thomas Jefferson? Were they all gifted marketers and salespeople? If they weren't, you wouldn't even know their names or the incredible impact they had on this world. Marketing and selling yourself ethically is what makes the world go round! Or, taking an example from the world of business, do you think Apple or Microsoft don't use the art of persuasion and attraction every second of every day? They use these disciplines like nobody's business! You don't like your iPhone by accident.

And here is a truth I've come to learn throughout my years. If you want to start a new business or you want to move up the ranks in your company and you're afraid of selling and marketing, it means two things: 1) You are not going to succeed at the level you desire, and 2) You are looking at selling and marketing completely wrong.

When you know you are the perfect candidate to fill a role, or you have a product or service so amazing that you are doing people a disservice if you don't get it into their hands, then you should feel obligated to sell it like crazy—or hire someone who is great at this job. And if you're still nervous about these activities, then maybe you need to sharpen your passion or improve your product or service.

The need to sell applies to all areas of your life. Let's take relationships, for example. If you are single, you want to attract the right person. And once you do, you want to persuade her to go on a date with you, and then a second date, and then, if you're in love, to marry you at some point. You're not persuading her unethically, but rather being your best self and allowing someone to see all the positive traits you bring to them or the world. I would bet that if you are afraid of marketing and sales, then you've already hit a roadblock in your life in other areas.

If you don't want to market yourself to other people and sell other people on the value you bring, then you need to look deep inside yourself and figure out why. Maybe you need to work on you, your product, or your service. Regardless of what you want out of life, without attraction and persuasion, nothing works. But it all starts with truly believing in the product and believing in yourself. And here is the best part: In this chapter, no matter how good or bad you are or think you are, I'm going to give you simple yet effective habits to help you become amazing. And it's a process that will be easier than you would ever expect. Because it all starts with being your best self and not another version of you. Let me explain.

MARKETING AND SALES AT ITS FINEST

Can sales be bad? Absolutely! If you're selling drugs, cigarettes, or something that can hurt someone, then of course it can be used in a bad way.

But if that's not your thing, and I doubt it is, then think of the power of attraction and persuasion when done properly and used to improve people's lives, including your own. When I'm on stage or when I'm on camera selling, and I know my book can take your life to the next level, I speak with true passion and purpose. When you know you're doing the right thing, you feel ethically obligated to get others to take action.

If you have a way to convince someone you love to stop smoking and save his life, wouldn't you do everything in your power to persuade him to do so? You should sell him, persuade him, and do whatever it takes to get him to quit. If you had a gambling problem, and I had a way to stop you from ruining your life, I'd do everything in my power to get you to stop. You need to feel that way about your business, your products, and yourself. When you can start to think that way, it will no longer feel like marketing and selling. Because at the end of the day, it's not about using a fast-talking sales pitch or false promises for selfish purposes. It's about attracting the right people and the right opportunities into your life. It's about persuading yourself to be the best you can be and persuading others to take the action you desire. So let's discuss a few different habits that you can integrate into your life and career to master the art of attraction and persuasion.

PEOPLE WANT TO BE UNDERSTOOD

So how do I persuade others to work for me, take my advice, buy from me, or learn from me? And how do I attract the right people into these situations?

Here's the number one thing that has allowed me to be on TV for over 15 years, to teach and sell all over the world, to attract the right people into my life, to close big deals, and have multiple million-dollar companies: People will learn from you, listen to you, love you, buy from you, and hire you when they feel understood, not when they understand you. Let that sink in for just a second, and say it again out loud if you want. Write it down, highlight it, and put a star next to it. "People will learn from you, listen to you, love you, buy from you, and hire you when they feel understood, not when they understand you."

People are more likely to take action with and for you when they feel understood by you. Yet, I've watched most sales and businesspeople completely miss this fact. They will do all the talking and rarely find themselves being absolutely quiet and listening. Most people get in a meeting and they just sell, and sell, and sell, wanting to be understood or prove they're offering a benefit, instead of first seeking to understand the customer or person on other side of the table. This is the biggest mistake most people make. They innately focus so much on explaining the value they bring and what's great about them or their product instead of focusing on what the other person or their clients really need.

When "I and me" are used frequently in a boardroom, on stage, or even in a relationship, you can already tell that the speaker is destined to fail. Conversely, the people who possess quiet confidence, close deals, have great relationships and great friends, all "get it"; they get that understanding others is the key to their success. People are attracted to them because they let others feel understood rather than trying to make others understand them.

Obviously, you need to use "I" and "me" in conversation to communicate your ideas. I use these words in this book, since it's the only way to relate my experiences and the lessons learned. This book, though, is not about me, but surely is for you. I want you to feel understood by knowing that I've been where you are; that I've encountered and overcome the obstacles that you're facing; and that if you learn from those experiences, you can accomplish the same great things.

Here's a simple example on feeling understood versus understanding. This may help bring even more clarity to what I am expressing. If you go to a car dealership and a salesperson walks up to you and says, "I've been selling at this dealership for eighteen years, and I'm the best in the office. I can see you are a smart shopper and want a reliable car so this is the brand for you. And just so you know, this car gets the best mileage and has a rear camera and it sure is fast." Is that going to make you feel understood or is that person just making a sales pitch composed of benefits and ego? He just wants you to understand how good he is and what he's selling. That's the type of salesman that you run away from, right?

On the other hand, imagine if the car salesman came up to you and said, "So what brings you out here on a Sunday? Are you having a good weekend? So what's your family like—how many kids do you have? What are your needs? What are your goals? What's important to you in a car—safety, comfort, convenience, fun?" Then he just went silent and listened. Think of the difference between these two sales techniques. The first guy doesn't know if you need a minivan for your five kids and a dog or if you're just shopping for yourself. He's already in his pitch mode before you get done saying good morning. He's already selling to you before he takes a minute to make you feel understood. Sales go horribly wrong when the pitch is just about pushing a product.

I can't stress enough that understanding how others think is the foundation of attraction and persuasion. You see, so many times in life we find ourselves just waiting for the other person to be quiet so we can talk. Is that us wanting to understand people or is that us wanting people to understand us? When was the last time you had a conversation with someone and you looked her directly in the eyes and you heard every word she said, and actually listened to understand everything she was expressing to you?

That's why it blows my mind when I walk into a big meeting and someone is trying to close a deal and all I hear is "me and I." There is a better way to make deals happen and to have people do the things that you want them to do! Because if you think about it, a lot of times selling is just giving people a solution to their problem.

My team calls me the "problem solver," and I've learned through years of experience that this is a much more effective way to persuade and attract than any other method. In a recent company meeting my event coordinator said, "When there's a problem or a conflict, Dean just knows how to come in and solve it." And believe me it's so much easier than people perceive it to be. I don't solve it by coming in and talking up a storm and insisting, "I can do this" and "Listen to me." Instead, I come in and I simply have the habit of listening to understand. I want to know why one person thinks the way he does and why someone else thinks the way she does. Not just the words they speak, but the meaning behind their words! And guess what? I learn something about the people in the room, and they literally tell me how to solve the problem or clear the confusion. Then when I solve it, I look like a magician when truly they provided me with the clues to know what to do. Your ears are a better persuasion tool than your lips.

In contrast, I remember being in my 20s and being all excited and wanting to close a deal or be in a relationship. I would just talk, and talk, and talk. I would walk into a room and be like, look at me, look what I bring, look what I can do, look what I can offer. I rarely tried to understand the other person's needs.

But time, experience, failures, and success have taught me a valuable lesson. Now I have an advantage and a success habit that most people don't realize they can access as well: Listening to what everybody else is sharing. Specifically, try to answer these questions by listening hard and deeply:

- What is their pain?
- What is their fear?
- Why do they think that way?
- What are their stresses?
- What are their limiting beliefs or empowering beliefs?
- What are their goals?
- How can I solve their problem and put them on track to their goals while still getting what I need?

I am sure you can see how this technique works in many areas of life beyond the conference room. The biggest conflicts between spouses happen when people try to make their own feelings understood, and they never listen to what their partners have to say. In our minds, we're going, "Yeah, yeah, yeah, but this is what I think." We wait for an opening, and then it's back to making our point.

Do you want to end conflict? Then listen. Enter the internal conversations in other people's heads. Let them feel understood. Then you can unite to solve the problem. You want to attract the right people, but you won't attract them by being the know-it-all—even if you really do know it all. You simply will not persuade others if you're the person doing all the talking.

THE UNFAIR DEAL CLOSER

Seeing issues from another person's perspective can help you sell in ways you've never imagined. Here's a multimillion-dollar success habit that produces amazing results every time: If you're having trouble figuring out what the other side wants, or having trouble "closing the deal," use this tactic, which typically silences the room and puts you in charge without playing the big-shot role. Here's what I've done many times, and it always works: I politely interrupt everyone and ask the question I asked you in Chapter 1: "Hey guys, I just want to get clarity here. Let's pretend it's a year from now and we're looking back. This deal went through and is going so well that we're here celebrating our one-year anniversary. Could you guys tell me what that deal looks like? Can you describe the past year to me?" Then just stop talking and listen.

People who were just pushing their own agendas or wanting to be heard or explaining why it should go their way literally become silent and thoughtful. They respond with uncomfortable silences, with "Damn good question," and even with "I never looked at it that way." And when I hear that last one, I'm like, "Then what the heck are we doing here!"

This technique works in many situations. If your child is trying to decide where to go to college, say, "I want to understand what you want. So let's imagine it's a year from now. You've been off at college for a year and you just came home, and it's been the best year of your life. What does that year look like? Describe it to me." The answers you get will help your child make that difficult decision.

This also works well when you're arguing with your spouse. What if you say, "You know what? I don't want to try and persuade you to my point of view. Let's imagine it's a year from now, and we've just had the best year of our lives when it comes to our relationship. What does that past year look like? Describe it to me. What do our date nights look like? What have we done with our children? How much vacation time have we had? What house are we in? Describe it in detail."

This is a powerful technique because it makes people think hard about the answer. You get them to think, maybe for the first time, about where they really want to be in a year. Most people really don't know what they want. They may never have thought this through. So it's an enlightening exercise. It even works amazingly well when hiring people. I won't hire anyone who can't provide an answer. If they don't know what they want, how the heck can I?

When you get these answers, you know how to close the deal or pass on the deal and run the other way. And when I don't get good answers, when people don't have a clue, or they're just too negative, I will politely say, "Hey guys, let's do this meeting again when everybody else knows where they want to go, because I know what I want out of this meeting. Specifically, I want this, this, and this. It'll be a great year if we all do this together. But if you don't know what you want, then it will be hard for us to agree. I don't think we should negotiate a deal until you know clearly what you want."

TRANSPARENCY AND TRUST ALWAYS WIN

Once you master the art of understanding rather than being understood, you can move on to working on your transparency and simply being you. I've gotten so much further in my life by not only listening but also by being open and not trying to become anyone but my true self.

When I was younger, I was driving in a car with a gentleman who was a bit older and much more successful than me. I was in my early 20s and was at the start of going from that broke kid in my heart to generating real income and believing in myself. I was at a phase in my life where I was doing pretty well from where I had started—I had a used car dealership and collision shop as well as 20 apartments and I was building new houses. I was starting to become a big fish in my little town of about 7,000 people. But I was hungry for the next level! So this gentleman was taking me down to New York City to pitch an idea and business model I was calling E-Therapy to a venture capitalist group. I wanted to create a business to connect therapists with patients who would receive counseling online. I realize this is no big deal now, but it was a pretty awesome idea in 1994. Nothing even close existed at the time!

I remember driving to New York City in his Jaguar and discussing weaknesses and strengths. He looked at me and said, "Dean, what do you think your biggest weakness is?"

I responded, "My biggest weakness is that I trust too easily, and because of that I have been taken advantage of several times. I have to learn to be more businesslike, be more shrewd."

He said, "So you think that your biggest weakness is that you are too nice and trustworthy?"

I said, "Yep."

He looked straight in my eyes and said, "That's crazy that you think that, because I think that's your biggest strength. You're twentysomething years old, you have no big business experience, no money to fund this idea you are proposing, and you have no college degree. Yet, I'm bringing you to New York and risking my reputation because you're so trustworthy and because you're so caring."

He continued, "By being honest, transparent, and a man of your word, you're going to get taken advantage of. But when you look back in life on how much you lose compared to how much you'll gain by attracting the right people and persuading them to take action with you because of your kindness and transparency, it'll far outweigh your losses." This was over 20 years ago, and he's still 1,000 percent right to this day.

By the way, that wasn't my true "story," it was a limiting belief I got from my dad growing up. He loved me a bunch as parents do, and he thought he was protecting me by giving me this belief. It died that day!

I realize now that when you want to persuade and attract the right people, the right money, the right job, the right business into your life, transparency always wins. Many times you'll do business with people who keep certain things hidden or try to mask who they really are. I decided at a young age that I was going to be me regardless of what the outcomes were. So maybe some would consider how I approach business to be too transparent, too trustworthy, but now I know that people want to do business with me simply because of that! Who cares if, on occasion, someone takes advantage of me? I remember when I first launched deangraziosi.com and I opened it up to the world, I was as transparent as possible. I wanted people's feedback on every video and every post I created. Sometimes I got feedback that wasn't very pleasant. But at the end of the day I was being the true me, and people appreciated that fact. And by listening to what people had to share, I got better.

When I started being completely transparent and speaking from the heart, my company zoomed to the next level. In this book, I'm "speaking" to you from the heart. I get to talk about my family, my personal struggles, my relationships, and my life. I know that in my business relationships and even in my personal relationships, the more transparent I am about my good and bad feelings, the better my relationships become. The more we open up and become ourselves, the more we bond. And that does nothing but help us get to another level. Authenticity and enthusiasm outweigh perfection and structure almost every time.

Now think about this concept as it relates to your business. How can you be more transparent in your business and in your career? I'm not talking about being someone who's always wearing their heart on their sleeve or boring everyone by constantly talking about their feelings. I'm talking about being honest, open, and authentic with the people of your business. Because you can't pretend to be someone you're not or even exaggerate who you are—false hype is just as harmful as being inauthentic. Salespeople who rely on hype instead of understanding the customer rarely succeed. As consumers, if we detect hype or BS, we tune out or we just leave, end of story! Transparency is a better strategy every time and in every situation. Whether we're talking about your business or your personal life, people can see through insincerity and falseness. Authenticity always wins.

SCARCITY MIND-SETS DON'T SELL

At their core, people either have a scarcity mind-set or an abundance point of view. People with scarcity mind-sets always see the worst in everything. An example of scarcity thinking is when people say things like, "We're running out of oil and the world is going to collapse. We're too much in debt and we'll never get out this mess. If I make money, I must be robbing it from somebody else. The American dream is dead. The days of being independently wealthy and creating your own wealth are gone."

We all have scarcity thinking deep down somewhere in our lives, so we have to be vigilant about spotting it when it affects our viewpoints and decisions. We have that fear of scarcity, that limiting belief, that doubt.

It's that inner villain we spoke about earlier in the book who whispers in your ear, "No you can't," or "It's not going to happen," or "It's too late." It can totally mess with your mind and get you out of focus. Or worse, it becomes a self-fulfilling prophecy: You focus so obsessively on these negative outcomes and that's exactly what you get.

Examine your own thoughts for a scarcity mind-set. In Peter Diamandis's book *Abundance*, Peter talks about oil and how some people say, "We're running out of oil. What are we going to do with our cars?" He writes, "Oil used to be the greasy stuff on camel's hoofs. What changed that was intellectual capital. Smart people figuring out how to process it, how to use it, how to burn it, how to build a combustion engine and power the world. If intellectual capital and an abundant mind-set got us there, why can't an abundant mind-set and thought process take us to the next level?" We have electric cars now and someday we might be running cars on water or solar power.

People with a scarcity mind-set often say, "If you get rich, you must be taking from someone else." Not true. If you get rich, you found a way to bring value to the world. I found a way to attract people to something that brings them to another level, that creates tremendous value in their lives. If you do that, if you create value, you'll create wealth. If you do great things with your money, help your friends, help your family, build security, donate to charity, do the things that give back to the world, then that's a wonderful accomplishment. That's living with an abundance mind-set.

You always want to avoid thoughts that come from a scarcity mind-set, that try to convince you there is not enough: not enough money, not enough time, not enough jobs, not enough friends. Whenever you notice yourself falling into a scarcity mind-set, try to do a 180-degree turn and change it to an abundance mind-set.

I've seen many struggling entrepreneurs who blame a hundred factors for their businesses not working. It's always someone else's fault or the result of a situation beyond their control. After listening to this litany of excuses, I always think the same thing: Their vision is clouded by a scarcity mind-set. They are innately negative about all things. Their customers felt it; their families felt it. There's a lack of congruence. These individuals see what is wrong in the world while trying to convince you what is right. It just doesn't work that way. Be aware of and use the strategies in this book to see the abundance in front of you every day. Change your thinking and watch your attraction and persuasion skills skyrocket.

SELL PEOPLE WHAT THEY WANT

I have seen huge companies and start-ups with passion fail, companies with lots of money raised never get off the ground, and inventions flop because the inventors were certain they had created something that people would buy because it was absolutely needed.

So remember this phrase for the rest of your life: People most often will buy what they want, not what they need. I have seen founders of companies who invest tons of money in creating exciting products but who never address whether consumers will actually want them.

And does this only happen in business? Do we sometimes think we know exactly what our spouse needs, what our children need, what our family members need, and what our employees need? And then we deliver that with an epic fail because what they really wanted was something completely different? We assume we know what they need, but deep down they wanted our love, wanted us to listen, wanted us to pay attention, or wanted us to stop being so distracted.

I know I make this mistake with my children sometimes. I focus so much on what I think they need, and I forget to satisfy what they really want. There are a lot of people that need to lose weight, but they actually want to eat fatty foods, and ice cream, and too much bread. People need to go to the gym, but if they don't want to, they'll never walk in the door. Some people need to go to marriage counseling, but they want to go to the bar and have a couple of drinks to numb the pain of a bad relationship.

No matter what your goal is—taking your business to the next level, starting a new business, or evolving through the ranks in your current job—remember that supplying what people want in most all cases will win over supplying what you think they need. Do the research, and understand what your prospect wants. What does the end consumer want that you can satisfy? What does your boss want that you could provide? What does the next level of your business look like from your employees' perspective—what will make them work harder and see your bigger vision?

I have a saying that I think will serve you well, even if you might question the ethics of it initially. But it's something that is very true, and I'd like to see if you can apply it in your life, in your business, and in your ability to create wealth: "Sell people what they want, and give them what they need." If you reverse this concept—if you try to sell them what you think they need—you'll probably fail. Better to hit the bullet points of what they want and wrap it around what they need.

That's what you see all the time in successful marketing and advertising. If people need to lose weight, just telling them they're unhealthy or that their weight can shorten their lives, may not be enough to get them to take action. They probably know they need to lose weight, but a good ad might spark the powerful want inside them.

"I want to feel sexier about myself. I want to be able to go to the beach, or to the pool, and feel confident in a bikini. I want to have my spouse look at me as sexy again, or look at me as the fit man or fit woman I used to be." When you tap into people's wants, you stir their emotions, and emotions make decisions. As long as you're emotionally engaging them in a process, or an action that can help their lives, do anything in your power to turn a proposed behavior into reality.

If you can do anything in your power to get your unhealthy, overweight friend to take action, lose weight, and get healthy, then you do it! But know if you just tell them, or try to market to them, or try to persuade them of what they need to do, you might fall flat. In your personal life, your business, and your wealth creation, people will buy what they want over what they need. Adjust accordingly.

TELL STORIES

You'll notice that throughout this book I use a lot of real-life examples to illustrate the points I am trying to make. And that's because I think examples—anecdotes, case histories, stories—are an essential part of persuasion. To make these stories effective sales tools, though, you need to tell them the right way. People often say to me, "Dean, you've been on stage and on camera forever. But unlike you, I'm shy. I can't persuade anybody; my message isn't going to attract anybody." I know I seem like an extrovert on camera, and I seem like an extrovert on stage in front of thousands of people. But truth be told, I'm a total introvert. When I go to my kids' functions and all the parents are there, I want to hide in the corner. And I'm being completely honest here; it's just how I am.

Knowing how to tell good stories, though, gives me confidence on stage. And not only that, but when you learn to tell stories well, you will increase your ability to persuade and attract people. If you can tell a story with a message woven expertly into it to illustrate key points, you will be more persuasive. Being a good storyteller can show your boss that you're more qualified than he might think. Or show your employees that you understand who they are. Stories can have all the impact in the world.

What stories from your past can you tell that will strike people as funny? What stories can you relate that reveal your work ethic or how smart you are? Do you have stories that will demonstrate what you can accomplish or what other talents you have? I suggest you craft and practice telling your best stories; the ones that can increase the power of your message.

I've been on TV for 15 years. And on every show I tell stories with an impactful message rolled into it. Next time you see me on TV or see me on stage, watch for the examples I integrate into my message. Stories have helped me transition from being the shyest kid in my class, who would skip school if I had to do a presentation, to a self-assured public speaker, who can get up on stage by myself and speak to 15,000 people. So what stories can help you make this transition?

Whether you are thinking, "This is awesome; I have lots of stories to tell," or you're uncertain if you have any good ones, take a moment and list the stories that could be good candidates. Remember you may be looking to share a lesson, overcome an obstacle, illustrate your dedication or hard work, or show how caring you are in a relationship. Take a moment and write what would come after the sentence: "I think there is a great story behind the time I did [fill in the blank]." Then dissect the story for the pieces you want to emphasize and share. When you tell this story to other people, remember to relate it to them, and make them anxious to hear the conclusion so they can benefit from the idea or learn from you. And as you're doing this exercise, keep in mind that enthusiasm and authenticity outweigh perfection and structure almost every time.

My storytelling skills were really tested a few years back when my family and I were on vacation in California and we were sitting outside around a firepit. My son was five years old at the time and the shortest kid in his school, just like I was. And I knew that one of his classmates was making it a little tough on him. Everyone was sitting around the fire after we had just finished making s'mores, and I could see sadness on my son's face. When I asked him what was wrong, he brought up going back to school in a few days, his small size, and how he wasn't sure he wanted to go back.

He didn't mention the kid or anyone making fun of him directly, but the writing was on the wall. Now I could have just said to my son, "Brody, I was small too. I know what it feels like, but it made me stronger, made me tougher, and I achieved so much because of it. You're going to be fine." That would be me trying to get him to understand me, my feelings, and what I went through. As I noted, this approach wouldn't create a connection, and it wouldn't help him feel understood.

If I would have said, "Don't worry about it; it's no big deal. You'll be fine," there would have been no emotional connection. So in my head, I immediately had to figure out how to provide an empowering lesson and have him see that he was created that way for a reason. How could I teach him to be strong without making it about me and at the same time make him feel understood? That's when a story popped into my head. And this one I made up as I went along.

I said, "Brody, have you ever heard of Toof?" Not tooth, but toof, spelled t-o-o-f. He said no, and then my daughter Breana perked up her ears and chimed in with a "No, who's Toof, Dad?"

"Toof is the one-toothed werewolf. He's only half werewolf, and his werewolf side only comes out during the half-moon, but boy he is ugly as heck when that happens. He has patches of long fur across his body, one tooth, he howls weird, and he's just funny-looking."

And they were like, "Really? So what happened with Toof?"

I said, "Well, you know, Toof went to school, and everybody thought he was a normal student, until one day there was a half-moon! And all of a sudden, Toof comes out of the bathroom with big patches of hair, one tooth sticking out a little sideways, looking really weird. So do you know what happened? Just like everywhere, at every school, and during every time period of life, there was a bully who picked on him. The bully called him funny-looking, and he called him bad names, and just made him feel sad, made him cry, and made him feel alone."

And my kids were looking at me with questions in their eyes: "What happened next? What happened to poor Toof? How old is he? Is he real?"

"Yeah, but then one day, Toof was walking to school, and he saw the bully that always made fun of him getting dropped off by his dad. What he noticed was that his dad was bullying him, and was really mean to him, and pushed him out of the car, and it hit Toof's heart. And he said, 'I don't care how he treats me. I now understand why.' And Toof walked up to the bully, and he said to him, 'Listen, you can be mean to me, but I understand why you are, and I'm sorry your dad treats you that way.'

"And he tried to give him a hug, and the bully kind of pushed him away. But then, all of a sudden at lunch, the bully sat with Toof. And they sat and talked to each other, and they eventually became friends. But that day, it wasn't really about the bully. What Toof realized is that he wasn't going to give anyone else permission to make him feel bad. That he was in control of his emotions and feelings.

"He decided to be happy no matter what other people said or did. He realized it doesn't matter what he looks like, or what his hair does, or that he's half werewolf and half human. What matters is how he feels inside, and that people's words on the outside can't affect him.

"And Toof got empowered, and all of a sudden the whole school started liking him. Soon his confidence grew, and he became head of the student council. And Toof went on to go to an amazing college, and get married, and be happy because he realized that his value wasn't in other people's thoughts, but that his value was who he was on the inside."

And oh my God, my kids went nuts! They loved Toof. They were like, "Toof is so awesome; I want to meet him. Tell us other stories!" And we sat around the campfire for hours as I made up Toof story after Toof story. In one story he got married, in another he had children. Then we named his kids Silly, Lilly, and Dilly, and all these incredible messages came from this story. But what did I do at the end of the day? I was able to give a message to my son that I wanted to communicate. I empowered him, and I empowered my daughter through a story with a powerful message. If I would have just said it without the story, it never would have sunk in. Needless to say, my son totally forgot about his school and height worries and the mean kid wasn't relevant anymore.

You have the same great stories inside you whether they're fact or fiction. Think about the stories you can tell your family, your significant other, your customers and business partners, and anyone else you encounter.

DON'T SELL PAST THE SALE

Have you ever closed on a sale? I'm not just talking about in business, but even as a kid when you convinced your parents to take you some place, drop you off at a friend's, or stay up late? Have you ever sold a house or a car? Have you ever sold an idea to your boss? Have you ever closed a sale in any sphere of life, but you kept talking so much that something caused the other party to change their mind to no?

Have you ever been on a date, and you wanted to go on another date, and you got a yes from the other person, but then you kept talking about it and for some reason the date didn't happen? I watched my father make this mistake when I was young, and I tease him about it to this day. When I was about 20 years old, we had a used car lot, and on Saturdays, my dad and I would both be down there selling cars. I always used to joke with my dad when someone pulled up to look at a car: "Do you want me to go out and sell it, or do you want to go out and scare him away?" And we'd laugh.

I was lucky enough to recognize at a young age what my dad did wrong. My dad would go out, talk up the benefits of the car, and the customer would say, "You know what? I'll take it." And my dad would continue to talk about the car and say something like, "Well, we even painted the whole thing recently!" Then the guy would say, "Oh, you painted it. I get nervous on new paint jobs. You know, I'm going to think about it a little more . . ." and the sale was gone.

I just recently experienced this same scenario with my daughter. She was asking me for something and kept asking and did a good job of persuading me to say yes. She wanted to go over to her friend Larson's house on a school night, and we really didn't want to allow that to happen. But she got her homework done, made a strong case for this visit being the exception to the rule, and finally, I said yes.

And once I said yes, she kept talking and talking and let it slip that she had a test the next morning very early, and that she hadn't studied for it yet.

And I said, "Unfortunately, Breana, you can't go now."

And she said, "But Dad, you said yes!"

And I said, "Breana, take this as a valuable lesson. Do not sell past the sale. When Daddy says yes, that's when you just be quiet and say thank you."

When the person trying to buy a car from my dad said, "Yes, I'll take it!" that's when he needed to stop selling and just say, "Thank you. Let's process the paperwork." When you want to persuade someone to take action, to buy your product, to loan you money at the bank, or get private money to fund your deal, do not sell past the sale. That's when it is time to be quiet.

I teach this all the time in my real estate education forums. If you go through why you want the house, what you think it's worth, and then you say, "The price I can pay is $100,000," it's time to shut your mouth, because typically, the first person who talks in the negotiation process loses. So silence is golden, at least if you time your silence properly.

THE POWER OF PASSION

Finally, I can't end a chapter about attraction and persuasion without discussing passion. When you're passionate about something, you care deeply about it to the point where it's on your mind all the time. People who sell with a fervent belief in what they're selling are more believable than those who sell with slick presentations or with statistics. When you're evangelical about your product, point of view, or proposal, people are much more likely to take you seriously. They're attracted to your sincere belief in what you're selling.

This is why I have had you think through so many exercises starting with the questions "Where are you?" "Where do you want to go?" and "Why do you want it?" Your goals and how badly you want to achieve them involve passion. Passion is the ultimate fuel for achievement and persuasion. I am not the smartest person in the world. I'm usually not even the smartest person in the room. But I've always been the most passionate about everything I did. And I found confidence when I needed it. Those two success habits, combined with letting people feel understood, allowed me to overcome many obstacles and become fabulous at marketing and sales. Think about what they could do for you!

Fundamentally and foundationally, passion, confidence, and helping people feel understood may be the secrets to my success. Shhh, don't tell anyone. All kidding aside, what I've shared in this chapter is what can get you where you want to go the quickest. If you master attraction and persuasion, you're going to achieve amazing things at a speed that will boggle your mind. For the rest of your life, if you just do the things I shared in this chapter, you will have exponential growth, guaranteed.

And there are a lot of books you can read about how to get somebody to say yes. But in my opinion, many of them rely on gimmicks and psychological tricks. That's not what I'm sharing here. No trickery. My goal is to help you become the person who attracts everything the right way, the ethical way. I want you to become the person other people look at and say, "Everything always goes right for her. She always attracts the right relationships, the right job, and the right business. She knows how to sell everybody on what is right, and everyone benefits. She is so lucky." But you know now that this has nothing to do with luck. It has everything to do with adopting the success habits that I've shared.

Chapter 8

AFTER THE "YES"

"A belief is a poor excuse for an experience. If you want to believe
something, that's a good place to start, but the most powerful thing
is to put yourself in the experience. If you think you know what
China is like, go to China and then you'll really know what
China is like instead of making up a story in your head."

— Tony Robbins, interview with Dean Graziosi

Attraction and persuasion are crucial to making your vision and your goals become your reality. Yet they are not the final pieces of your dynamic success habits. When you add one more habit to those game-changers, the trio can become the foundation for any start-up business to succeed or give you the boost to reach a new level in your company. This secret success habit is managing people's feelings after the "yes." Let me explain.

But first, let's summarize where you are at this point.

- You have discovered the clarity of where you want to go in life.

- You have identified and purged the inner villain.

- You have replaced a limiting story with a limitless story.

- You have come to understand the avatar of the best you.
- You have discovered the one truly monumental combo that can take your wealth to the next level.

The most accomplished people in the world use these millionaire success habits in their business lives as well as their personal lives.

But this chapter is dedicated to a secret success habit most people overlook or maybe never even think of—and this oversight causes them to fall short. It's a habit that sets supersuccessful people apart, since it helps them understand what needs to happen after the yes: the after-sale relationship, the after-sale feelings, and the after-sale reciprocity.

I looked back at my blessings and the ability to generate hundreds of millions of dollars through all my businesses and my brands, and I realized a lot of this success was because I obsessed about how my clients felt after they said yes. As minor as this may feel right now, believe me it could be the difference between decent success and blockbuster growth.

Applying a very tactical but simple process, you will understand how your clients or other people in your life feel and what they deserve from you after the yes. Throughout this chapter, I'm going to lean more toward wealth creation and business than other forms of success. But this strategy can help in every area of your life.

For example, think about attracting and persuading someone to marry you. What happens after you make this relationship sale, after the yes? Have you ever heard someone say, "Oh my God, my husband was so kind, so sweet, so romantic, so charming, and then we got married and everything changed"? Have you ever heard people express their excitement about creating a partnership? They were going to start a restaurant or start a new online business together, and the relationship was just magnificent. And then they launched the business and in five or six months they're in court battling to dissolve it.

Have you ever been charmed by a salesman, a product, a company, or an online sales funnel—where you felt amazing, where you felt understood? They did all the things I taught in the previous chapter: They knew what you wanted, they were listening to you, and they delivered exactly what it was that you wanted. But then after the sale, you never heard from them again. In fact, when you tried to call them, you couldn't get through or you talked to someone who was disinterested or unhelpful.

Everything I shared up until this point will create unimaginable momentum, but if you want to maintain success, evolve it, and take it to heights you've never even dreamed of, you need to understand how to bond and build relationships after someone says yes. The following is a cautionary lesson about what happens when you neglect this success habit.

Several years ago, my good friend Joe and I decided we wanted to help out billionaire Sir Richard Branson and his charitable arm, Virgin Unite, an incredible foundation doing magnificent things all around the world for those in need. It is such a good organization that when Joe and I helped raise a million dollars, 100 percent of that money went on the ground to help. Richard pays all the expenses of Virgin Unite out of his pocket so all donations can go to the people in need. Amazing!

So we went to work, raised the money, and ended up going to Necker Island (Richard's private island in the British Virgin Islands) and spending a week with him. We did this for a couple years in a row. I got to sail around his island, boat race with him, snorkel, eat dinners, etc. It was great to get to know, love, and understand this man who's done so many great things. He started Virgin Records, Virgin Airlines, Virgin Mobile, plus a plethora of other companies and helps so many people in the world who need it.

So with the work we did, and the money we raised, and the significant amount of my own money I put in, I felt great, like I was a part of something big and significant. But I have to tell you, after I donated the money, the communication with the organization ceased. This had nothing to do with Richard personally, and the organization itself truly appreciated all we did. But they never even thought about the after-sale relationship. I never heard from anybody. I never saw where the money went, I never got pictures of schools, and I never heard about the kids that it helped.

At one point I paid for a whole bunch of clothes for homeless kids in America, and I knew the clothes were distributed across the Midwest. But after I donated, I never heard anything else from the organization. I felt disconnected. And what happened was that I drifted away from helping that charity, even though I loved what it was doing and I truly love and respect Richard Branson. And I ended up moving on to help other charities, but this time I explained the need for follow-up and follow-through when we had the opportunity to talk.

One of John Paul DeJoria's claims to fame is his obsession with understanding people—understanding his employees after they've said yes to coming to work for him, as well as understanding the needs of his clients who are buying his tequila and his shampoo and making sure they want to come back.

John Paul once said, "I'm not in the selling business; I'm in the reselling business. I want to make people happy so they continue to buy and buy again." If you want intimacy back in your relationship, bring that same thought process and watch what happens! Do the same things you did to win your spouse over in the beginning and watch things heat up. Business is the same way.

If you were part of my real estate education or bought one of my *New York Times* best-selling books on how to invest in real estate, you know that after you bought my book you would get a video from me every single week on how to improve your life, deliver capabilities, and deliver inspiration every time.

I didn't charge for it. I didn't tell people I was going to do it. I just delivered it. I made sure my students got e-mails after the sale to make sure they knew that I cared and I appreciated their business. This was part of my "after-the-sale" relationship building; I was expressing appreciation that they had faith in me.

And guess what. They felt it, they recommended me to others, they bought more products, and they wrote great reviews. Not because I bribed them, but because they knew I cared.

For the people in my high-level mastermind groups (like the group I have with my good friend Joe Polish, where people pay $100,000 to be with Joe and me a couple of days a year), I make sure that they know that after they cut that check, I care—I am going to deliver massive value, and I care how they feel.

You know that people will forget your name. I forget names all the time. People forget what you do for a living. People forget where you went to college. People forget how they first met you. But what they won't forget is how you made them feel. You see, we go around our whole lives looking to feel better. Why do you do anything? Why do you want to make more money? Because you want to feel better or you want to feel a certain way. Why do you want to fall in love? Because you want to feel amazing reciprocal warmth and connection. Why do you have a drink? Why do you exercise? Because of the powerful feelings attached to these activities. So remember this truth: "When it comes to your clients, it's all about them, and it's all about how they feel, especially after they said yes to purchasing your services, purchasing your company, purchasing whatever it is you have to sell. It's not about what you think they want. It's not about what you think they deserve. It all comes down to how they feel."

As I'm writing this section of the book, I had a reminder as bright as the sun about why it is terrible to not comprehend how someone feels. It was breakfast and my kids and I were sitting around the table. My son has this magical memory, and he happens to love specialty crayons right now. I'm not talking about the typical red or green. He likes the fancy crayons like English Vermillion, Dark Venetian Red, and Permanent Geranium Lake! So we were sitting at the table, and there was a pack of 50 on it. I pulled out a crayon and said to my son, "What color is this?" And he named it. I said, "Wow!" Then I pulled another one out, another one out, and with all of these crazy names he got 50 in a row right.

I was shocked! I was ready to fall off my chair. My daughter, seeing the praise my son got, said, "Let me have them. Let me study them." So she looked at them for two minutes and while she was doing it, I said, "Hey, guys, we all have unique gifts and unique abilities. That's just one of Brody's. I could never do that, but Breana, there are unique gifts you have that Brody doesn't."

She said, "Okay, now ask me." She got the first one wrong and she got a little sad and said, "Let me study them."

Well, it was five minutes before school, so I said, "Breana, there is no time to study them; you have to go to school."

She got sad, started to cry, and said, "Dad, it's all about Brody. You play with him every day in the morning and not me."

Thinking I was doing the right thing—and failing to recognize that I was not acknowledging how she felt—I said, "Bre, that's an absolute lie, and you know that it is. Don't tell yourself a lie, and don't tell me a lie. I work every day to make sure my time between you and your brother is completely equal. So you told yourself a lie. You told me a lie. I want you to take that back, and I want you to go get ready for school."

Completely sad, she cried and walked away. It was the first morning in her nine years of life she left without saying "I love you" and giving me a kiss. After she was gone for about a half hour, I felt terrible about what I had done. I had ignored her feelings! I had ignored how she felt. It didn't matter if it's true or not; if she felt that way that means it's real to her!

It hit me so hard that I jumped in the car, went to school, and politely asked to pull her out of class. I walked outside in the courtyard and sat down on a bench with her, looked her in the eye, and said, "Bre, your dad made a massive mistake. It doesn't matter if I think it's true. I know I spend time with you and your brother equally. But I dismissed the way you felt. I dismissed your feelings. I basically said, 'Tuck them down,' and that what you feel doesn't matter because your father knows the truth, and I was completely wrong. All that could do is hurt our relationship and make it so you don't open up to me in the future. And I want to give you my word that I'm going to work hard to never do those things, and if I do, I'll make sure I fix them right away. And I apologize."

My daughter's smile was so unbelievable. And a thousand pounds fell off my shoulders because I saw in an instant that all she wanted was to be understood. She didn't care about the facts.

Therefore, obsess about how your client or the people in your life feel after they say yes. When you care post-purchase or post-sale just as much as you did pre-sale or pre-purchase, that's when you are putting to work one of the biggest secret success habits to massive wealth and business and life success.

CAMP OUT

My son used the phrase "epic fail" last week. I've heard that term for years now, but you know when your seven-year-old uses it that it's officially a trendy phrase! Here's the definition of an epic fail in life and in business: When you don't "camp out" in the mind of your client, or your spouse, or your children, or your employees, or your employer, you have epically failed!

What exactly do I mean by camp out? Figuratively, it means that I want to set up my tent where they live. In other words, it means I want to walk in their shoes.

If you camped out on a friend's couch for two weeks and you got to see firsthand their routines, their habits, what they worry about, what their goals are, and what they hate, you would know that person 100 times better than if you knew them only through a handful of transactional conversations.

So I want you to use this analogy and remember that when you camp out in the minds of your clients and everyone you care about, you are moving toward your next level of abundance. You see, people spend copious amounts of money on marketing, advertising, attraction, and persuasion just to get the client to say yes, but after the sale is over, many individuals forget who that client is as a person and what he wants.

Here's a scenario that illustrates how easy it is to forget. When a start-up happens, everyone is hungry and eager. Your employees are dedicated to understanding the wants of the clients, but then business starts to boom. Now you have to hire more employees, a CFO, a personal assistant, salespeople, and a customer service team. And as your company grows and business is going well, you join the local country club and move into a larger space in a better location.

This scenario plays out in all types of businesses. Your law firm began with four clients and now has 100. Your online business started with 10 buyers a month and now has 500. As a doctor you opened your doors and had four patients a week—and now you have four patients an hour. And guess what happens next? Your company or your job is evolving, which means you're busier, and you have less time in the day. Or your thoughts are increasingly focused on growing your business, rolling out your marketing, or on all the other extracurricular activities that your growth has created.

In many instances, you neglect or forget what's going on in the mind of your current clients; you stop camping out in their thoughts. You stop paying attention to their fears, what they want, and what they need from you. Instead you are focused on processes and systems. And of course you need all of that in a business, but when you don't camp out in the minds of your clients, they feel disconnected, and you've blocked yourself from the highest level of success.

And camping out can be used in any area of your life—with your boss, your employees, your parents, your spouse, or even your kids. In terms of this last relationship, I can't emphasize enough how crucial camping out is—and I'm not talking about going to your local state park. Get to know their lives. I have friends that keep themselves so busy that they miss the chance to bond with their children. And then when they *do* want to be with their children, they find out they've missed their chance because their kids are older or less interested.

How do you think it would help your relationship with your kids if you knew all of their friends' names? What if you knew what goes on at recess, what class they struggle in, what teacher they like, what teacher annoys them, what's trendy among their age group, or what boyfriend or girlfriend issues they are having?

You see, we have this tendency to be in physical proximity to our families but not camp out in their thoughts. We often finish their sentences rather than let them tell us what's on their minds. Or they come home from school and we say, "How was school?" And they say, "Good," and walk into their room, and the conversation is over.

Instead, what if you look your children in the eyes and ask them questions that you know can engage you both in a conversation and further the relationship? What if instead of "How was school?" you asked, "At recess today did you and Scott play football, or did you play soccer, or did you stay inside and read? Oh, you read today because it was so hot outside. Are you reading that cool book *Where the Wild Things Are* still?"

Or if you have older kids, and you know that your daughter is frustrated with her job, what if instead of "How is work?" you ask something like, "Is Mr. Smith still making you work late? Have you taken that trip to Vermont you promised yourself in July?"

All of a sudden, you're no longer just talking to hear yourself talk and asking generic questions. Instead, your kids know that you care and that creates massive connection.

Now maybe you don't have kids or you are wondering why I shared so much about parenting. It's because kids touch our hearts, and you should be trying to touch the hearts of everyone from your spouse to your clients, even though they have already said yes to you. If you don't understand their fears and camp out with their issues, they are going to move on to somebody else who will show them they care.

One of the worst things I see, especially in bigger companies, is when a committee tries to decide what other people want and need. I know I stated previously that people will buy what they want, not necessarily what they need, but let's talk about what takes place after they have become your client or customer.

When your company gives a lot of refunds, receives numerous returns, fails to have people make repeat purchases, or doesn't have many long-term customers, the problem is a failure to camp out in people's minds. Instead, you have started to assume what they want and what they need. When a committee tries to solve the problem and stops listening to the client, it is destined to fail.

To avoid this outcome, here are some tactics to camp out effectively:

- Send a survey to your customers about what they want and need.
- Ask in person what they require.
- Create an ethical bribe to get them to tell you what they want and what they need.
- Follow relevant trends and data via social media to determine where your clients are clicking and on what sites they're hanging out.
- Look at the analytics for your website; identify the particular parts of the site that get the most traffic.
- Don't pretend to know what your client needs or make guesses without any feedback or data.

All of these tactics should help you listen and camp out in their minds. Let them tell you what they want and provide it to them.

RECIPROCITY

What is the definition of reciprocity and how does it fit in with the "after-the-sale" relationship? First, in the dictionary it may say one thing, but I believe in a somewhat different definition; let's call it no-strings-attached reciprocity. It means providing value to someone else without asking for anything in return or doing something before someone does something for you.

Most people think, "I'll do something if there's something in it for me. If I help that person can they help me?" I've been blessed to develop amazing relationships with amazing people by doing something for them and expecting nothing in return.

When you give to others without the need for them to give back, that is no-strings-attached reciprocity—it forms the foundation for many successful people and companies. Whether you believe in "Do unto others as you would have done to you" or karma, be the one who makes the first, generous move. Make this who you are rather than how you intend to get ahead. If you do, watch as the gifts, the breakthroughs, the opportunities, and the promotions start flowing your way.

Use reciprocity after the yes and create unexpected rewards for good behaviors. Think about this: How often do you tell your spouse, kids, employees, friends, and family that they have disappointed you? How often do you share what went wrong, and even possibly what kind of discipline there will be because of it?

Conversely, how often do you give a gift or even just a kind word to people who do the right things? When was the last time you said to your spouse, "Thank you for being such a great provider. Thank you for being such a great mother or father." Or when was the last time you told your kids, "Thanks for making your bed today. Thanks for being so polite the other night when we went out to dinner and you looked our waitress right in the eyes when you spoke."

And it's no different in your business or career. When was the last time you said to your clients, "Thank you for being a part of our company. Thank you for sticking with us. Thank you for giving us money. Here's a gift to show my appreciation."

For example, if you rent one of my 400 houses around the country, when you pay rent on time for six months, you get a letter that includes a $50 Starbucks card. The letter reads, "You have a choice to pay your rent on time or late, and you choose to pay your rent consistently on time, and I just wanted to say thank you." People don't expect either the letter or the gift, and they respond in so many positive ways: tenants stay longer, complain less, and often want to buy the house from me. The letter creates a connection. This isn't trickery, I truly appreciate them, and I let them know it. By doing so, we move beyond being just tenant and landlord—a purely transactional business arrangement—and build a real relationship. Yes, they are paying me money, and I am providing them a home. That could be enough, a fair exchange. But my ROI on renting single-family homes is significantly above industry standard, and my tenants know that I care even after they give me money.

That's your goal: Let the people who have said yes in your business and your personal life know that you care. Here's how.

This is a challenge for you that I know will give you back gifts that you can't yet foresee: This week, create five handwritten letters of gratitude to people who have made an impact on your life. When was the last time you wrote a handwritten letter? If you can't write legibly, then type it and e-mail it. But let me assure you, the impact of each letter will be incredible. Send them to clients, a mentor, a teacher, your husband, your wife, your mother, your father, your siblings, your children, your employees, your manager, or your boss.

Here's an example of a simple, unexpected note of gratitude that you may send: "I just wanted to let you know that today I was sitting here thinking about the evolution of my life, and I'm not sure I'd be where I am today without you keeping me accountable, being tough on me, being so sweet, being so loving, providing love in my life, or being a client who pays me for services that we render. And I'd like to say . . ." Well, you get the point and can fill in the blanks and tailor it to a specific individual.

Do me a favor and take that challenge this week, write those letters, and mail them. Or if you prefer, write them digitally and e-mail them. Better yet, send a gift with your note! Send flowers to someone with a card and discover how grateful people are to receive an unexpected gift; this is how reciprocity is created.

Do this, and the emotion of love will come back to you in waves. If you make this sort of selfless gesture in your personal life, why wouldn't you do that in business as well? Why wouldn't you do that with your clients or coworkers? Why wouldn't you do that with your boss? Why wouldn't you do that with your employees?

Building reciprocity fosters a long-tail relationship. This means they will use your service, respect you, appreciate you, and refer you for many years to come. This is the opposite of a one-time transaction or short-term relationship. Building these long-tail relationships is a core success habit of most supersuccessful people.

LEARN WHAT MAKES YOUR PEOPLE TICK

If you own your own company and have employees or manage other people who lack motivation or have poor morale—or they're not getting their jobs done for any reason—consider spending some time just trying to understand them and their world. They said yes to working for you or their employer. Focus on how they feel, and you can get results that are unimaginable at this point. What if their obstacles and challenges are nothing like you think they are? What are their goals? What do they talk about at lunch? What do they think of you and your management style? What do they talk about when they go home to their spouse?

Now let's flip it around; you said yes to working for another company and want to grow in that environment. Say you're in a challenging job with a tough boss. Ask yourself these questions:

How does your boss feel about her job? Is he really the arrogant boss who disdains his people, or is he just misunderstood? What are his stresses? What are her worries? What challenges is he facing in his life? How does her boss treat her?

You will get a whole new level of understanding if you make the effort to answer these questions. Then use what you've learned to let your boss feel understood—communicate that you are part of her solution, not part of her problem.

Take the same lessons I shared earlier and camp out in the mind of the person you want to work with and you will see things from a new perspective. Eventually you might come to know them well enough to finish their sentences. The end result is that you understand how to be a part of their solution, not a part of the problem.

STRIVE FOR RELATIONSHIPS, NOT TRANSACTIONS

Here is one of the most important success habits shared in this chapter. If you want a next-level business that thrives in today's environment, remember: When it comes to your clients, be in the relationship business, not the transaction business. People will refund a transaction, but not a relationship. Let me explain this quickly. If you have a transactional relationship with the owner of your local diner, you go there and the conversation goes like this: "Hey, where do you want to sit? Here's the menu and the specials. What may I get you?" He delivers your food with a smile, you eat, get the check, and you leave. Nothing wrong, food was fine, yet that's purely transactional, there's no heart and no personal relationship.

But what if the owner actually spent time getting to know you and building a relationship. What if the conversation was more like, "Hey, Dean, good to see you again. How's the family? You guys have to bring the kids in soon. We'll make them those special sundaes again. They sure loved them last time. You want your favorite booth? Green tea, right? Okay you got it!" Now which of those two restaurants are you most likely going to return to for lunch? Which one would you still go back to if for some crazy reason you had a bad meal occasionally? That's right, the one that you have a deeper relationship with. People bail on transactional relationships fast; they hang tight when it's a real relationship and they know you care.

If you're running a business where your relationships with customers are purely transactional, those customers know it. Maybe you're just pushing product through, or you only care about sales, your refunds are high, your customers are complaining (or they're not referring you), or you just can't seem to generate momentum. It's likely because you really don't show you care about your customers on the level they need to be cared about. Without realizing it, you view customers from a transactional perspective, not from a relationship one. Securing customer loyalty without a relationship is a difficult task in today's connected world.

In contrast, if you understand how your customers or clients feel, know where they are coming from, realize how they found you, recognize what they like and don't like about your product, and grasp what their personal needs are, you will develop a bond with them that transcends the transaction. And once again this builds a long-tail customer rather than a one-time transaction.

NO MORE ASSUMING

Another huge mistake you can make after the yes is assuming you know what people are thinking or feeling. We do that in our personal lives as well as in business, and it can cost you money as well as create unwarranted stress. Let me share a story that had a huge impact on me and helped me learn this lesson of not pretending you know what another person is thinking but making the effort to actually know. My first book, *Totally Fulfilled*, hit the *New York Times* bestseller list in 2006, and the following year I wrote *Be a Real Estate Millionaire*. However, this time I did something different in the way I promoted that book. It was sold in bookstores and other retail outlets like *Totally Fulfilled*, but I also did an infomercial selling it directly to consumers. It became a massive hit; my biggest book sales to date. In fact, that first show ran every single day all across America for almost 18 months. We were all over TV selling thousands and thousands of copies of *Be a Real Estate Millionaire* weekly. But it almost never happened because I assumed I knew what a key team member was thinking.

I made a deal to have someone interview me on camera. He was great at it and came highly recommended. At the time I had already been on TV for seven or so years with infomercials. But this was the first time I was going to do a sit-down Larry King–type interview. Watching Larry King interview Joel Osteen one night gave me the idea to do that type of show. I knew that if Larry King had said, "Love Joel or not, if you want his brand-new book, call the number below and get it at a discount right now," it would have been a massive hit! It became all I could think about. So I was ready to replicate that type of show with a great host, and I found someone I thought would be perfect. I made a deal with him and a shoot date was set.

The day of the shoot I arrived at the studio and I was a little nervous, because I wasn't using a script. Instead, I wanted to speak from my heart. I wanted to share real stories and real emotion in an unscripted, back-and-forth interview. Keep in mind that this was at the beginning of the recession. The economy was tanking, mortgages were being foreclosed on, and I was going on TV to sell a book on real estate investing. Everybody told me I was crazy. Friends and even family were telling me, "No one's going to want to figure out how to make money in real estate. People are losing their homes; they just want to survive right now, Dean!"

I stayed positive and ignored the naysayers and continued on schedule to launch this book and infomercial. What made my nerves even worse was overthinking. On the way to the studio to record the infomercial, I became increasingly anxious. Would I sound good? Would I be able to share from my heart and not freeze up?

So I arrived a bit nervous, walked into the studio, and the TV host kind of snubbed me. I was taken aback initially, and I jumped to a conclusion: "This guy thinks I'm crazy for doing this too."

Then the TV host said to me, "What questions do you want me to ask you?"

I replied, "I really don't want any questions. I just want you to try and prove me wrong. Try and prove that I'm not the real deal, or that I don't know real estate, and that now is not a good time to invest. Let's make this interview as real as they come. If I'm the real deal and speak from the heart, people will feel it." Again, I felt as if he thought I was making a mistake; he gave me a skeptical look and walked straight into the makeup room. It was almost as if he was rejecting my book and my message. And I'll admit, I allowed those feelings to fester inside me. I was upset enough that I was a moment away from canceling the whole interview. I even started thinking, maybe another time, maybe I wasn't prepared enough.

I had created a story in my head about this TV host. I was all worked up, thinking, "This guy doesn't believe I'm the real deal. Does he think this is a joke?" I became even more nervous and agitated.

Then we sat down on the interview set, and he looked at me and said, "Dean, I'm sorry if I'm acting weird. I'm just so intimidated by you. You are so good on camera—you're a damn legend in this arena, and I've been a huge fan for years. I'm excited to do this interview. I'm just a little nervous and, unfortunately, getting over the flu."

Now I want you to think about what I did. I was stressed for an hour thinking the TV host snubbed me and didn't believe in me. I made up all these stories in my mind about how the host thought I was a joke. And I was flat-out wrong! What a waste of mental energy, right? I felt so silly. But at least this story ends well; I went on the air, and spoke from the heart. He did a magnificent job interviewing me, and this infomercial became the biggest and best show I'd ever done. It was a monster hit. That show alone sold hundreds of thousands of books, and I got to help families all over America safely invest in real estate.

So why that story, and what does it have to do with the after-the-sale secrets to more success? Because, at the time of that story, I was already a seasoned business owner, a millionaire with many great accomplishments. I already lived by the rule of "No assuming." Nonetheless, I made assumptions that simply weren't true. So keep reminding yourself of this no-assumption rule, and recognize that if you're making these types of assumptions, you aren't as relationship focused as you should be for next-level growth.

Think back and ask yourself how many times have you made this same mistake with a business relationship, a spouse, a child, a coworker, a boss, or an employee? Your mind starts chugging like a runaway freight train, and these wild, manufactured thoughts cause all this extra stress in your life for no reason. Well, if it can happen in your personal life, then it can surely happen with your clients. Do you think you know what they are thinking or do you really know? Do whatever it takes to really know and watch the growth in whatever area of your life to which you apply this philosophy.

Chapter 9

THE POWER
OF HAPPINESS

*"If you actually are paying attention to serving, creating, and doing
the things that you want to do, you have no space to listen to that
negative story. It fades so far into the background, that it becomes vir-
tually nonexistent. If any of us pause long enough, that negative voice
comes back in. If we're not actively engaged in what we're doing, our
attention has no other place to go other than to listen to that voice in
our mind that says we suck, that we can't do it. It's a really fun and
cool game to train yourself to stay engaged, which keeps you taking
action, and then the by-product is confidence."*

— Marie Forleo, interview with Dean Graziosi

As your success, income, and responsibility grows, you can't
neglect your happiness. If you are not consciously defending it,
it can slip away. I'm going to share with you the 10 Happiness
Habits that can make happiness the core of success (rather than
success the core of happiness). Yes, you read that correctly: happiness leads to success, not the other way around. In our society,
we often think that if we've got tons of money, are the head of
a profitable company, and have a lot of fame as well as fortune,
we're going to be happy.

In fact, one of the biggest things that stops people dead in their tracks from living an actual fulfilled life is the assumption that if they find success, happiness will follow. Take your own life, for example. Have you ever thought that if you got a certain job or started your business, then happiness would result from it? Have you ever felt that once you made a certain amount of money, or once you have a wife that loves you or a husband that loves you, or once you have children, or once you lose weight, then you'll be happy? Well, I hate to break it to you, but many people who think this way eventually find out that they're wrong.

I would be doing you a huge disservice if I failed to let you in on this secret. And yes, you can attract next-level wealth with the right habits, but why deny yourself happiness? Wealth without fulfillment is emptiness. Let me help you achieve it all.

What if we've had it backward for all these years? What if happiness is the prerequisite for everything else? What if it is the prerequisite for success, abundance, prosperity, weight loss, passion, intimacy, and love? What if most of us don't really know how to be happy, but instead we think we'll figure it out once we get somewhere? Think of what we tell ourselves: "All I need is to get my business up and running, and I'll be happy." Or: "As soon as I buy that dream house, I'll be satisfied."

You see, most of us let our desire for external things guide us. We think once we have that new house or that new job, then we'll be happy. But guess what? The excitement of external things fades. Have you ever thought, once I get a raise or to that next level of income, that is when the fun begins? Then it happens, and you spend accordingly, get some new stuff, upgrade your apartment, and think, *I'm making more money so now I'm happy!* But then a few months pass, and the additional income and what you bought no longer satisfies you.

As much as I am an advocate for growing your wealth and your success through the right habits, no amount of money will make you happy unless you find internal satisfaction. But combine that with more money, and it's time for next-level and real fulfillment.

A friend told me about a couple who for their entire adult lives wanted to move to the West Coast. The wife just wanted to watch the sunsets every day as they sank over the ocean. So the couple saved up, worked for many years, and once they retired, they finally moved to California. So every night they got to sit out on their deck and watch the sun go down over the Pacific Ocean, and it was just an unbelievable goal they had reached. Naturally you would assume their lives were complete, and they could live happily ever after, right? Wrong! After 18 months of living in that house, they were fuming, and decided, "We need to get blinds installed on these windows! Every night the sun is glaring right through and blinding us when we're trying to cook."

You see, the outside world can only give you temporary happiness. We all want that next level of income, the ideal weight, perfect health, a great lifestyle, more money, true love, intimacy, and passion. Trust me, I get the desires that exist and the accompanying perks. But all that goes away unless we learn how to be happy on the inside. And here's the crazy part: If we find happiness on the inside—not an easy task—then suddenly all of those other things we want are more obtainable. When you learn to create happiness internally, those things become a by-product of the happiness you're creating, which is the opposite of what most people think. Most people believe success, money, fast cars, and diamond rings come first and then happiness will materialize. That is completely false, and the source of so many people walking around depressed.

So let's look at happiness and what I've learned about it through all my years of writing books, reading other great books on success, and being friends with billionaires and presidents and world-changers. From these experiences, I've created a list of 10 specific habits and thought processes that I think are the fastest and quickest way to happiness. As I always say, I just want to give you the recipes, ingredients, and instructions that get you to your definition of success the fastest.

HAPPINESS HABIT #1: DEFINE WHAT HAPPINESS LOOKS AND FEELS LIKE TO YOU

Imagine that we're sitting in a restaurant right now and I ask you this question: "From the deepest part of you, what makes you happy?" Would you have an answer? Do you know what it would be? I believe that's a hard question for all of us. And I think it is a difficult question because so many times we try and compare our definition of happiness to others. Just because someone else's definition of happiness is a sports car and a mansion, doesn't mean it has to be your definition! Honestly, if you were to ask me that question just five years ago, I probably would have fumbled to come up with an answer. Back then I don't think I was crystal clear on what happiness truly meant to me. It would be easy to say, "Being with my kids," and even though that is true, that was a default and not a truly thought-out answer. But I want you to get crystal clear on what makes you truly happy!

Take the time right now and think through or start writing down ideas about what makes your heart smile, your eyes brighter, and causes you to be alive with joy. What truly makes you happy? Come on, do this. Don't default to a few answers that have become your reflexive response. Think back to when you were a kid, or earlier in your life. When did you feel at peace? What lit you up? What made you smile? Is it spending time in the woods with your kids playing games and breathing fresh air? Is it going to a sporting event or going fishing? Do you like being by the ocean and feeling the sand between your toes? I personally love being in the woods—I relish big trees and a mountain stream. And it's probably because I grew up in upstate New York and my grandfather took me fishing a lot. He was such a great role model and someone I loved dearly. When I'm around nature, I'm truly happy. If I were to take an entire day and go out into the wilderness with big trees and a beautiful clear-running stream, that would provide me with an inexplicable sense of happiness.

When I'm with my kids and when I feel like I'm guiding them through life the right way, that too fosters happiness. When I'm inspiring people to become their very best (like now, I hope), and when I'm teaching on stage and on camera—all these things give me a deep level of happiness. So what's on your list?

More specifically, what's on your list today? If I were to have created this list 5 or 10 years ago, my answers would have been different. Some were materialistic, and some were embarrassing. So make sure you're thinking about your present happiness.

Also, don't confuse happiness with goals. I still have materialistic goals, financial goals, and achievement goals. I'm not stopping my evolution. But I know the difference between goals and what makes me happy. I want to make sure you do too.

The search for happiness starts by thinking through and defining the term as it applies to your current life. So try this: Jot down things without overthinking them. Don't limit your list to things you do, but also include the thoughts that make you happy, blessings that you can be grateful for, and activities that bring you joy. Write, write, and write some more! Then look back at your list and circle three to five items that you feel strongly about, and those are typically your top ones.

HAPPINESS HABIT #2:
MAKE THE PRESENT YOUR FRIEND

And no, I don't mean the present underneath the tree at Christmas time. I'm talking about the present day, the right now, this very moment you are living in. You have to make it your friend. So many of us go through life looking forward to tomorrow, to next week, to next year, instead of making friends with the right now. We think to ourselves, "When I get this promotion, when I start my own company, when my company's profitable, when my wife truly understands me or my husband just gets me, when my kids are out of diapers, when they go off to college, when I lose weight—then and only then I'll be happy!" That kind of thinking is just an excuse for pushing happiness off to some vague time in the future. But when we do that, guess what? It may never get here. That is why we have to live in the now. Why not decide to be happy now?

When you say the words "when/then" too many times—as in, "When I get that promotion, then I can finally relax and feel great about my life"—all you're doing is putting your happiness on hold until tomorrow because you're mentally living in a time other than right now. How many of us are waiting to be happy until that one certain thing happens? What if we threw away that mind-set and just made today our friend? What if today was an incredible day? What if we no longer lived in the past or the future but rather decided to be happy right this second? What if we started doing more of the things that make us happy and focused on more of the thoughts that bring us joy, today? Right this moment! You can decide to do this; it's your choice.

How many times do you get stuck thinking about what could go wrong in the future? How many times have you thought, "When I do this, then this might happen next month or next year"? Then what happens? You get on this slope of negative thinking and you just go snowballing down the hill of thinking what could possibly go wrong someday. You're predicting the future; and not only that, you're predicting a negative future! The truth is, you don't know where the future is going and how things are ultimately going to end up. Of course living too far in the future with the wrong thoughts diminishes your happiness today.

Choose the present and choose it now! Realize that each day happens for a reason and that each moment must be seized with a present mind-set. As simple as this advice sounds, consider the implications: What if you appreciated being alive and healthy and all the opportunities you have at this very moment?

When you can let the past melt away, you can stop focusing on a fictional future and learn to live in the moment—that's where gratitude and happiness begin. As Eckhart Tolle wrote in his fabulous book, *The Power of Now*, when you live in the "now," you will finally find inner peace and happiness. So no more delayed gratification! You have the right to be happy today.

HAPPINESS HABIT #3: STOP OVERTHINKING

Have you ever heard the saying "paralysis caused by overanalysis"? What stops us in our tracks from living the life we desire is simply overthinking. I've witnessed this repeatedly in so many different circumstances, especially starting or going to the next level in business and wealth. What ends up happening is that we overthink, overanalyze, and find ourselves stuck.

It doesn't matter what your goal is, you can overthink it to death. I've watched this in my real estate education classes for years. I'd go to an event, and I'd meet people and shake my students' hands and sign books, and so many people would say to me, "You know what, Dean, I'm dying to do that first deal, but I'm not done reading contracts, and I need to know every detail first. Before I get started, I need to get my MBA, save up until I have a nest egg, find a partner [or fill in the blank]." And so much of what they are usually talking about is stuff that I've never even done! And I've done thousands of successful real estate deals. If there's a recipe for success, all you have to do is follow the recipe. There is no need to make a dish from scratch, right? Don't overthink things, because you'll never do anything.

I've seen single people who desperately want a romantic relationship overthink themselves right out of that relationship. "Should I become involved with her? Well, I could try, but then she could end up straying. She could end up breaking my heart. Do we have the same religious beliefs or spiritual beliefs? If not, then that could really cause problems. You know what? It's better if I don't get involved."

You've given up without giving it a shot! What if that person was the person you were meant to be with and you ignored the chance because of overthinking?

So obtain the knowledge you need to build confidence, but then don't get bogged down in endless questions, second thoughts, and circular analysis. If your heart is telling you to act, if your subconscious is telling you to go for it, stop over-thinking and start taking action.

HAPPINESS HABIT #4:
FOCUS ON A POSITIVE OUTCOME

This is a powerful way to bring happiness into your life and get what you want in advance. And I know it sounds simple, but I can't tell you how many times I've heard someone say, "Oh, Dean, you're too optimistic." Am I too optimistic or do I just understand how powerful our subconscious is? Listen, your energy is going to go in any direction you aim it; you get to choose if it is spent on the positive or the negative.

I know so many people who focus on what could go wrong in life rather than what could go right. One day they may feel a little run-down, and they conjure worst-case scenarios: "What if this is really me getting sick? What if it's the flu; I never got a flu shot? What if I have an illness that could kill me? I don't have health insurance—man, I am in trouble!" Guess what? People like this will talk themselves right into getting sick! Why not put all the energy into focusing on a positive outcome and perfect health and more wealth, happiness, and abundance? Concentrate on thoughts of good health and a long life.

Consider the results of studies about driving on long roads where there is only one tree: Most, if not all, of the accidents on these roads involve someone running into that one tree. Because people may be rushing through traffic or lose control of the wheel and think to themselves, "I don't want to hit that tree. I don't want to hit that tree. I don't want to hit that tree." And what do they do? They hit the darn tree.

The world has programmed us to think a certain way about situations we face. When something comes up, our minds immediately want to go to, "Oh no, this isn't good! What if this happens or what if this happens or, oh gosh, what if, what if." The antidote: become a keen observer of your thoughts. It's worked for me. And now, when what-if thoughts try and sneak into my mind I say, "No, no, no. I'm not going to let my mind go there." Yes, I could focus on the negative and be stressed and worried about what could happen, but I decided years ago that I was no longer going to do that. You can focus on what might go wrong or you can focus on what might go right. Why not invest your energy in what can go right?

I used to focus on the wrong outcomes, and this story from my personal hell illustrates the dangers of this focus. For years, I woke up at 2:00 in the morning because my mind was racing with thoughts. And for years I just thought this early-morning waking was a reason for my success. I'd wake up and I'd start thinking about all the things going on that day, and I'd think about what could go wrong, and I'd try to find solutions to them before the problems even were reality! Half the time I wouldn't be able to fall back asleep because I would get obsessed about these imaginary bad outcomes and become stressed. Then one day, I said to myself, "No more! I'm going to start tricking my mind and my subconscious by changing those negative thoughts I have when I wake up. From now on, I'm only going to focus on a positive outcome to these situations rather than creating negative outcomes in my mind." And what happened? I was able to visualize success and happiness and finally started getting my much-needed sleep. It took some time to make the transition from negative to positive outcomes, but when I replaced that disempowering habit with the empowering habit, it eventually stuck.

Trent Shelton is a former NFL player who is the founder of RehabTime, where each week through social media he delivers powerful, inspirational, and uplifting messages. Trent has transcended his career as a football player to become an amazing motivational speaker and inspirational leader. He may have been in the spotlight as a football player, but he has a much more visible and prominent role now as millions of people see his videos and posts each month. He gets tens of thousands of positive, uplifting posts from people expressing their gratitude for his dedication to their greatness. With so much exposure, though, comes some negativity—the haters.

When I interviewed Trent, our conversations provided many great lessons, including his own happiness habit that helped him deal effectively with the pessimists and naysayers, both online and in his life.

"First, I've come to associate a hateful post from someone as a disillusioned fan who is unconsciously still in need of some hope or motivation. It's so easy to scroll down and see a post under a video I sent out that can immediately affect my mind-set. I'm human just like everyone else. But when I simply gave that negative post a new meaning, it created a new behavior in me. No longer did I see it as 'I did something to create this'; rather, I see it as 'This person still needs help and hopefully he will come around.' But I'm not in control of them; I'm only in control of what I do. I let the tens of thousands of positive posts from the people who get inspired by my words be my fuel. And to protect myself even further, I'm very picky about who I follow, what I do, what I watch, and honestly, even the conversations I have . . . I'm very selective about certain people when they call me, because I know certain people either want something, or they want to bring gossip, or want to bring drama, so I always tell myself to protect my peace. So I will do what I must to put barricades between me and their negativity. Protect your peace every day and watch your happiness and joy grow.

"And I have another habit to start each day off the best I can. When I wake up, I put myself in the Championship Mode mind-set, as I like to call it. I give thanks for the opportunity for life, for another day to give it my all. It's my biggest thing for protecting my confidence and protecting my peace, because so many times, we don't realize the opportunity we have, to give our greatness to the world every single day. God gave each of us greatness inside us, and we can't share it and use it if we are not at peace. Do what you must, protect your peace, and show the world what you are made of."

So be like Trent and don't let the naysayers in any area of your life bring you down. Switch it up and try to find how to give it a new meaning. "Protect your peace" are words Trent often uses, and so should you. In so many cases suffering is a choice. Therefore, do what you must, create new habits, and avoid suffering whenever possible. You are amazing; let the world see this incredible part of you every day.

HAPPINESS HABIT #5:
LET GO OF SPECIFIC OUTCOMES

This is a game-changer. It's not easy, but it's damn effective. Too often, we predict what different outcomes should be, and we get hung up on our predictions. "If I put this money into this deal, and I partner with this person, we should make x amount of money, and here's exactly how it will look." Then if it doesn't turn out like that, happiness goes away. You think to yourself, "That's not what I wanted! That's not what I predicted! This isn't right!" Sometimes you order steak, and the server brings you chicken, and all of a sudden, you're angry. "This is not what I wanted! I can't believe they did this!"

Here's how we make the same mistake in relationships: "We're going to be married next year, and we're going to honeymoon in Hawaii, and this is the way it's going to be." And when it doesn't turn out that way, we immediately get angry or our joy in the relationship diminishes.

Remember what Tony Robbins said: "What if life happens for us, not to us?" Imagine you're paddling downstream in a canoe, and all of a sudden, the current takes you off course. You could resist it and say, "I have to paddle upstream against this strong current and get back on the track I expected." But wouldn't that take a tremendous amount of effort? What if when our course is altered, instead of being angry, we said, "What if this little change in direction is a strategic part of my next level of life? Maybe this is happening for me and not to me. Maybe I should just ride the current out and see where it goes."

Many times when an entrepreneur starts a business, the original idea doesn't work. So then the entrepreneur changes course and finds success in a totally unexpected direction. For example, that's how Twitter was born, almost by accident. Twitter was originally started by its cofounders to be a podcast company where you could call a number and create a podcast. It wasn't even called Twitter. Then, iTunes announced that it was going to make podcasting available on all major Apple devices, and suddenly Odeo (the company now known as Twitter) was screwed! They had brainstorm meeting after brainstorm meeting to think of a new direction for the company and eventually came across the idea we all now know as Twitter! And that success would never have happened if the entrepreneurs had given up because their original concept didn't pan out.

When you're fixated on "riding the current" to one specific outcome, you become unhappy when things don't work out. When you're mired in unhappiness, you're never going to be successful. Instead, you lose confidence and walk around depressed. After I learned this lesson, it changed everything in my life. If I start a business and it starts to go in a direction I didn't expect, I just ride the current! Maybe this is the direction that will lead me to success! When you let go of a very specific outcome, the heavy weight of expectation comes off your shoulders. You will become a different person immediately, and your happiness will skyrocket.

HAPPINESS HABIT #6: DON'T BE AFRAID TO FAIL

We were raised to think that failure is bad. But truthfully, failure is the cornerstone of success. I'm looking at a quote on the wall right now by Winston Churchill, and it reads, "The definition of success is going from failure to failure without losing your enthusiasm." When was the last time you embraced failure in your life?

Usually if you're not failing, that means you're not pushing yourself hard enough, and you're not trying new things. It means you're stuck in a rut and you're just going with the flow or you're not straying from your well-worn routine. But here's the thing: you'll never achieve your goals on autopilot.

So I say fail often and change the meaning of failure that is in your mind. I want you to be able to say proudly, "I failed today; I tried something new." I ask my kids all the time, "Did you fail today?" When they say no, I respond, "Well, you didn't step out of the box or you didn't try anything new." I'm trying to reprogram their perception of failure, to help them perceive it as a prerequisite for success.

When you embrace failure, you will no longer feel sad when something doesn't go as planned. I've asked countless thousands of my clients through e-mails what's holding them back from getting started on their dreams. Fear of failure is a common answer. But what if you just got rid of that fearful attitude? When that happens, you replace your fear with an acceptance of changes in your life. Wayne Gretzky said it best, "You miss 100 percent of the shots you don't take." Embrace failure as a necessary part of success, and aim to do it daily.

HAPPINESS HABIT #7: LET GO OF GRUDGES

Another way of stating this habit is: Try not to take things personally. I know this is a tough one. But when you hold a grudge, you are holding that inside you at the expense of your happiness, health, and success. Have you ever held a grudge against a parent, boss, or relative, or somebody who did something horrible to you, and you obsess about it all the time? Just so you know, that grudge isn't affecting the offending party. As much as you boil and stew, your grudge-filled thoughts don't harm a hair on anyone's head. They do hurt you and your future success. You have to let go of all grudges, which I know is easier said than done.

Growing up, I had my own issues and craziness with my parents; I sometimes felt I was on my own and didn't have their support. Without anyone knowing, I held on to grudges for a long time.

I dreamed about them, I thought about them, and I allowed them to make me resentful. But all this obsessing did was hold me back from that next level of happiness. Then one day, I just let them go and said, "I wouldn't be the man I am, I wouldn't be the father I am, I wouldn't be the motivator I am had anything happened any other way. Those things happened exactly the way they were supposed to, and I forgive the people involved; grudges gone!"

When I let those grudges go, my happiness rose to a new level. Letting go of past grudges was one of the most liberating things I've ever done, and I urge you to take a look at your life and find the grudges you can release. If you do, you'll free yourself to be the best you possible.

HAPPINESS HABIT #8:
BE GRATEFUL FOR WHAT'S IN FRONT OF YOU

We all know that being grateful is the cornerstone of happiness. It's one of those things that you have to be consciously aware of daily. You could be struggling, need money, have debt or overdue bills, or be going through a divorce, but there's always the opportunity to find gratitude for things in our lives.

I know life can be like a kick in the teeth sometimes. But gratitude can overcome anything, and the best way to find it is to start by focusing on small things of which you're appreciative. You can be grateful for a smile from a stranger, a hug from your child, or a look from your spouse. Be grateful for living in a place where you can define yourself as you choose, where you enjoy the freedom to become your best self. Be grateful for the blue sky or the white clouds or the flowers or the green grass. Heck, be grateful for your heart beating and never having to think about it.

Again, success without fulfillment and happiness is a massive failure. So I encourage you to spend today finding gratitude in the small things and let your gratitude grow from there. When you can train yourself to be grateful for a simple lunch or for a hug, then these little things add up, and you become more meaningfully grateful daily.

HAPPINESS HABIT #9:
DON'T SETTLE FOR "GOOD ENOUGH"

Don't settle for things being just okay. This acceptance will take away your happiness in a flash. Don't say things like, "My relationship is good enough." Instead say, "My relationship might not be perfect, but I'm going to work hard at making it better." Strive for greatness in every part of your life. When you settle for just okay, whether it relates to income or a job or a relationship, you lose out on much of the joy life has to offer.

Say no to just being okay. Get that terminology out of your life, because subconsciously, that means you're telling yourself, "You're not good enough. You don't deserve better. Other people get to be happy and get to live life abundantly, but you don't. It's good enough for you just where you are." The heck with that! Stop telling yourself things are okay, because you're subconsciously ruining your chances for happiness and for the joy and fulfillment that lie beyond.

You don't have to say, "My life is perfect right now." You could just be honest and say, "It is okay today, but I'm going for more." And I know you are going for more, so keep going! Just okay is not good enough, not for my students and not for anyone reading this book. There is that next level of life, and it's your turn to grab it.

HAPPINESS HABIT #10:
BE PART OF SOMETHING BIGGER

This is about seeking a spiritual connection or developing a relationship with God or any higher power. You must allow yourself to be a part of something bigger than you are that lifts you to the next level of faith. Explore whatever type of spirituality fits your beliefs and traditions. It could be general spirituality, Zen Buddhism or other organized religions, or your personal relationship with God. When you attach yourself to something bigger than yourself, your happiness is amplified.

I know you bought this book to discover the habits that create wealth and abundance, and I urge you to go for it—make all the money you desire—but I also implore you to take this chapter seriously and make happiness the foundation of your life. It will make success come easier and faster in any area where you choose to apply these 10 Happiness Habits. If there's any chapter that I'd urge you to reread, it's this one—commit these habits to memory and to heart. I also suggest that you implement each of the 10 habits gradually over the coming months. Maybe focus on one each week for the next 10 weeks. Now go smile!

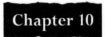

Chapter 10

THE QUICK HACKS
TO SUCCESS

"The movie Rudy just happened to connect to the fiber of the American underdog. The idea of being the underdog is such a powerful, powerful thing. If you're the underdog, you have that chip on your shoulder, you always work hard, you'll only accept excellence, you keep striving toward excellence. You're not going to try to be perfect—you're going to try to have a perfect moment, but you're not going to be perfect. That's not saying you're not going to struggle. I think the struggle comes in finding the right people to be around."

— Rudy Ruettiger, interview with Dean Graziosi

This chapter is going to be like a lightning round on success hacks that you can adjust to fit into your life at a moment's notice. Of course, there are thousands of habits, daily routines, or "hacks" that can help you along your journey to success. These are some of my favorites, and you can incorporate them into your life easily, quickly, and with a far greater impact than you might think.

TAKE CREATIVE TIME DAILY

We often get into ruts or routines, and we live the same schedule day after day. Sometimes we feel like we're on a hamster wheel or that we're just running in place on a treadmill. When this happens, your creativity, new ideas, dreams, visions, and inventions don't get a chance to flourish.

Set aside 10 to 30 minutes each day, and just think creatively. Don't respond to e-mail, don't read over your to-do list, don't text or look at social media. Just think. I do this after I work out in the morning and before my kids wake up. I focus on what's next for my life. What should I say in my books? What new idea can I share with people today that will have the most power to transform lives? What's my next TV show going to be?

As you allow yourself to exercise your creativity, you'll get the juices flowing. I don't care if you think you're not creative; you are. If you're like most people, you don't give yourself credit for all your innovations. You've invented a new relationship, a business, a career, a game you play with your kids, a more efficient way of doing your yard work, a character that makes your spouse laugh. Nothing in life comes to us unless we think of it first. Look around you. That lamp, that chair, that painting—somebody thought about them first by being creative, and then those items became reality.

If you forget to take creative time every day, you're not feeding part of your soul, and you don't want it to wither. Sometimes I'll do a whole day of just being creative, where I spend time finding those things that spark my mind and fire me up and keep me looking forward to that next level of life. All of us have our own definition of creative time. It can be painting, writing, sculpting, inventing, digital design, or 1,000 other things that get your creative juices flowing. Whatever it is, schedule the time and do it daily.

OBSERVE OTHER JOBS FOR GRATITUDE

What the heck does that mean? I know we spoke about gratitude earlier, but I want to give you some additional ideas for being aware of it and expressing it. Whether you are expressing thanks for something big or small, you need to find a way to get this feeling out into the world. But sometimes it's hard, right? You're busy, you're doing 10 things at once, and finding gratitude isn't always at the top of your mind.

So what I do is observe other people's jobs to create a kind of gratitude consciousness. I don't care what you do for a living—I know it can get stressful. More than that, it can be overwhelming or it can make you feel like you're doing something that's trivial or mundane and that you're not making a difference. So when I see people hard at work, getting their hands dirty, I mentally say "Thank you" to them. I send my thoughts of gratitude and appreciation.

Here's an example. I live in Phoenix, and in the summer it gets brutally hot. I was driving around recently and saw five guys working up on a roof in 106-degree heat. So I looked at them and I sent love. I'm not trying to be foo-foo or New Age here, but this is just what I do. I think to myself, "Good for them. Thanks, guys." They're taking care of their families, they're making a house in my neighborhood look better, and at the same time, it reminds me that I'm so grateful for what I get to do for a living. Every day I see hardworking people doing difficult jobs, and I feel gratitude for my life and send that appreciation to others.

SET GRATITUDE ALARMS

Since cell phones can do pretty much everything in life except go to the bathroom for you, I love using the daily alarm to remind me to stay grateful. This is a cool little trick I learned from my good friend Brendon Burchard. In the craziness of our day, not only can we forget to be grateful, we can get frustrated, overwhelmed, annoyed, or even become pessimistic or unable to smile. So I set the alarm on my phone to go off every day at three different times, accompanied by a description that pops up when the alarm goes off. At 10 A.M. the alarm sounds, and it reads, "Be optimistic, enthusiastic, and loving." At 3 P.M. it goes off again and reads, "You can handle anything." And then again at 7 P.M., when I am typically home with my family, I see, "You are truly blessed. Be grateful." I can't tell you how many times I've needed those exact messages at those exact times. These little reminders typically make me take a 30-second break from whatever is going on and appreciate everything I have in this world. And as a bonus, the alarm and message often snap me into a better state.

STASH CASH

Trust me on this one: You must make it a habit to put money away. I don't care if you make $500 a week or $500,000 a week, save some of it. There are certain people in the world, and maybe you know some, who will spend as much money as they make and more. If they make a dollar, they're going to spend $1.25.

But you've heard this advice before. Parents, financial advisers, and spouses may have all insisted that you start saving. This success hack, however, isn't as much about money as it is about confidence.

When you have money put away, it does something for your confidence. You will know in the back of your mind that you can weather any storm. If you have a bad month, a bad three months, break your leg, can't work, you can handle it. You possess peace of mind knowing that you and your family are going to be okay until you're back on your feet.

On the other hand, if you have no savings, you're always going to worry about your future, even if only subconsciously. And that is the worst feeling in the world. All it does is tug away at your confidence and peace of mind. You'll start thinking, "If

I have another bad couple of months, I won't be able to pay my rent. I have nothing saved for my retirement, and I have nothing in savings. I have nothing to fall back on!" So I would encourage you, no matter what your income, to make it a habit of stashing something away every single week of your life, even in the bad weeks. It's not about the money you're stashing away as much as it's about the feeling of confidence that helps you make better decisions moving forward.

Have you ever heard the saying "Scared money makes no money"? For me this is true. If you have no money stashed away, you're going to make decisions very cautiously, avoiding risk to feel safe. Because of this you might miss out on taking an educated gamble that could lead to a big payoff. If you have no money stashed away, you're going to stay at that job you hate because you have no cushion. But if you stash money away for three or four years and your boss comes in and finally treats you so badly that you can't take it, you at least have the option to quit. But if there's no money, you'll swallow your pride and take the abuse. I don't care if you save $10 a week, $100 a week, or $1,000 a week—whatever amount you can put away, do it. It will give you more than just a savings account.

SPOIL YOURSELF RANDOMLY

This might seem to contradict my previous point. But hear me out; you can save and spoil yourself. You just have to choose wisely about how you spoil yourself. I don't have hundreds of cars and thousands of shoes, because to me, that's a waste. But I do spoil myself and my family with the things that really matter to us and that we derive value from.

For example, I know I spend three times as much as the average person on our household groceries because everything in my house is organic. I don't want my family eating food chock-full of chemicals.

I will occasionally take the family on incredible trips, stay at the best places, and we pamper ourselves. I love experiencing a great meal with my family no matter the cost. These are my rewards for my hard work, and they make me want to achieve even greater success. So when I say spoil yourself, that's what I'm talking about. Treat yourself to things that evoke a positive emotion; and if this spending creates a lasting memory at the same time, wonderful.

If you stash cash and spend less on things that don't mean much to you, when it's time to spoil yourself on the things that really matter, you'll have the money to do it. Spoiling yourself can empower you, give you glimpses of what could be the norm, and push you harder to implement strategies and make decisions to better your life.

INVEST IN YOURSELF

I truly believe that we die when we stop learning. When it comes to life, we're either climbing or we're sliding. If you want to make more money, and have more money in retirement, more time for you, and more freedom, then never stop investing in yourself. Gaining more knowledge will transform your life experiences into wisdom; and wisdom will provide you with the insight and guidance to reach your next level. I currently spend well over $100,000 a year on continued learning, and you reading this far shows me that we are kindred spirits. But please remember what I shared earlier about bad advice. Make sure you are learning from someone who has done what you want to accomplish on a grander scale. Get a mentor or a coach. Do an internship. Digest knowledge from those who have the path and the plan to the success you desire.

DRAW ENERGY FROM YOUR FREQUENT SMILES

I am optimistic and I love people; it's as simple as that. But I know it can be a challenge to maintain this positive, friendly outlook. Sometimes we get so busy and caught up in our own worlds that we put our heads down and ignore people who we think don't matter because we're too busy to notice them. The delivery truck driver, the building custodian, and the restaurant server may go unnoticed. But then, someone with influence walks into the room, and only then do we put on our friendly faces. I promise you, I have never in my life been one of those people who treated a server badly. I'm always nice and polite. But I decided 10 years ago that I'm not just going to be polite, I'm also going to be consciously aware to smile and make eye contact with everybody I interact with. This isn't just a decision to be "nice"; it's a choice to plug into the power source provided by an upbeat, human-centric attitude.

Now, you can't be "on" all the time. But you also don't want to be the person who treats somebody well because of what you think you can get out of them. Instead, wouldn't it be better to make an effort to appreciate everyone daily, and give a quick smile as often as you can? Think about it: How much energy does that take? Not much at all, yet it will actually improve your state of mind and boost your energy while potentially making someone else's day.

FIND THE GOOD IN THE BAD

If you can create a habit to find good when things go wrong, your life will be transformed. So many people have things go wrong in their lives, and they wallow in them for years. Until someday down the road they say, "You know, it's a good thing that relationship didn't work, because I found the love of my life." Or "You know what? It was actually good that my first business failed, because I learned from it, and that experience helped my next business succeed."

How many people do you know who have avoided committing to relationships because they had their hearts broken years ago? Or do you know someone who won't start a new company because a business venture failed years ago? I believe everything that happens in our life happens for us, and there is a lesson and something good in all of it. If you can create a habit of finding that good sooner rather than later, you'll change your life.

BOUNCE BACK FAST

I've been successful for lots of reasons, but my ability to bounce back from setbacks fast is near the top of the list. Why not be the person among your peers, coworkers, or employees that rebounds from failure or overcomes obstacles faster than anyone else? I have self-programmed this habit or "hack" of fast rebounding, and it has paid huge dividends. How long do you linger on things when they go wrong? How long do you play the situation over and over again in your mind? Learn from it, but pick up the pieces and move on with that experience in hand. The people who fail the fastest are the ones who find the solutions the quickest.

THINK SOLUTION, NOT PROBLEM

It's unfortunate that when something goes wrong, people obsess about why it happened, whose fault it was, and "why me?" Honestly, what good is that thinking in most cases? Yes, learn from it, but train your brain to be solution oriented. Let's take the simplest example on the planet. What happens when a glass of milk spills? Yes, you can obsess and say, how did that fall, who made it fall, will it stain the floor, will it smell, or think something along the lines of, "Why always me? I'm in a hurry and don't need this." But someone with a solution-oriented thought process would simply get a towel, pick up the glass, and get a new glass of milk. Use your energy wisely; learn from mistakes but then move on fast with solutions.

Develop a habit that when stuff goes wrong, you immediately ask, "How do I fix it? What steps can I take right now to lessen the damage?" Make it a habit to put all of your energy into the solution, not on why it happened or who's to blame.

ASK HAPPY PEOPLE

Every time I see people who are always in a good mood, always smiling, and always find the good in things, I strike up a conversation with them. I'll say, "What do you do to be happy?" As you might have guessed by this point, I love asking people what makes them happy. Sometimes you get a funny one-liner as an answer, and you just have to chuckle and be on your way. Other times you might get a thoughtful answer that has a lasting impact on you. When you see happy people, talk to them, and find out what they are doing to stay that way.

My wonderful friend John laughs more than any single person I know. He owns and runs a multimillion-dollar company, has tons of obligations and pressure, and has three young children, but he finds the simplest things funny, and his laughter is contagious. So, of course, I asked him what it is that makes him happy. He told me, "I personally think every day how lucky I am to have been born when I was, to live where I live, and to have the family I have." So as you see, nothing groundbreaking; John doesn't possess a magic happiness button. He found a way to be happy with a routine of gratitude.

GO TO YOUR HAPPY PLACE

I touched on this in the happiness habit chapter, but this success habit boils it down to one particular happy place or thought. Sometimes we find ourselves in funks and need quick hacks to set us free from our negative moods and set our minds and souls straight. For me, it's thinking about being a child and being with my grandmother. She was this warm, comforting light in my life, and when I was with her it felt like a warm hug wrapped around my body. She taught me how to cook Italian food, and I'd sit with her on Sundays for hours while she made the tastiest Italian dishes you could imagine. Things like that are my happy places. So when I need them, I go to them. I urge you to find your happy place and make it a habit that when you're having a rough day, you remind yourself to imagine this place. Once you get out of your funk, you can start thinking clearly again.

LIVE LONG AND PROSPER

This signature phrase from *Star Trek* is worth applying to your life. If you don't have a healthy body, it's hard to have a healthy life and healthy thoughts. An Indian proverb says, "A healthy person has a thousand wishes, but a sick person only has one." How true is that statement?

This isn't a health book, and I don't claim to be an expert. But knowledge of healthy lifestyles is easier to find now than any other time in history. Search it out and create habits that get you in optimal health. Why make all the money and attain all the fulfillment and abundance you desire if you can't be the parent, grandparent, leader, or spouse you know lives inside you?

To live long and prosper, you've got to exercise. It may be hard to start this habit, but once you make it a part of your life and you feel and see the benefits, you'll be hooked. You can find amazing workouts to fit your body and your fitness level online. Heck, you can hire a coach to keep you accountable and have him or her help you with a routine. But whatever you have to do, make it happen. I find that a few things keep me exercising. First, I want to be an example to my children. I want them to see me making exercise a part of my life and not treat it like a chore. I know this to be true: Kids do what you do, not what you say. Also, I want to be an active dad and, someday, an active grandparent. I'm sure you want the same.

Here are a few other ways to make exercise a habit. First, create a fitness challenge with a friend, whether it's based on weight loss, pants size, a 5K, or a before-and-after picture contest. A challenge makes it more likely you'll get engaged with the program and stay there. Next, I recommend mixing it up! Don't do the same thing every day! Go for a walk, run, ski, swim, bike, do some weights, row a boat, play tennis, or do short sprints.

Just get in the habit of doing something different daily. When you exercise, you do everything else better. You make wiser food choices, you refrain from adult beverages more often, and you even start to sleep better. On top of that, you start looking better. It's truly addicting! So, why not start this habit today?

TAKE TIME TO UNDERSTAND

When someone does something to make you feel slighted, underappreciated, snubbed, or even disrespected, you become upset. That's understandable. But many times, we don't understand how they really feel, and we are simply assuming their negative intent. And like I stated previously, this can cause us to waste energy, thoughts, time, and focus. It happens sometimes without even knowing it, and we have to stay away from this energy and time grabber. We are so much better off not wasting our time on the perceived sense that someone is doing us wrong.

I had this happen with my daughter's friend's father. Every time I saw the guy, I felt he was snubbing me. I remember thinking, "Well, he must have a problem with me." He never smiled and barely said hi when I tried greeting him a few times. I convinced myself that he was snobbish or opinionated, and foolishly never talked to him about this subject. Finally, one day I just decided to sit down and chat with him. He and I talked, and I discovered that I was completely wrong about the guy! He was just shy and a little insecure. He turned out to be the furthest thing from pretentious: a humble guy and a great dad. He just lacked the confidence to communicate well with people he barely knew.

Forcing myself to understand a situation before I react has been transformational. Make it a habit to pause in any circumstance that offends you, no matter how bad the offense may seem. So much energy and stress can be avoided if we try to understand why people are doing what they do; or, if necessary, we can avoid this wasted energy by deciding it is not going to affect our mood, no matter what. If you find out your spouse lied to you, your children lied to you, somebody at work is trying to undermine you, somebody at the gym is making fun of you, or someone went behind your back, stop and take a breath. After any upsetting event that happens in your life, taking a breath and refusing to react in the moment can lower your stress. Make the effort to understand where that person is coming from. Look through their eyes and then respond. Letting yourself go down a rabbit hole of assumptions is one of the largest energy-drainers there is. So make it a habit: decide not to do it.

DON'T JUDGE

Easier said than done, I know. But when people ask me about times in my life when the biggest shifts or changes happened, I always reflect back on the moment when I completely let go of making judgments. Can anyone be perfect? No, of course not. But can you get pretty darn close? Heck, yeah! And the results are life-changing.

When we judge, we are literally expending energy, thoughts, and time on something that's none of our business, or that we often lack sufficient knowledge of to make a judgment. As a child I grew up around people who were very judgmental, and I think some of that attitude seeped into my young adult attitudes, even though I would've considered myself a nonjudgmental person. Then one day it hit me: I was making judgments about people, and I had no idea what kind of circumstances were causing them to act as they did. Sometimes you may see overweight people and, as your default reaction, you assume they're lazy or just have no control when it comes to their eating. When you see alcoholics, you think they have no self-discipline and that they should just stop drinking. When you see individuals who are grumpy or disrespectful, you think they are bad people. These default mechanisms live inside all of us. But when you get rid of your judgments, a whole part of your soul opens up for new exploration and new growth.

As you can see, I love sharing by example. And I want to make this point in my children's lives at a young age, so they can be judgment-free their entire lives. For the last five Christmases, after the kids open their presents and we have our morning routine, we jump in the car and drive to downtown Phoenix, armed with bagged lunches that also contain $100 bills. We drive street by street, alley by alley, to find the homeless people on Christmas morning and hand each one of them a lunch bag. We then say, "Merry Christmas," and as we pull away, in so many cases, they are crying or shocked or saying, "Thank God and thank you." And it's about more than the food and the money. It's about having the chance to feel that someone cares. And my children are old enough to realize that people will say, "Why are you giving money to the homeless? They should work, they're lazy, they have options, they will use it for drugs or alcohol." And maybe that's the case in some instances, but who are we to judge?

Rather than pulling away from someone who's barely dressed, completely dirty, or smells horrible, the lessons I'm able to share with my children are the ones I want to become permanent in their souls. I get to teach my children that we don't know if homeless people's families threw them out, if they were molested, if they were beaten, if they have a severe learning disability that no one noticed. I share with my children that there are a million reasons the homeless person could be where they are. Some of them may be on drugs and may use alcohol, and maybe that's the only thing that quiets the noises in their heads. I always tell my kids that we have no idea why they are there, but we can wish them well, let them know someone cares, pray for them, and find gratitude for the blessings we've had in our own lives. Yes, this is a lesson for my children from a dad who had a tougher childhood than they are experiencing. And yes, I may be doing this to help create adults who have empathy, caring spirits, no judgment, and gratitude. But at the same time, I continue to do things like this to cement those values into my own life and heart. So stop judging, and watch your heart, mind, and world open up—and your income increase in the process.

HELP THOSE WHO ARE WORSE OFF THAN YOU

This may seem like the same advice that I offered in the previous habit, but bear with me and you'll see the difference here. I had a friend of mine introduce me to Joel Osteen a few years ago, and when we met, he invited me to fly to Houston and attend a service. I remember being in awe of the size of the church and how beautiful it was and also how many smiling, happy people were attending. I got to sit next to Joel's wife and mother and truly enjoyed it all. I must confess it was the first time I had been in a church in quite some time. As I watched Joel share stories, he told one that really aligned with my heart, and it was something I knew to be true. This was a while ago, so I'll share as closely as I can remember. He said something along these lines: "When you think things are really bad in your life, when you think you don't have enough money, love, health, or maybe joy, go help somebody who's much worse off than you are. When you think your relationship is bad, go to a place where battered women need help, and go donate your time or donate money. When you are feeling you deserved that raise and feel slighted, go visit a homeless shelter. Our problems are our own, and they are relevant, and we still feel the pain. But it is impossible to feel sad or depressed and grateful at the same time. Make it a habit to help those worse off than yourself, and even more so when you are feeling down. When you help others who are worse off, your gratitude will rise and push your stress away. It's a win for everyone."

Helping others isn't a totally selfless act. As important as it is to lend a hand to those in need for its own sake, realize that you're going to benefit too.

DO YOUR BEST ALWAYS

I know so many people who hate what they do for a living; they are dreaming, hoping, and trying as hard as they can to find the career or business they know they will love. But until you find that thing you love to do, use this quick success hack: do the absolute best you can, even if you hate it, until your next level kicks in. Yes, it doesn't matter what it is, always give it 110 percent. Remember my earlier story of billionaire John Paul DeJoria, who swept floors in places the boss couldn't even see, and it set a success habit he followed for the rest of his life? Even though you may not like a particular task or job, do it amazingly well, and the habits learned will be priceless.

When I was in high school and during the few years following, I used to fix wrecked cars in a collision shop with my dad. It was dirty and smelly work that, on many days, gave me headaches from the chemicals. My nails were dirty, my clothes looked like crap, and the truth is that I hated it. But you would have never known how I felt by how I carried myself. If anybody walked into that collision shop, I know they thought to themselves, "Damn, this guy loves his job!" What they saw was that I did that job to the best of my ability every day, and with a smile to boot.

My first big real estate deal was made possible by someone who had often visited the collision shop. We would chat and laugh, and I think he really liked my enthusiasm. One day I told him my story about some real estate deals I was working on and how I was juggling money but still making it happen. He ended up lending me over $80,000 because he saw my enthusiasm. Would I have received that investment if he had walked in and I had a crappy, negative attitude? The guy wouldn't have given me the time of day! Yes, I hated fixing cars, but my habit was to do the absolute best that I could until I reached the next level of my life. This one instance was a shift in that direction. The real estate deal resulted in over $1,000,000 in sales. True story!

I love to share examples from my own life that reveal the power of the right success habits or "hacks," as they've become part of my life and routine. But I'm not the only one creating these hacks and habits; they are also the habits of the highest achieving, most successful people on the planet.

I met Josh Bezoni a little over nine years ago in Hawaii at a weekend mastermind. At that time he was running a decent-sized company and doing fairly well in the nutrition space. We hit it off and had great conversations. We stayed friends and communicated through the years. Then Josh hit hard times with his company, and it went out of business. I flew to meet him in Colorado about six years ago when this was happening, and I remember walking through his old office. It was like a ghost town, empty desks everywhere, and it was truly sad to see. I could feel that my friend was doing his best to put on a good face, but he was heartbroken.

A year or so later Josh invited me to a small event he did in Austin, Texas. It was really his coming-out party in a sense. He had spent sufficient time trying to learn what had gone wrong, getting over the negative stories and self-doubt in his head, and he was ready to jump back into the entrepreneurial world, even though he literally had no money to start over.

Fast-forward from this moment of reinvention to today, and Josh is the founder and CEO of BioTrust Nutrition, one of the world's leading premium nutrition brands. His company does hundreds of millions of dollars in sales, employs many great people, and provides outstanding products, some of which I use daily.

What happened? How did Josh move on from failure and the overwhelming stress of closing a business, with no seed money to start to a dominating world brand? His answer was, "I discovered through my success and failures, through trial and error, that I had to change and create new habits."

Over the years, he's been incredibly successful in many roles—entrepreneur, nutritionist, and philanthropist. So while I was writing this section of the book, I called Josh and asked if he would share his new habits or success hacks with us. Josh was so excited to share the routines that changed everything for him that he made a recording and immediately sent it to me.

He shared a lot of hacks, and there's not enough space here to include all of them, but let me give you a "taste" of some of them:

- Hire people who have already done what you want to do. Josh referred to this as his number one success habit, and he talked about how this is exactly what he did when he started BioTrust Nutrition. Most people think they can train people to do a job, but there's no substitute for experience—especially when they have it and you don't. Josh shared, "Don't hire great soldiers that you can train to be great in their positions, hire generals who know their roles better than you do and let them hire the soldiers underneath them."

- Delegate anything that's not your unique ability. Listen to Josh explain why this is such an important hack: "For ten years, I was stuck in a company that I owned, and it was almost like a prison. I was doing all the work . . . I had a very small team, and I was making good profits, but my life was completely miserable. I was working 80 hours a week. I could have easily taken some of the profits and delegated and hired more people, but I felt like I had to do it all or it wouldn't get done right. When that original company closed and I had time to examine what went wrong and what could go right in the future, I knew this had to change. When I started BioTrust I came out of the gate delegating everything that wasn't my unique ability, and I watched the magic unfold in front of my eyes . . . I was also more successful because I was a happier person, and I wasn't doing things that I didn't like . . . accounting and HTML programming and all these things that I had tried to do in the past.

  "When I focused on my unique abilities, which are hiring the right people, creating the big vision for the company, and putting the right teams together, I made the biggest impact possible and watched all areas of my business and personal life go to the next level."

- Feed your daily motivation just like you feed your body. What Josh means by this is that you have to do something every day to remind yourself why you're doing what you're doing. Here's how Josh describes his application of this habit: "Sometimes I make my own inspirational audio; sometimes I read. Sometimes I listen to Tony Robbins and other inspirational thought leaders. Every day I feed positive energy and positive information into my brain and remind myself what my goals are . . . Life can get hard sometimes, none of us are immune to that, no matter what level of success you are currently achieving. So we can decide to focus on what's not going right, or we can get daily motivation from any source possible and get our thoughts focused on a better version of ourselves. If you are going to think, it may as well be about why you want more and the positive thoughts about how you will get there."

  From afar, I was a witness to how Josh's changing habits allowed him to not only rebound, but to create a business and a life that is truly abundant and inspirational. Josh made mistakes, felt he let others down, believed he wasn't good enough. Is that unlike any feelings you and I have had or are having right now? No, of course not, because we are all so similar. Yet some people choose to stay in that place of despair, to keep the same routines and repeat the same patterns day after day, year after year. Unfortunately, life doesn't one day become amazing by accident. You have to decide it is going to be amazing. Josh is a shining example of someone who knew what he wanted, learned from his mistakes instead of wallowing in them, shifted his habits, and achieved greatness.

- Focus with passion on one thing, and only one

thing. This is a hack I believe in with all my heart, and I think you will too when you "hear" Josh describe it: "I'm kind of ADD and so I'd start a hundred businesses if I could. So I have rules in place where I can only have one thing, and I can tell if it is running by itself and is a success. I don't move on to something else, so it's forced focus (my term for this approach) because entrepreneurs will go all over the place and have a hundred projects and none of them really take off. So, it's a hard discipline, but you have to have forced focus."

Use Josh's success hacks, the ones I've listed, or modify and create some of your own. These small but impactful habits or hacks can be incorporated into your life starting right now. And like I said earlier, it's not about adding more time or more habits into your day, it's about replacing current habits that simply are not empowering your future. If we work on our habits one day at a time, then life will never be the same again.

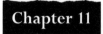

Chapter 11

THE CHALLENGE

"I'm going to go out and do it, and show myself that it's possible, be-cause possibility is very contagious. If you show yourself that something is possible in your life that you once thought was impossible, that's going to give you confidence throughout your whole entire life. And so every single week, I try to do something that pops into my mind as, 'Easier said than done,' or 'That's impossible,' and I go out there and do it. And I show myself that it is possible, so that helps me overcome fear."

— Trent Shelton

You have been exposed to the success habits of the world's richest as well as most fulfilled human beings on the planet. Now it's time for you to reach new heights. You can have everything you've dreamed about: wealth, a great job, a terrific business, and incredible relationships. It doesn't have to be a "wonderful thought" anymore. It can be your reality, and all of it is within reach. So what's holding you back?

Well, if you're like a lot of people, you read these words, got inspired, started dreaming about what's possible, and glimpsed where you might go. Maybe you even had a clear and powerful vision. Your thoughts might have included all the positive things that could happen if you don't let the villain within sabotage you and if you change your story from limiting to limitless.

You can envision how this type of change would affect your life. You get the success habits, happiness habits, and success hacks. It all makes sense, and you're inspired by the stories I've told you—stories of people just like you who have transformed their lives. Some of my stories might even have made you think, "If this guy can do it, I surely can."

So why the heck would you or anyone ever struggle to get started? Because the idea of making changes in your life can be overwhelming and scary. Your subconscious found a place to be safe and doesn't want to stray. But safe doesn't mean happy, fulfilled, or financially prosperous. And that's just what's going on below the surface! On a conscious level, you've got a lot going on. You've got bills to pay, jobs to do, chores to tackle. As much as you want to start making these success habits part of your life, you've got to take action. You've got to do stuff.

I get it. I've been stuck in that place between thought and action. The good news is, I know how to get unstuck, and I'm going to share that with you right now so this book isn't just a good inspirational read, but your road map to action.

FIRST STEPS

Have you ever tried talking yourself into changing through sheer willpower or pep talks? That approach can usually work for a little while, but it's not enough. You need to focus on one small step at a time and also on what's doable and feel the change you're imagining. This is where your motivation will come from; this is how you'll kick-start yourself into action.

So here's how to start a small, doable sprint. I bet you can imagine doing anything for 90 days. It's a tiny slice of your life; think of it as a testing period where you'll see results that will become addicting. So let's break it down to 90 days—what I like to call a sprint. As essential as it is to visualize what your life will be like in 12 months and even 12 years from now, you need a sprint to reinforce change today. I want to chunk your to-do list down to a bitable size. Go ahead and imagine it's 90 days from today, and you've made some astonishing shifts in your life. Follow the process I shared in Chapter 1. Pretend it's 90 days into the future, and it was just the best 90 days of your entire life. What does that look like? Whom did you say yes to? Whom did you say no to? Did you ask for the raise? Did you quit your job? Did you register your new company's name, hire your first employee, start the marketing ramp-up for your current company, or hire a CFO? What does the greatest 90 days of your life look like? You can focus on your income or career and you can also project these 90 days into any area of your life. To help give you even more clarity on how to do this sprint, answer the following questions in writing from the perspective of 90 days into the future, looking backward:

- What specifically happened during the past 90 days? What has changed in your job, your business, your relationships, and your community?

- What success habits have you introduced into your life? What habits did you replace that weren't serving you well?

- How did you get those new success habits into your life? What actions did you take to make things happen? What did you say or do that created this change?

- With all of your positive shifts and accomplishments, how do you feel emotionally? Where is your confidence level, your happiness level, and whom do you see when you look in the mirror?

- Whom are you spending more time with—or less time?

- What is your state of mind like? What are you grateful for?

Imagine it is as if you were there in the future looking back. Then use your pen or the keys on your computer to write down the specific actions you need to take to make this imagined scenario your reality.

Remember, these action steps are only for the next 90 days. They're not designed to achieve your ultimate goals. They're just to get you moving in the right direction. So think about what you need to do to get that great job or a promotion or start a new business. What will get you moving in the right direction? Answer that and you've given yourself a map and transportation to get to the place you want to be.

Here is the linchpin to make this 90-day sprint become your reality. Stop doing so much busywork (tasks that are meaningless to your goals) and make sure more than 50 percent of your daily activities focus on the action steps to meet your 90-day goals. Yes, it can be that simple. Get off the treadmill and start running up a ladder, as the following example illustrates.

FROM THE MACHINE SHOP TO THE PENTHOUSE

Matt Larson was a machine-shop worker in his early 20s, struggling with depression. He looked at his fellow workers and spotted a guy in his 70s who was only making about 10 percent more than Matt was earning. For Matt, that was his future. He was a smart guy who worked hard, but he wasn't making much money.

He got one of my books, was inspired, and chose to get involved in real estate. Matt did this despite receiving criticism for his choice from friends, family, and his girlfriend, who called him a dreamer and ended up breaking up with him. Like many entrepreneurs, Matt had to go against the grain and follow his gut, despite how overwhelmed he felt when he did so.

I met Matt, did some personal mentoring, and taught him exactly what I'm sharing with you in this 90-day sprint. I told Matt that he was looking for too much, too quickly, and that he was in danger of returning to his old routines because he was so overwhelmed. So let's look at 90 days, I suggested. Let's pretend it's 90 days from now, and it was the best 90 days of your life. Looking back, what do you observe?

Matt responded that he'd be doing five wholesale real estate deals a month and making $70,000 monthly. He added that he saw himself as being more confident and not feeling insecure.

More than that, he observed that he wouldn't have to worry about his bills because they were all paid on time and that he had helped his parents to retire. They were getting on in years and stressed about having to keep working.

Finally, he said, "I'd like to prove to my friends that I'm smart enough to do this, and I'd like to look in the mirror and know that I am in control of my own destiny."

I said, "Okay, dude, what do you have to do to make that happen?"

Matt's action steps were different than he had thought. He realized that much of his time was consumed by busywork, and one of his first listed actions was to hire a great personal assistant to take everything off his plate that didn't have to do with making money.

He also listed his need to get up an hour early to hit the gym in order to feel healthy and have the energy to get through the day.

He decided to stop having cocktails when he was stressed, as well as avoiding the negative people in his life. In the extra time that he possessed because of his intention to hire a personal assistant, he would create a unique marketing plan to target real estate customers using direct mail, Facebook, and Craigslist.

Matt focused his time on implementing these action steps in his 90-day sprint and ignored all the time drains that were essentially busywork. At the end of the 90 days, he reached every one of his goals: his parents retired, he did even more deals than had been in his ambitious projection, and he found an amazing personal assistant who's gone on to be someone who runs his company.

Matt has gone on to do over 3,000 real estate transactions, and he's one of the greatest real estate investors I know. And he was an inch away from doing none of these things because he received negative responses to his plans and because he was overwhelmed with the difficulty of changing his life. No one in his family had ever made money, gone to college, or even owned a house. But Matt pushed past these obstacles, in large part because the 90-day sprint gave him a short, doable process to get him on the path he wanted.

YOU HAVE MASSIVE POTENTIAL

Maybe you're thinking to yourself, "Dean doesn't know me. I'm not special like Matt. This may work for other people, but I'm not so sure it will work for someone like me." Well, here's the truth: You've got incredible potential. I write this without having ever met you, but I know from experience that every person is capable of making small shifts in his or her life that can lead to big success. The question is, will you realize your potential?

I absolutely believe you will, but first you have to get past one of the biggest delusions that most people have: Others are gifted and have advantages, making their road to success easier than your path. Yes, there are supertall people who have an advantage playing basketball. Yes, there are brilliant people who are natural mathematicians and can do complex calculations in minutes that most of us would puzzle over for hours.

The words "gifted" and "lucky" get thrown around a lot, yet when you do your research on those who excel, who go to the next level of life and reach their full potential, you see two very important things that most high achievers have in common. They believe in themselves and their vision, and they practice hard. They use grit to get the results they desire rather than standing on the sidelines wishing they were "gifted."

Tiger Woods is no longer the most dominant athlete in the world, but no one in the history of golf ever played at his level when he was in his prime. Was Tiger just another gifted athlete? Did he get lucky? Or maybe his success had a lot to do with the fact that he practiced his craft every day from the time he was five years old. When many NFL athletes vacationed in the summer until training camp, for many seasons Peyton Manning stayed home and watched tapes and practiced.

The same holds true for any person who created wealth and abundance. Did they succeed because they were special, gifted, or got lucky? Or was it because they were willing to roll up their sleeves and take the right actions? And do it over and over, even when they hit obstacles.

Why am I sharing this? Because the success habits I've described don't work unless you work them. The difference between those who take advantage of them and those who just think about taking advantage of them is that the former exhibit grit. To me, grit is stick-to-itiveness. It's persistence. It's being willing to go the extra mile to get what you want.

How badly do you want that next level of life? Do you get depressed knowing there's more that you can accomplish, yet haven't?

The good news is that you don't have to "settle." Not another day. You don't have to go through life asking, "What if?" You don't have to fret and fume about your unrealized potential.

You can have everything you want and deserve, but to achieve it, you can't give in to the naysayers. And it won't happen by just hoping it will. As the Nike saying goes, it's time to "Just Do It."

COUNTER THE CRITICS

Those who achieve the most are the ones who push through obstacles, even when no one else believes in them. They do what it takes to steadily put these success habits in place, and if something doesn't go exactly as they planned, they don't get discouraged or give up. If you look at businesses that have had massive breakthroughs, most of them at one point were on the brink of failure, if not bankruptcy, and most founders of these businesses were told their ideas would never work.

You see, critics are judgmental types of people that successful people make a habit of ignoring. Critics are often pessimists who gave up on their dreams; their bitterness causes them to tell others why they can't do, have, or be something. If you'd like a more abundant life, then you must believe in yourself, and not rely on others for encouragement or support. Sounds harsh, but it's your path to freedom. Once you break through, you can expect a new group of supportive people to appear in your life.

I'm not suggesting you should hate the naysayers you know, but you must go against your peers if they insist you can't do something. They may be friends, family, work colleagues, and others who tell you can't succeed for their own reasons, not based on who you are and what you're capable of achieving. You may have to stand up to some of your peers and say, "I appreciate your opinion, but don't tell me what I can't do." Maintain faith in yourself that you can do anything you set your mind to. Find the "why" of your life like we talked about in Chapter 1, and stare at that goal no matter who gets in your way and no matter who says it's foolish. You see, once you know where you want to go, you've got to do everything you can to get there, despite what others might tell you.

In fact, you may have to do the opposite of what most people around you are doing, and it will probably feel odd. But if you continue to do what the people around you do, you will continue to get what they get! And if they're not living the life that you desire and deserve, then you have to do the opposite. You're going to have to differentiate yourself from your peers, and I'm not saying you should do it with an elitist mind-set, or by letting your ego be in charge. Instead, your true purpose needs to be in charge.

BEST PRACTICES

Michael Jordan is the greatest basketball player to have ever played the game, and he said, "You can practice shooting eight hours a day, but if your technique is wrong, then all you become is very good at shooting the wrong way. Get the fundamentals down and the level of everything you do will rise."

I've talked a lot about the value of persistence and grit, about practicing and using new skills until they are a part of you. And as I've emphasized, some of the mega-successful people I know have achieved what they've achieved through sheer determination. They put the success habits to use over and over and over until they were part of their DNA. And yes, practice makes perfect. But as stated clearly by MJ, you have to be practicing the right types of things.

My son is only seven years old right now, and he's been playing baseball since he was three. And I must say, the practice that he's put in has made him one heck of a little ballplayer. This previous season he went 25 for 29, and barely missed a ball in the field.

Watching this evolution and the praise he gets, my daughter Breana decided that she wanted to play softball. So a year and a half ago she joined a team, not knowing anything about the game. She jumped in, practiced, and had a really solid first year. The second year, it moved to kids pitching (rather than coaches pitching). If you've never watched girls' softball, you might not realize how complex the pitching motion is. There's the wind-up, the push off, and the releasing of the ball off the hip. It's something I still can't do great, but am trying to learn for Bre! But three games into the second season my daughter realized, "We don't really have one really good pitcher on our team," and the games become very boring because of it. At their age, if a girl can't throw a strike, the teams hit the five-run rule, and it's off to the next inning. Sometimes it's like watching paint dry or grass grow.

Whether it was to stop the games from being boring, or to be more in the spotlight, my daughter said, "Dad, I want to pitch." Keep in mind she'd never pitched before. I said, "The only way this can happen is if you prove to me that you really want it, and you practice—you show your grit."

So we watched a bunch of YouTube videos, we got the right format, the right form, I set up a plate behind my house, and my daughter went to work pitching every single day with me!

Finally she reached the point where I told the other coach, "I think Bre could be ready for a couple of innings." And it just so happened to be during a game when our pitching was falling apart. So they put my daughter in and she struck out the first batter. She ended up doing amazingly well that game, and they won. She went on to do well for the next few games.

But what I noticed was that Bre had a couple of weird habits that I hadn't seen in any YouTube training videos, so I hired a coach. When he showed up, he came in and messed with her flow. He changed the way she held the ball, and he changed the way she was stepping.

Now you may think to yourself, "Why would you mess with somebody who's doing well?" And that's a great question! It's because the coach I had hired explained to me that her method will get her some strikes, but if she wanted to get better (and she did), that style will never let her evolve past being a great nine-year-old pitcher.

He explained that if she's 12 with that pitching style, then she'll get clobbered. So as frustrated as my daughter was to make that change, I encouraged her to do it. She was putting in the practice, so she may as well be doing it the right way. Do you know what happened in the next game that my daughter pitched? It was her worst outing ever.

She was pitching with the right form, but she couldn't throw a strike. She got done with that game and cried, and was really mad at me for messing with her pitching style.

And what I explained to her is what I'm explaining to you right now: You can practice the wrong way and still be okay, but you can only reach your full potential by practicing the right way. Yes, it wasn't easy for a nine-year-old to digest this truth (I hope it will be easier for you). If I had let her put the time, effort, and energy into practicing the wrong way, it would have taken even more time to unwind those wrong habits she was forming. Eventually Bre understood this notion of practicing right, and now she is practicing every day with the right form, and she's getting in the groove of a pitcher who could go on to compete at any level she wants.

Remember, too, that the habits that may have helped you achieve something at one point in your life may not help you today. The habits that took you out of Egypt are not the habits that'll take you to the promised land.

I hope that my coaching "messes" up your current game the way it messed up my daughter's. As you start putting your new success habits to work, you'll see the difference between old and new. At first, these new habits may feel uncomfortable, like an awkward golf swing. But the little bit of discomfort that you experience now can result in the rest of your life being filled with abundance, joy, and wealth. And once you're on your way, you'll bring others with you.

Malcolm Gladwell wrote the famous line, "You don't master anything without putting 10,000 hours in." This is true mastery! But turn this around and ask: What things have you done wrong for 10 years that you've mastered? Maybe you've mastered making yourself feel insecure, or feeling regret, or not taking advantage of the opportunities that are in front of you? You've mastered the art of playing it safe, of avoiding trying something new, of telling others what to do but not listening to their ideas.

Whatever limiting habits you've mastered, it's okay. We've all done it, but luckily it won't take you 10 years to make a shift to get rid of them. But it does require action and some grit to go for it. I love Tony Robbins's quote, "People will overestimate what they can do in a year, and underestimate what they can do in five." I'm not saying it will take five years for change, but imagine the change that can happen in your life when you model those who are achieving at the highest levels. Simply put, you need to start adopting the success habits when you wake up tomorrow! At that moment when you roll out of bed and start the day, start implementing habits so the trajectory of your life can shift, even if it's just an inch a day.

But inches add up, and as you get further down the road and further away from the things that don't serve you, you draw closer to your purpose and the goals that you desire. Again, this isn't a magic money machine. You can't hit a button and money falls out. But if you apply these success habits, make the shifts that stick, and then practice them with grit, you will receive the closest thing to a money machine that exists in the world.

Remember when you first shift a habit and the new way of acting seems weird, keep this thought in the back of your head: "I'm not doing this to impress my peers. I'm doing this because this is my path, this is my destiny." Be assured, each time you practice a proven success habit, it will feel less uncomfortable, and it will eventually become more and more familiar—and soon will turn into an unconscious habit.

THE BETTER LIFE CHALLENGE

I know you want more, and you are willing to put the time in to achieve it. The proof of that is right in front of you, and if you're persistent about reading a book until the end, it says a lot about you and your future. You're not the sort to give up.

I know I've given you a lot to think about and do, but sometimes all you need is that "one thing" you got out of a book that makes all the difference. On many occasions in my life, one shift was all I needed to course-correct. One slight shift in direction today makes all the difference tomorrow, and a year from now, and 10 years from now.

So right now, I want to challenge you to do something that will start that shift in motion and not let you fall back to your old habits and the status quo. I spent many days and nights researching and thinking through the best way to get you started on your new course and how to make it stick. One way is doing a 90-day sprint. It takes away this big, heavy chore of change and chunks it down to a doable goal. But I wanted something even easier to implement that you could do in minutes a day in addition to the 90-day sprint. It would be something that would anchor the shifts you need to make, and you would barely notice they were happening. The result is a process you simply can't miss, an added feature of this book that will make what you learned stick and jump-start you into action. Oh, and yes, I am ethically bribing you use it as well. Bribes to get you to take action are not beneath me.

To help catapult you into your new life, I have created the Better Life Challenge at www.thebetterlife.com. I designed a specific quick action for you to do each day for 30 days. In just minutes a day, you will start reprogramming your habits effortlessly. Your mental energy and confidence will grow by leaps and bounds daily. You'll feel empowered, fueled to achieve your 90-day sprint goals, and on course toward the life you once thought was unreachable. This challenge is specifically designed to ease you into it and not make you feel like you are making massive changes or sacrifices.

Here are some of the quick challenges you will have during the 30 days:

> **Day 5: Random Act of Kindness:** In today's challenge do a kind act for a stranger. Buy lunch for someone randomly, clean out a garage, carry groceries, help a homeless person, or take five minutes to listen to someone who looks like they need it.
>
> **Day 15: The Not-to-Do List:** By doing things we should not be doing, we are robbing ourselves of the time needed for those projects and efforts that can catapult us to the next level. What are you doing now that should be eliminated? Today we are going to create the top five things you should "not be doing."
>
> **Day 17: The True You:** If you didn't feel you would be judged, and had no money concerns and no time concerns, what would you do to create income? What is your dream job or business? What would you love to wake up to every morning and do?
>
> **Day 20: Courage Day:** Today it's time to be courageous and take action toward that "one thing" that you've been thinking about doing for years. No more hesitating.

And the best part about it is you will not only have the ability to transform your life in 30 days, you can challenge friends and family to do it with you and share the results on social media. All of which earn you points, and those points can win you incredible gifts. Basically, these are huge ethical bribes to get you to take action. If you're ready to stop thinking about a better life and start living it, then go to www.thebetterlife.com and join the challenge today.

NOW IS YOUR TIME

I know this may seem to be a crazy time to be alive, but in reality, now is the best time in history to put these success habits to work for you. Remember, uncertainty, wars, depressions, oppression, epidemics, and "crazy times" have been around for thousands of years. But we must remember that those who had the right success habits prospered in every era. Now is the greatest time, because it is the time you are alive and reading this. You can't postpone putting these habits into action for one more day, one more hour, one more minute. If you say now isn't a good time, then what you're really saying is there will never be a good time. A month can fly by. And so can a year or 10 years. Don't find yourself somewhere in the future trying to discover another book that could save you or take you to that next level. Don't wait 10 years to go to an inspirational live event and try to start fresh at that point. Don't let someone else take your idea in business. Don't let someone else take the job you want. Now is the time—your time.

My grandmother's best advice to me, the grandmother who saved me, was, "Don't stress about the things you can't change." I'd fail a test and she'd say, "Can you retake it?" I'd say, "No." She would then say, "Then forget about it. Take another one, get a better score, and your grades will average out okay."

Don't stress about the things you can't change from your past. Your past was simply research and development and the fuel for the great life ahead of you. Just let most of the past die and only bring along with you the things that serve your bigger future. It's crucial that you focus only on the things you can change and how you can create a better life for yourself now. You have the road map to implement strategies and habits that can take you to where you desire.

Can you implement all of them overnight? Absolutely not, but very quickly you will be astonished by the changes in your life as you make one small shift at a time. Start right now while you have momentum by taking the Better Life Challenge. Turn the wheel of life just an inch today, and another tomorrow, and watch as your life takes form as the life you always desired!

Your journey can begin today on that road to your next level of life with abundance, prosperity, and happiness. This isn't a quick fix, but these are the strategies that have allowed not only me, but also the most successful people in the world to move to the next level. And now you have them in your hand.

You now possess the habits for your success. Dig in. Take action. Be gritty over gifted, and show the world what you're made of.

PRODUCTIVITY AND THE ART OF ACHIEVEMENT

Before I start this new bonus section on productivity, I want to ask something of everyone reading this. And that is to play full out!

Now what does this mean exactly?

It means that when there is a lesson or two in this chapter, actually take the time to do them. If there is a place where I suggest you ask yourself some questions, give yourself 100 percent honest answers.

You see, the fact that you're this far along in the book tells me you are not just a dreamer but a doer. So let's do it. All of it. What we get out of experiences is in exact proportion to the time and effort we put in. So if you want to pivot in your life toward a bigger, better version of you, then play full out. You can start by following a few simple instructions in this book.

And as you're reading the words on these pages, try and anchor them with emotions, tying them back to the change and goals you desire most. Because one of the greatest things I've learned in my years of being an entrepreneur is that information without emotion is useless. If you want these words to truly sink in, apply feelings with the education. This will make the lessons stick.

Chapter 12

IT HAS TO BE A HECK YES OR A HELL NO

As valuable as the success habits in this book are, they won't change your income, make you a millionaire, or change the quality of your life unless you actually use them. You can't just think about them or plan to implement them at some time in the future. You have to put them to work for you and do it regularly and reflexively. Only through practice will the millionaire success habits you're being exposed to become your norm—and show you what your true potential really is.

Look, I know how hard it can be. With all the thoughts running through your mind, it's easy to say, "I'll start putting these habits into practice when time allows." Maybe you're having a busy weekend or the kids have you running around like a crazy person. Maybe that job of yours has you a bit stressed out, and on top of that, family and friends need your time as well. With examples like these, plus the things that are actually specific and personal in your life, you may wonder how on earth you're ever going to find the time to take your dreams seriously. I mean, there are only so many hours in the day, right? And you wish desperately that you could achieve everything you've always hoped for, but it just seems impossible to dedicate the time it takes to make it happen.

But here's the crazy part . . . and I want you to take a minute to really let it sink in.

Oprah Winfrey, Richard Branson, Bill Gates, and all of the world's most successful people—all, without a shadow of a doubt, have ONE THING in common with you. They all have the same 24 hours in a day that you do. The same 7 days in a week that you do. And the same 365 days in a year that you do. The only difference is that they've mastered a skill that allows them to achieve amazing things. Do you want to know what that secret skill is?

PRODUCTIVITY. By far one of the greatest success habits you can master is the art of productivity and getting stuff done.

I can almost hear what you're saying. "I don't have time for this right now." Believe me, I get it. I'm busy too. For a point of reference, let me share a bit of my schedule so you can understand how much I relate to what it's like to try and fit it all in.

THERE'S ALWAYS TIME TO BE SUCCESSFUL

During a 15-day period while finishing this book I did the following:

- I launched new Millionaire Success Habits live events in two cities per week. I had to align new partnerships, create trainings, and build the processes to achieve this.
- I created a brand-new, 90-minute online training for a new product.
- I created the agenda and a complete new presentation on marketing for my GeniusX mastermind group.
- My buddy Joe Polish, who co-founded GeniusX, and I had a two-day meeting with the group. Membership in GeniusX costs $100,000 per year, so we had to be spot-on and deliver massive value for the members. And we did.

- I had three team meetings and created a new system for higher-level productivity.

- On the home front, I coached five football practices, three baseball practices, and attended three football games.

- I also had date nights with each of my kids. I make sure I take them out individually in addition to family time so that we strengthen our bonds.

- I flew to Utah for a day of consulting and closed perhaps the biggest deal I've ever done.

- In Utah, I spoke on stage at an event focused on my friend Tony Robbins. I had to prepare that presentation as well.

- I flew to Long Beach, California, to speak at *Success* magazine's yearly event.

- I was a keynote speaker at the Electronic Retail Association's event.

- I worked out 13 times, ran Camelback Mountain 7 times, and recorded my best time.

- I finished at least two hours of live video training and shot over 30 videos for several different companies.

- I brainstormed with my buddy Trent Shelton regarding the layout and promotion of his first book.

- My infomercial with Larry King launched in five different states, and I laid out and then created the next-generation course for making real estate profits from home.

- I went on Facebook and Instagram Live about 15 times.

And that was in a period of just 15 days! I didn't share this to brag or to say how great I am. That is never my intention. I shared this list so you can see what it's possible to accomplish once you master productivity. Yes, you're busy, and I know how hard it can be to imagine doing more. The fact is you can achieve so much more if you train yourself in productivity habits. And if you truly want more out of your life, this is the best training you can do. It's like building muscle. If I go to the gym once, I'm not going to get in shape. That's why I go every day. If you want to master productivity like millionaires, billionaires, and some of the greatest minds on the planet, you have to practice being more productive every day.

Here is a little secret. It's not as hard as you may think. It's just that you have never been exposed to true productivity processes. At least until now. Listen, I love doing a lot of things. I love learning. I love growing as a human being. I love teaching others, and I actually love my business. And most of all, I love spending as much time as possible with my kids. If I'm not productive, these things can't all happen, so that's a powerful motivator. So the question you have to ask yourself before becoming more productive is not "What do I have to gain?" The real question is, "What do I have to lose?"

Why not right here, right now, make a commitment to mastering productivity so you can get the most out of life? Can you do that? I'm guessing that was a "hell yes" if you are this far along in the book. This book isn't about entertainment; it's about you reaching your next level. If you don't use it that way, then you may as well stop reading. Without action it is just another stack of papers on a shelf. So I want you to declare to the universe that you will do what it takes to exponentially grow your income, dramatically improve your health, strengthen your relationships, and live life on your terms!

IT *IS* ALL BLACK AND WHITE

So what's the secret to massive productivity and making that be your reality? It comes down to two words: binary thinking.

Binary thinking is like binary code (which is made up of ones and zeros). Binary thinking is the same way. Things are either black or they're white. It's a yes or a no. You're either climbing or you're sliding. The value of binary thinking is that you get rid of the gray area that lives in between. "I'll get to it next week" is a gray-area statement. Let's face it, will waiting until next week move you toward your goals or away? Eliminate middle-of-the-road thinking and speaking. Leave no room for second-guessing. If you're waiting until next week to start your business, face your fears, or even to implement new habits, then you are moving farther away from your goal. Every minute you wait, your bigger future slips a little farther out of reach.

For instance, a majority of the people I get to meet in person tell me that they're interested in developing an additional income—maybe a home business, a real estate venture, or an online business. When you apply binary thinking to this goal, you engage in activities that either produce measurable amounts of results to get these side incomes going or you don't. You ask yourself questions like, "Is this action taking me closer to that side income or taking me away from it?" The answer to that is always clear. There is no gray area and no middle ground.

I'm going to help make this easy for you to adopt because it's vital to your success. So let's start by practicing binary thinking in a small way. Pick one or two different activities you do on a regular basis that you feel are related to your success or financial growth.

Write them down if you'd like. Then think about them one at a time and ask yourself: Does this activity drain me or does it excite me? Remember, we're practicing binary thinking so there are no "in between" answers. The answer can't be "It kind of drains me a little, but I think I should still do it." You must pick a definitive answer. Does it drain you? Or does it excite you? If the answer is that it's draining you, then continuing to do that activity will diminish energy, enthusiasm, and excitement and not move you forward toward your goals. When you realize what it is costing you, then you can make a fast and clear decision to change a behavior or even stop doing it altogether. I hope this gives you a glimpse of how clear things can get when binary thinking becomes the norm.

PRODUCTIVITY HABIT #1:
YOU'RE EITHER CLIMBING OR SLIDING

To develop this habit of binary thinking, you need to be okay with asking yourself the tough questions. And then be okay with the even harder part—being brutally honest with yourself about your answers. Questions like the ones below could be good examples for you to start with:

- Is this person or relationship moving me forward or backward?
- Am I simply busy or does this activity make me massively productive?
- Does this activity make me money or is it actually preventing me from reaching my next level?

Why are these "tough" questions? Let's take a look at the first one. Think about directing it toward someone who is really close to you. That could be a scary and tough question to answer honestly. Let's say a close friend perceives himself as a realist and thinks you're a hopeless dreamer. He may tell you to stop reading all those self-help books or criticize any desires you have for your own thriving business. Maybe every time you are with him you leave discouraged and questioning your own value and capabilities.

So here is that tough question from before: "Is this person or relationship moving me forward or backward?" The answer is clear that this person is moving you backward and not toward your goals. At the end of the day, we are the sum total of the people we let influence us. You could say, "Well, he's been my friend a long time and that's how he is." And I get that! But you're reading this book because you want the habits for success and productivity that have shaped some of the most successful people on this planet. And letting that person influence you negatively is the complete opposite of what you need to climb faster in the direction of your next level. That's why these are tough questions. Because you must be honest if you want to break free.

Before you start getting nervous about ending a bunch of relationships, here's some good news. I'm not telling you to divorce a spouse or stop talking to siblings, parents, and friends. What I am telling you is that you can't give them your energy; you can't let them suck it out of you with their misguided cynicism. You can't let their words and their fears steer your ship. Remember, Joe Polish says that two types of people exist: battery drainers and battery chargers. Be careful of the battery drainers, since they're the ones who will suck the life right out of you. So if you do find yourself with a relationship that isn't serving your dreams and desires, you can take the binary thinking one step further. You can ask yourself, "Is this a relationship I should just end or should I create boundaries and roadblocks to keep their negativity from affecting me?" You can take it from there.

Now consider the second question: "Am I simply busy or does this activity make me massively productive?" This is a tough question because no one wants to admit they are "just busy." That would make you feel like everything you do is all for nothing. But again, we must be honest and have no gray areas. So let's say you're a "hustler," and you're always busy. It's easy to have the perception that you are heading toward your goals when you are always moving at full speed. But are you? Are you like a sports car roaring down the road with no GPS? You're going faster than everyone else, but not getting closer to your true goals and desires. Are you like a hamster on a wheel, spinning furiously but stuck in your cage?

When you know the art of productivity, you will stop racing to get things done that do not serve your bigger future. You will see why successful people seem to get done five times as much as the people who are "just busy."

Whether the above accurately describes you or just a small bit of it rings true, I want you to know I'm not about just pointing out the problem. Soon you're going to learn the process for how to become more productive than ever. First, though, I want you to look at the third question related to your busy life: "Does this activity make me money or is it actually preventing me from reaching my next level?"

Think about what you do daily. Perhaps you enjoy spending the afternoon sipping coffee at Starbucks. Great, but what do you do while you're drinking coffee? Are you just exchanging gossip with friends? Are you daydreaming or people watching? Or is this an opportunity to be creative, to craft your marketing campaign, or maybe even go deeper on that invention you have been thinking about for years?

You probably do a lot of stuff that makes you feel like you're active and engaged—and this can absolutely foster the illusion of productivity. But if the stuff you're doing is not making money or creating the foundation to make that happen—if that's one of your goals—then to be blunt, you're just fooling yourself. You must ask that tough question. Is this activity making me more money or is it not? You must increase your money-making activities and decrease the busywork that doesn't make you a dime.

I see people all the time who are excited that they've started their own business, yet months and even years can go by without them making any real profits. Why? One main thing is they are not asking themselves this tough question. They're focusing on the "hustle" and not the outcome. They spend hours posting on social media to "make their brand look good." They post funny quotes, they make cool videos, and they get more followers. But they never actually do the things that produce income. If they asked themselves that tough binary question, they would realize they need to spend more time on the moneymakers like marketing and sales.

So here's what I want you to do. Commit to asking yourself these tough binary questions. Commit to being honest with yourself about the answers and to becoming massively productive rather than busy. This is fundamental to obtaining the life you want, the income, the joy and the happiness.

Keep in mind the "big why" that I hope you discovered during the seven levels deep exercise. Compound those emotions and desires by always remembering "where you want to go." Whether you want more money, more freedom, more control of your time, or to help others in your life, plant that picture firmly in your mind. Then get to asking those tough binary questions; answer with a yes or no and watch your productivity start to soar. One quote that always inspires me to stay on track—as I said earlier—is this: "You're either climbing or you're sliding."

Let's go a little deeper and apply the principle of binary thinking not only to your actions, but also to your thoughts. Imagine asking yourself, "Am I free or am I enslaved?" Does that seem extreme? Maybe, but it allows you the ability to make a powerful point that will stick. For every thought you have, ask yourself if it makes you free or keeps you trapped. Yes, it takes discipline. I've shown you throughout this book that you have to be able to cultivate discipline to stay in control of your life. And it's not hard to do it if you stop listening to your own BS.

For instance, let's say I decide to stop making offers on houses I want to buy because I convince myself that not a single good deal remains because the media, friends, and other investors are telling me so. In this case, I would literally be not taking action on something solely based on other people's opinions that have converted my thoughts. Those thoughts enslave me because I'm not in control—not to mention that I'm not making the money I'd like to make. The truth is, as I write this book, there are more deals being bought and sold now than any other time in history. But we can so easily sell ourselves on these lies we hear from other people; and if we do, our thinking gets fragmented and then our discipline goes out the window.

Believe me, I know how hard it is to change our habits, to change the way we think. But every time the voice in my head tells me, "Do it later," I fight back by ignoring my thoughts completely and immediately taking action—no matter how painful or uncomfortable it may be. And every time I do so, I find myself reaching a whole next level of life.

So why not start implementing these habits the second you put down this book, no matter how inconvenient a time it may be? You know the areas of your life that need help the most.

Start there and ignore the thoughts begging you to wait until "later," and decide to take action today. Because in the end they're nothing more than that: thoughts. The discomfort will fade, but the habits will stick. And those habits will take you from where you are to where you want to go—faster than you can possibly imagine.

To add a little more urgency to this way of thinking, let me ask you how fast the last five years of your life went by. If you're like me you may be thinking, "Damn, that went fast," and heck yes, it did. So there is no better time than now to get started. Don't say to yourself, "I'll practice that habit of Dean's tomorrow, next week, or next month." No. As they say, there's no time like the present. As busy and as stressed as you may be, you have to start working on you *now*. In fact, the more complex your life is, the more you need these changes, and you need them fast. Face this challenge head-on; don't allow it to be the habit that "could have" changed your life.

PRODUCTIVITY HABIT #2: ARE YOU IN CONTROL?

When we discipline ourselves, we are controlled by no one. This is why cultivating discipline is so important. Let's say you're starting a consulting firm to help companies market through social media. If so, as we talked about earlier, the only thing you need to focus on when starting out is marketing and selling your new service. So do your best to schedule your day around those two things. Then stick to the schedule at all costs. Create strict deadlines for the things you know need to be done.

What you shouldn't do is stray into the area of negative talk and distraction. Let's say you ask seven friends about the types of businesses that "they think" could benefit the most from your social media marketing service. The truth is you'll probably receive seven different opinions. This isn't being disciplined at all! Instead, you're fragmenting your attention and activity causing procrastination and eventually hitting a standstill.

Have you ever been in a relationship and decided you wanted to end it because it was no longer fulfilling your soul or heart? But before you stopped seeing that person, you asked 10 people about their thoughts on the matter and half said end it and the other half said you have to commit no matter what? Then you ended up doing nothing but staying in a relationship that no longer fulfilled you. You lacked the discipline to take action because of confusion and the distraction placed on you by other people!

Let's go a little deeper into the concept of discipline—it's not that scary when broken down. Imagine going to the gym, sitting on a bench surrounded by exercise equipment, and saying to yourself, "I want to be in shape." But instead of hopping up and doing something, you simply stare at others wondering what's the best workout routine for you. Then you decide to check a few e-mails and scroll through your music thinking about what you should listen to. Then maybe you go grab a bottle of some sports drink and start reading the ingredients. And then all of a sudden you look up and it's time to leave. As you walk out you think, "I'll get to it next time!" Compare that to another person at the gym who showed up, put earbuds in, hit Play on the music, and got after it by doing a great exercise routine.

If you took a step back and seriously looked at that person, you would recognize that he or she has great discipline. And even more, when you realize how integral discipline is to sustained success, you will feel urged to adopt more of those principles.

Let's be honest: for most people, "discipline" is a scary word. Heck, that word always used to scare me. But I was looking at it wrong. We may think it will take all the fun out of life, but in fact, it's just the opposite. Discipline is simply creating a habit out of an action that will get us where we want to go.

David Kekich wrote in his Kekich Credos, "Living life the hard way is easy and living life the easy way is hard." Think about that one. It's hard to get up early, practice gratitude, drink something healthy, and go to the gym every day. But the result makes living life so much easier—health, energy, stamina, and fewer doctor visits. It's much easier to get up late, scarf down a donut, turn on the negative news rather than practice gratitude, drink a coffee for energy, and head off to work with no exercise. But later in life when your health is an issue or you hate the fact that you're overweight, you realize that creating and sustaining discipline may be the biggest make-or-break decision in your entire life!

Plus, in most cases, when you feel overwhelmed, it's because you didn't ask yourself the tough questions, which results in a lack of discipline. You're probably working on so many things that really don't matter and don't drive you toward the bigger, better, wealthier version of yourself. That can be frustrating, and as a result, you procrastinate and stay stuck. When you cut those things out of your day and out of your life, space opens and the feeling of being overwhelmed starts to fade.

Discipline becomes even easier when you reduce your tasks to their most basic elements. People write 300-page books on how to make money in real estate by using a strategy called wholesaling, but when you really boil it down, that only works if you are focused on three main things: 1) Using unique marketing to find hidden deals. 2) Making multiple offers until you find a deal cheaper than others can. 3) Handing that deal off to a cash buyer for a profit. People will cloud their minds, occupy all their spare time, and obsess on so many things in real estate that don't matter unless deals are being done. If you don't focus on the important parts above all else, it simply won't ever work.

My goal is to lead you down the path to be ready to actually schedule time for implementation and growth. Whether you need time to implement the success habits I'm sharing in this book, or to start marketing your new company or making offers on deals, you must have clarity on your goals, focus on the main things that matter, and then be disciplined enough to actually schedule the time to follow through.

Start right now. Take out your phone or whatever you use to schedule your days. Now let's schedule the time each week for your growth. Like Tuesdays from 2 P.M. to 4 P.M. is the time you spend crafting a marketing campaign on Facebook for a new company. Schedule it, set an alarm, and during those two hours focus 100 percent on only that topic and the solutions around it. You will get more done in those two hours than most people do in 10 if you're clear on the intentions, focused on the important things that can move the needle, and disciplined to make it happen when you say you will.

Here are a few more tips for imposing discipline on yourself. First, pay close attention to the people with whom you associate. Tony Robbins has said that you're the average of the five people you hang around most. If those five people energize you, challenge you, and inspire you, they'll hold you accountable for getting things done. And of course, the wrong people will help produce the complete opposite results.

Second, lay out your day. Don't just hope you'll have a good day. Create a schedule that imposes discipline on what you do and when you do it. The greatest minds and most successful people in history almost always plan tomorrow, today.

Third, focus your thoughts. What you think is who you become. If you tell yourself, "I'm never going to do this," then you won't. If you tell yourself, "This is going to be a little tough, but I'm going to make this happen," then you will. Google other people who have done what you're attempting to do and read their success stories. Take advantage of what you learn from these stories to refocus your thinking on solutions and success.

Fourth, take action and get results. I know I've said this before, but I've seen so many people who talk about all the great things they're going to do but never do it. So make it happen. B follows A, day follows night, results follow action (and keep reading—there's more about taking action later in this section).

Put all this together and you have a disciplined, conscious way to get what you want most. You surround yourself with the right people. You schedule your day to get things done. You focus, and you have the right thoughts. Even when the bad thoughts intrude, acknowledge them and say, "No, I'm not playing with that thought anymore. It doesn't serve me well." Switch to thinking about positive driven thoughts and remaining focused on success. That will lead you to action, which leads you to the results you're looking for.

PRODUCTIVITY HABIT #3: GET REAL ABOUT TIME

How much time do you need to spend putting these productivity habits into practice? You might see this as requiring a huge investment of time, or you might think that if you adopt my habits, you can put in a few hours a week and magic will happen.

The fact of the matter is that time and effort are bendable and results are less about minutes passing by and more about the level of commitment to that time allocated. Let's get real about time. When most people are working, they usually can do no more than two hours straight before their attention becomes fragmented and they start to mentally wander. There are exceptions when inspiration is at high levels—when you look at the clock and say to yourself, "I can't believe it's already eleven. Where did the morning go?" You're so focused that the hours are zipping by. But many of us spend our days dabbling without even paying attention to it. For example, you know you're dabbling rather than working at a high level when you look at the clock more than once and say to yourself, "I can't believe it's only eleven; is this day never going to end?"

So do your best to get in the habit of doing two-hour sprints rather than daylong slogs. Put all your energy and enthusiasm into those two hours. If you find yourself drained after working this intensely, take a break. Go for a walk, stretch, get some tea, et cetera. Recognize that putting in more than five hours of real productive work in a day is not sustainable.

Now, what do I mean by that? You're thinking, "Dean, I work way more than five hours a day." But I'm talking about productive work. Not busywork. Not personal stuff but rather head-down, powering-through-your-to-do-list work. And right now your goal should be very productive two-hour sprints. Then, you can build your stamina to an ideal of five hours of productive work daily. If you can do that, no one will touch you. You'll take your productivity to a whole new level.

Here's a secret weapon you can use to create even more momentum in your life. Just realize there are basically three types of days you can have. The first type is the one you dread, a day in which you feel insecure and afraid to take on any project: "Man, I hope this doesn't go wrong. What if my idea doesn't work? What if everyone hates it?" This "what-if" thinking sends your brain into panic mode and ties your stomach in knots. Nothing creative or groundbreaking comes from days like this.

The second type of day is uneventful, pretty much routine, and that's neither good nor bad. If someone asks you how the day went, you may respond, "It was okay." Who wants a life that's "okay"? Who wants a status quo life? Who wants to fall into a routine where nothing memorable happens?

When you experience the third type of day, though, it is magical. You're on fire. You're courageous. You're confident. You take control rather than let events control you. Your enthusiasm is contagious. If someone comes to you with bad news, you say, "Okay, we got this." That's because your mind-set is solution oriented. Instead of denying there's a problem or procrastinating, you tackle it head-on and then back to the task at hand.

Make a conscious decision to have more of the third type of days. And don't think for a second that you're incapable of having them. People aren't born energized and enthusiastic—I know I wasn't. You have the ability to create it using the tools and habits that have been shared throughout this entire book. So make this can-do, I-will-control-it mind-set yours. Recognize why you want to achieve great things and use that to power your way through all the things that get in your way.

Another secret weapon in your fight for productivity is creating systems. I have a system when I sit down to write a new book that breaks it down in tiny bite-size pieces so I don't get overwhelmed. I have a system that helps me find real estate deals that are not for sale to the public yet. I have a system for a morning routine, how I exercise, and heck, even how I eat healthy. Yes, they took me a little time to figure out and create, but once I did, overthinking and procrastination went away. I could just follow the system. In any successful business there are Standard Operating Procedures (SOPs). What these do for companies and can do for you is take away the guessing and allow the proven system to create faster results and more effective action consistently.

I also have a system to increase my productivity in all the work I do. Writing my to-do list at the start of the day is part of this system. I also write down my ideas about what I want to communicate or accomplish later in the day. Having these idea reminders makes the day feel much less overwhelming, and it ensures I address the things that are important for me to achieve. It's time to develop your own systems and use them as your blueprints for higher achievement.

The third secret weapon is proactive planning. This is a fancy way of saying "spend more time thinking out the plan than actually working on the plan." Many times, people slave over creating business plans, but they don't realize they are lacking the pre-planning vision and creativity. If, however, you start that plan by taking notes and letting your subconscious be your guide, you'll create a far better plan faster. Let all those thoughts that pop up when you're taking a shower or just before you go to sleep flow out. Jot them down on a piece of paper. You'll discover some amazing concepts this way.

For example, I had a tight deadline to create a new training program. I laid it out and completed all the slides in one day—an activity that could easily have taken a week or longer. How was it possible to get it done in a day? Because I planned ahead by thinking through it, then writing notes to myself about what I wanted to be in that training, and I drew from all those ideas. I visualized in advance what I was going to do in the first training, second training, and third training. I let my subconscious take control, which means I trusted my gut.

When we're kids, we're good at relying on our instincts. School, society, and other factors cause us to become less reliant on instinct. But here's the truth: Your gut knows what your head might not. Trust it. Let it form the plan through your thoughts and notes, so when it's time for execution, you've got the steps you want to take mapped out in rough form.

Knowing what you need to do, in what order, and then making notes about implementing it helps you figure out what not to do as well. It will highlight the areas where you shouldn't waste your time and energy. This is where your not-to-do list can originate.

I've given you multiple secret weapons to increase your productivity. But before I share more productivity habits, I'd like to explain what productivity really means, since people often get it wrong. The more accurately you define it, the better you can overcome the obstacles to working at a high level of effectiveness.

THE TRUEST FORM OF PRODUCTIVITY AND WHY YOU NEED TO MASTER IT

From a binary-thinking perspective, productivity is either something that moves you forward measurably toward your goals or something that kills your momentum. If you're like most people, you probably do a lot of different things simultaneously and call it multitasking. In most cases this is not being productive, because you can't do two things at once effectively—and therefore it doesn't move you forward. If you doubt that, answer this question: If you're meeting with someone and the other individual is talking, and you glance at your phone to check a text, do you really remember everything the person shared? Maybe a few sentences or a few key points here and there. But let's be honest, your brain can't focus on two things at once. That's a proven scientific fact.

The truth is that we spend a lot of time doing things that don't matter. If you don't believe me, start documenting what you do hour by hour for a week. Note whatever activities you're engaged in—from online activities to phone conversations to meetings to paperwork to lunches to picking up the laundry at the cleaners, et cetera. After you have completed your list for the week, use binary questioning and ask yourself, "Should I be doing this? Or is it a waste of my time?" "Are these things moving me forward toward my goals or keeping me stuck?"

Once you've completed this exercise, I promise that you'll look at your supposedly busy, crazy life and say, "Wow, what the heck am I wasting time on these things for?" Suddenly, you'll find that a block of time will open. This is time you can use to take action toward your bigger future!

Another thing that truly slows people down is the idea that "everything has to be perfect." We all think we're being perfectionists, but our obsession with dotting every "i" and crossing every "t" prevents us from focusing on what truly matters to move the needle forward. It causes us to overanalyze to the point of paralysis.

Let's say you're contemplating starting a real estate–investing business, but you're on the fence. You say to yourself, "Well, let me think about that. Is this the right time? Could it really work for me? Am I going to have to figure out every contract and every deal before I start? And then what if the regulations in my state don't allow me to invest in real estate this way? I'll just decide next week." It's official: you have overanalyzed, and you probably will never take action on the steps you'd need to take to make a real estate–investing business a reality.

Whether you have ever thought about real estate or not, I hope you see how clear this can be in any business or venture in your life. Let's take it a step further for the sake of a deeper example. In real estate investing, here are some of the tasks that new investors engage in: Surfing online, asking friends advice about it, browsing social media to see what other people in the field are doing, driving around looking at properties, visiting The Home Depot or Lowe's to purchase equipment and materials, getting logos and business cards made, and overstudying contracts.

However, the only main things a new investor should be focused on are: *creating unique marketing to attract the buyers and sellers, making offers, building a buyers list, and selling houses.*

Those last four tasks in italics are the only things that really matter if you want to get momentum and profits from today's real estate investing. Again I'm using real estate as an example because it has been a key moneymaker in my life and something I train other people in. But this applies to every single business in the world. There are lots of moving parts in any company, but only a handful create the kind of impact that leads to success. Concentrate your time and energy on what is crucial to making money. You can hire people to help you do the other tasks. If you're starting a software business or an online training company or anything else, boil down the top three or four things that most of your focus should be on and just do those things. As simple as this sounds it's what most people do not do.

For me, marketing is a crucial activity in every business I own. If I'm not a good communicator, especially on video, then it doesn't matter how great my products and trainings or methods might be, they won't sell. If I got in front of an audience and said in a monotone voice, "Hi, everyone, my book is really great. You should get it," not a single person would listen to me! If I acted like a robot, who would pay attention to what I had to say no matter how good my book was? I've focused on improving my video performance and on creating the best training courses possible. Consider this book you're holding. Would you have bought it if I hadn't gotten you motivated to take action through a video or my marketing? Maybe not, and I wouldn't have the chance to positively affect your life.

You may be thinking, "Well, Dean, you have a gift to motivate and sell." Let me simply say I was the shyest kid growing up, deathly scared to talk in front of anyone. The fact is I wasn't good at a lot of things. I suck at contracts, I hate filling out receipts, and I hate all the organization it takes sometimes to complete real estate deals. There are so many things I'm terrible at and quite frankly hate to do. I used to think I had to get good at all these things or else I was doomed. For instance, I was sure

I couldn't succeed at real estate because I didn't understand all the terms people were using. However, I did 500 real estate deals before I understood many of those terms! For quite a while, I felt inferior because I was so focused on getting good at something that I truly hated and really didn't matter. There are great car salespeople who don't understand the first thing about engines yet they are still crushing it! So why would I let something as minor as real estate terms slow me down?

I realized that to be productive, I just needed to get great at a few things. If I could do these things at the highest level, I could be successful. I became highly proficient at finding deals others couldn't. And I became adept at finding buyers who have cash and wanted to buy my properties. And those were the only two things that mattered. In fact, those were the only two things I had to know to make my first million. I stopped getting distracted by things I sucked at or that didn't have the most potential to make me more money.

In fact, you need only do a couple of things really well to become ubersuccessful. So what should you be doing? Pour your time and energy into high-priority tasks that are absolutely essential for success. If your business will live or die based on the team you assemble, dedicate yourself to assembling a dynamite team. If you need to generate x dollars in six months to make your business a "go," make marketing and selling activities the ONLY THING you focus on. Everything else can be done by others or ignored until you have time to address those issues.

Remember: Productivity is about doing. To get good at these activities, you need to schedule them. How? Here are three things I want you to do right now:

- Look at the tasks you need to accomplish in the next two weeks that will build the right momentum.
- List the logical order in which they need to be done and set hard deadlines.
- Chunk big things down.

The first two are self-explanatory, but what do I mean by "chunk big things down"? In other words, don't give yourself big, vague activities: "I'm going to go out and find cash buyers to buy houses I find." When things are too big and vague, they're not actionable. When you chunk big things down, you're breaking the actions into smaller, more doable components. For instance, instead say, "Post unique Facebook and Craigslist posts to find buyers." This is something you can plan, schedule, and take immediate action on.

Like we discussed earlier, you must dedicate hours during which you will do nothing but work on these tasks in their proper order. Using this real estate example still, you would decide you're going to put ads on Craigslist and Facebook and you're going to do it next Tuesday at 11 A.M. while taking a two-hour lunch. You're going to spend an hour on each one, and you're turning your phone off and eliminating any other distraction so you can get your most important things done in record time.

This is such a huge component of being massively productive. You chunk activities into bite-size tasks. As you do, you'll start getting phone calls. You'll get a buyer. And all of sudden, you'll be like, "Oh my gosh. This is real. This really can change my life! What's next?" Then you pick the next activity and follow the same process.

Remember: setting dates and deadlines are crucial because doing so creates a sense of urgency. When do entrepreneurs and successful people work best? Under pressure. It's not about waiting until the last minute. It's about providing yourself a tight but reasonable window in which to get important stuff done.

PRODUCTIVITY HABIT #4: IT'S GOOD TO BE SELFISH

Now that you have a sense of what true productivity is and is not, let me share a habit that took me a while to learn. And this is going to seem completely counterintuitive, so bear with me a second. We believe that we're being our best selves when we're doing things for others. And while doing things for others is truly amazing, it isn't the quickest way to the best version of ourselves. In fact it actually hurts the people you love and want to help the most. Let me explain. We're at our best when we're being selfish. But not with the way we act or the way we talk—with our time. When you are able to look at your time and become selfish with it, ultimately, it's what benefits those we care about most.

In order to accomplish this we have to think of selfishness from a different perspective. Rather than looking at it as a negative, we have to spin it to a positive. If you take your income to another level, if you're able to pay off debt, if you're able to write checks to solve life problems, if you can help a loved one retire, if you can save enough money to send your kids to college—how are any of these things selfish? Imagine if being a bit more selfish with your time could allow your income to increase and your problems decrease. What if it allowed you to spend more quality time with the people you love?

By selfishly reducing distractions, you can have it both ways—great success and a great balanced life.

Here is another anchor to help this thinking: If you choose to allow yourself to be distracted during work hours, you lose your ability to create a legacy for those you love. Rather, by being strategic and taking more of your time back now, you'll soon be able to give even more of you back to those you can impact most.

And to reduce distractions, you must decide who gets your attention during work hours and commit yourself to the people and tasks that can help get you to the next level. You must work on the ability to stay focused in a world full of distractions. You can't control the economy or your competitors or the stock market, but you can control how you spend your time. Remind yourself that distractions will cost you millions.

Consider how much time and money distractions cost you. If you spend 30 minutes daily messing around on social media, that translates to three and a half hours weekly—time that could be devoted to next-level objectives. Talking on the phone, texts, e-mails, and social media notifications all add up and eventually cost you more money than you could ever imagine.

Do you feel like you should be accessible at all times? Don't! Only desperate people are accessible every hour of every day! Don't be that person who when your device beeps or chimes or vibrates, you immediately look to see who liked your Facebook post or commented on your Instagram. If you're dedicated to becoming highly productive, become stealthy at it. People will soon notice that you don't text back immediately or respond to e-mails instantly. The smart ones will recognize that you're busy and committed to your next level.

You also must make sure you never live in a reactive mode but rather a proactive mode. This is especially good advice when it comes to computers and phones. Use your computer to get the information you need to learn, not because you're bored or want to be entertained. Promise yourself that you're not going to go surf or look at negative news headlines. Don't go check your bank account, then end up watching 100 YouTube videos on how to pop a huge pimple.

I truly believe that e-mail is one of the biggest distractions that you'll encounter on a daily basis. When people e-mail you, they are asking you to jump. And our usual response is, "How high?" But the truth is that you don't have to jump. You can reply when you want to. You can use an autoresponder that communicates: "I reply to e-mails every day at 2 P.M. and at 7 P.M. Other than that, I'll be working on my bigger future." This is something I have seen people do, and I think it is brilliant!

And it's not just digital media that distracts you. It can be anything! People will call you up to have coffee, lunch, or drinks multiple times throughout the week if not every day. And if you want to see them, great! Say, "You know what? Tuesday I'm working all day, but I could do Wednesday at five. Do you want to do that?" It is about picking out the time for nonwork activities strategically. Learn to say no more than you say yes and you will thrive!

And please, never try to rationalize your distractions. Never tell yourself that you don't think you're making much progress, so you might as well spend an hour on a social media seeing what your friends are doing. This type of thinking will lead you down a negative spiral right out of confidence and back into the life you are trying to get away from. You will never reach your full potential with this type of thinking.

PRODUCTIVITY HABIT #5:
IF ONE MAN CAN, YOU CAN

Don't fall for the lies. In many businesses, one of the biggest challenges is finding good deals. And people look at the great dealmakers and say, "Well, they're the lucky ones, and I'm not lucky like them." When they look at others who have made it, they attribute their success to where they live or who they know or sometimes just plain luck. Or they believe they've been successful because they're smarter. Or they're convinced that they've hit it big because their parents gave them money to get started.

The truth is that all of these are lies. You know how you become successful at dealmaking? By making deals! This means you do the work, testing and tweaking your approach until you get it right. Dedicate one hour per day to selling and by the end of 30 days, you'll be so good that the lies will no longer possess the power to derail you. It doesn't matter what you're trying to achieve. To get good at it, dedicate yourself to the task and don't get distracted. It's like anything else in your life. It's one step at a time. You just have to decide to do it.

Related to lies are the money barriers—the things that stand between you and making the income you want. They include:

- Lack of a plan
- Lack of a skill
- Lack of confidence

- Fear or worry about "what if"
- Lack of a target
- Lack of a system
- Perfectionism
- Procrastination
- Distractions
- Learning through your own trial and error

So how do you overcome money barriers? By using a super-simple binary checklist. It's a list of a few questions you need to ask yourself weekly. Here's the one I offer to real estate trainees:

- Did I make any offers?
- Did I cultivate more buyers?
- Did I tweak, expand, or focus on my marketing in both of the previous areas?

You can adapt this type of checklist to any business venture. It's a way to hold yourself accountable for being productive. Be aware that if you're new to a field, you may have doubts. For instance, new real estate trainees will tell me, "I haven't done a deal yet. I don't know why it's not working." And my first question to them is, "How many offers have you made?" Inevitably, the response is something along the lines of, "Oh, I haven't made any offers. I've been spending my time going over the contracts." Or "My friends tell me now isn't a good time to do real estate."

Start saying no to all the crap that doesn't help you get to where you want to go. When you eliminate the extraneous, you have more time to focus on mission-critical matters—the stuff that will lead you to your better future. I hope the message is getting clear to concentrate on your list of the mission-critical tasks and prioritize them.

Next, let's look at what you're worried about. Let me put this in context. As you know, we're driven by two things: pain and pleasure. As a result, we make decisions that help us move away from pain and toward pleasure. If we're in pain because we're poor and can't afford to send our kids to a good school, we naturally want to generate more income so we can afford to send them to the best school—that gives us pleasure.

But something stops us from making the transition from pain to pleasure, and that is worry. Worry can stop you in your tracks, and it can keep you stuck for a week, a month, a year, or even longer. It can prevent you from taking a good relationship to the next level or it can keep you trapped in a toxic relationship. It can stop you from leaving a bad job to start a business that you've always dreamed about. It can prevent you from telling your parents hard truths, and it can keep you locked into a self-destructive pattern of behavior like drinking, gambling, or doing drugs.

The good news is that we don't have to live with this worry. I can't tell you how many people have told me that they'd like to follow my suggestions and make more money, but then they add, "I just have so much stress and worry in my life right now. I have to wait for a better time."

No! Again, you don't have to live with this worry. When I'm teaching and I present my materials for how people can make money from real estate, I know exactly what questions are on people's minds: What if it doesn't work? What if I fail? What if I find a deal, but I don't know how to close it? What if my spouse thinks I'm an idiot for doing something like this? And in many cases these worries go back in time; they are rooted in our child psyches. They may not even be conscious, but when we try to do something ambitious, it triggers an old childhood fear and we get stuck.

Let's say you're contemplating making a big change in your professional life—you're thinking of starting a business or switching companies or even switching fields. Imagine what you might worry about as you consider making this change. If there's a financial risk, you might say to yourself, "If I do this, I may end up going broke, and I'll lose everything." If you are considering taking an exercise class, you may think, "I can't do this, I'm too old. I'll embarrass myself." Or if you're trying to decide about ending a toxic relationship, you worry that "It may be a bad relationship, but at least it's a relationship—and who knows when I'll ever find someone else."

Yes, those worries are oppressive in the moment, but you have to think beyond the common immediate fears and imagine if nothing changes and you have the same worries a year from now or five years from now. Nothing new has happened, you've refused to take any action, and you feel as stuck as you ever did. You're still not making the money you've always dreamed of, you're still 30 pounds overweight, and you're still bored to tears by your job.

If you're honest with yourself, you know how this feels—it feels like crap. Let yourself experience it now, because that's exactly how you'll feel if you keep allowing worry to control your life.

You're worth more than your worry. I'm sure you don't want to be enslaved by it, but that's what's happening. Perhaps this is because of some traumatic past experience that is affecting your behavior in the present. Whatever is causing you to get stuck in worry, it's not worth it. A bigger, better version of yourself exists on the other side of that worry.

There's a great book by Ryan Holiday called *The Obstacle Is the Way* that addresses this issue. Its premise is that your paradise, or what I refer to as your next level, is on the other side of your worry, but you can't see it because you're letting the worry get in the way. You may believe that you can find your way around your fear and anxiety, but you actually have to go straight through it.

Byron Katie, who is tremendously insightful about relationships, has a terrific approach to managing worry. She maintains you need to subject that worry to the following four questions:

1. Is that worry true? Perhaps you respond yes, perhaps no.

2. Is that worry absolutely true? When you put that worry under the microscope of "absolutely," you may find proof to the contrary.

3. How do you feel when you tell yourself this worry-story? The odds are that as you think about the story behind the worry—how you're always fretting that you're going to make a mistake or that others will speak negatively about you—you'll realize that the worry doesn't carry as much weight as you thought.

4. How would you feel without this worry? Imagine if you didn't have to live with your worry-story—what would your life be like?

This last question requires some explanation. If any of you are familiar with the Harry Potter movies or books, you may recall that Dumbledore had an instrument that could extract memories from people's heads for viewing. Think about extracting your worry-story and then banishing it from your mind. Or what if you could reverse it? Instead of saying, "I don't think this can work for me; I've tried in the past and failed," you said, "Yeah, I tried in the past and failed, so I now know what not to do, and this time I will crush it."

You don't need to worry that the time isn't right, that the economy has to change, that you need to wait until you receive a loan, that you can't move forward until you save x number of dollars. You control what you do, not your worry.

I get worked up about this subject because I allowed worry to waste years of my life. I worried that I wasn't smart enough to get to the next level. I have dyslexia, and I didn't go to college. Who am I to think I can write a book? I remember struggling in reading class, so it's quite a leap to consider writing a book. Who the hell do I think I am to even contemplate such a venture? I should be grateful to have what I have, right?

Wrong. I got rid of the story where I worried about whether I was smart enough. Once I did, the worry was gone, and I was free to write, to excel at public speaking, and to reach the next level.

PRODUCTIVITY HABIT #6: PAY YOUR SUCCESS TAX

Have you paid your success tax? Wow, I sure know I have! And I would bet you have too in many ways—you just haven't looked at it this way. Okay, I know you're probably thinking to yourself, "Dean, what the heck is success tax?"

Well, before I give you my definition, let me tell you a quick story.

As many of you know from reading this book, watching me on social media, and simply following me for years through Weekly Wisdoms and other things, you know that growing up, I wasn't the smartest kid in school. I wasn't born into a wealthy family. I barely graduated high school, and college was never even a question.

But luckily, at a young age I knew I was going to push, scratch, and claw my way to success. I knew that if I worked hard, never gave up, and always dreamed big, I would accomplish more than any teacher ever thought I would. It's why I sold bubble gum in middle school. It's why I sold firewood in my early high school years. And it's why when all my friends were going off to college, I was working with my dad at his collision shop in Marlboro, New York.

In fact, I was working so hard that my dad renamed the shop Paul & Dean Auto Body. Wow! I guess I officially made it right? I wasn't even out of high school yet and I already had my name plastered on a business right downtown! Some friends were off to college, some were joining the military, and others were doing construction, but I had my name on a successful business. In my mind I was crushing it.

But then it all changed. Shortly after I graduated high school my dad went through a divorce that really hit him hard. So hard in fact that he mentally "checked out" of the business and kind of checked out of life. I remember getting a call from him, and he said, "Dean, I'm sorry, but I'm getting rid of it all. I'm closing the shop. I'm letting the bank take our house. Do yourself a favor and go see if you can find a job up at the Triple

R Industries"—the only factory in our little town. And just like that, my world stopped.

Whereas a few months ago I'd felt like somewhat of a big shot for having my name up on a building, I now felt hopeless. The future didn't seem as bright as it had earlier. Friends were still working construction and thriving in college, and I had just lost what felt like everything.

I took as many supplies as I could from the body shop and moved them to an old broken-down barn that was on the property where I was living. I put in a woodstove for heat and installed the compressor along with my tools and went to work.

I remember thinking at the time that I was finished. I was a fraud. Who was I to think I could be a success? The business is done and now so am I! I may as well just give up.

Have you ever felt like giving up? Have you ever felt like the moment you are in or were in was the hardest thing you've ever faced and that you would never come out on the other side? Well, did you come out the other side? If not, I'm here today to tell you that you will.

Looking back now, I realize that the moment I moved into that shed may have been the lowest part of my entrepreneurial life, but it was the start of me paying the success tax I needed to pay to be where I am today.

So let me put success tax in a way that is easy to understand. And this is something I truly believe. What if all the crap, all the struggles, and all the BS we go through are actually designed to show us if we are worthy of success? What if, when you go through those trials, you're actually "paying your success tax"?

As silly as it may sound, what if there is a success auditor in the universe that is keeping tabs on all the crap people are facing and rewarding those who face it, learn from it, and come out on the other side? I truly believe that it is those people who grind when no one is watching, who hustle in spite of what others say, who persevere and push on through all the worst of days who are rewarded with the success they desire.

Then what if all your struggles were designed for you, there to show that you are worth the success you crave? What if it all happened exactly the way it was supposed to, and the "Success Auditor" was checking off all the boxes that said, "Hell yes, she deserves success"?

I paid my success tax that year. And in many years to follow. I worked hard, I dug deep, I hustled, and I came out as a better version of myself. This could have never happened without those roadblocks along the way. So why don't you take a step back and look at all the rough parts of your life. And look at them as they really are: nothing more than you paying your success tax.

I tell my kids all the time that they have to honor the struggle. I believe that is how the world rewards people with success. Right now my daughter is practicing like crazy to be the best pitcher in her softball league. While everyone else is out enjoying summer break, eating unhealthily, not working, my daughter is practicing three days a week to be the best pitcher she possibly can be. What is she doing? She is paying her success tax!

Here's another way to look at this. I want you to take a second and write down on a piece of paper or on your phone, "I Want Bigger Problems."

"What the heck, Dean! I definitely don't want bigger problems!" Well give me a minute and let me see if I can change your mind.

If I were to give you the choice of having one of the problems below be the biggest problem in your life, which would you choose?

A. I ordered chicken, but the waiter brought out steak.

B. My accountant messed up, and my real estate deal only profited $60,000 instead of $70,000.

Which one would you choose?

Norman Vincent Peale said the following about problems: "Problems constitute a sign of life. The more problems you have, the more alive you are."

If your biggest problem in life is that your server brought you the wrong meal or that someone cut you off in traffic, then you aren't pushing yourself to the point of becoming the best you possible! If my server brought me the wrong meal, I would simply say thank you and smile. I know this is a silly example, but it's a serious point. I want to encourage you to desire an upgrade in your problems.

The bigger your problems are, the more risks you are taking, the more you are thriving, and the bigger results you are getting for you and your family. If your true desire is to reach the best version of you, then you have to want bigger problems.

Now I'm not saying to go out and cause problems. I'm simply saying that when you start to upgrade your life, upgrade your risk-taking, and upgrade your business, health, wealth, et cetera, you have to expect—and actively desire—an upgrade in problems.

Spin it and throw a positive message behind it! "I am going to pay my success tax and take on any problem this world throws at me no matter how big!" You should write that down somewhere! Put in your journal or on your phone and look at it every day! Make it your new mantra!

And instead of feeling defeated when things aren't going your way, look to the sky and say, "Oh, I see what you're doing, Mr. Auditor! I am going to pay this success tax, and I am going to thrive!" Because when we choose to consciously stop self-suffering, we are able to experience life the way it was meant to be. And how long does Tony Robbins say it takes to make a decision or to make a change? An instant! So decide right this instant that you are going to stop viewing your downfalls as the lowest part of your life and start viewing them as the success tax you have to pay to enter the land of true potential.

When you start to look at the events in your life in this way, you will experience a level of freedom and release like never before. It can feel as though 100 pounds have been lifted off your shoulders and you can finally unleash your true self.

ACKNOWLEDGMENTS

I believe that we reach our full potential and the level of life we desire by taking in information and gaining knowledge through experience, failure, and success. We evolve exponentially when we take action in the world, and all that knowledge and information becomes deeply embedded wisdom and gut instinct. At the start of this book, I dedicated it to my dear friends, Tony Robbins, Joe Polish, and Dan Sullivan, because of the positive impact and shortcuts to success they have given me. But I also appreciate them for their journey, for their bravery of taking that knowledge, discovering the wisdom behind all of it, and then selflessly sharing it with the world.

I've learned from great teachers like them, as well as Dale Carnegie, Earl Nightingale, and Napoleon Hill. To that list I would add Eckhart Tolle, Wayne Dyer, Michael Singer, Brendon Burchard, David Bach—I could add many more names, but there isn't space enough to include all of them. Their transformative words, once absorbed into your very soul, make it difficult to determine where their ideas end and yours start. As I wrote this book, as I wrote certain sections, I asked the question, *Where did this come from? Did I discover this through my own trial and error, through my failures, through my own success, or did I adopt it from others who've trod that path before me?*

And at the end of the day, you realize that's what true deliverers of wisdom want. They're delivering you the road map to allow you to go faster once you integrate them in your own life. And I want that same for you. I did my absolute best throughout the book to share when I knew for sure where a given piece of wisdom or an exercise came from. I'm sure I missed acknowledging the source of some concepts, so here I'd like everyone who's been a part of mentoring me, from past business partners, authors, friends, and loved ones, to someone on the street who shared a good thought, to know that it's the cumulative efforts of all of you that allow us to achieve success faster instead of trying to figure it out more slowly on our own.

I also want to acknowledge the people who helped me put this book together. When running multiple companies, trying to be the best dad in the world, doing real estate deals, traveling the country speaking and doing masterminds while still coaching Little League and softball, time can be in short supply. Without my nephew, Tanner Sheldon, helping me put this book together and coordinating a lot of the pieces; without Bruce Wexler helping me create clarity in each chapter and ensuring that the material flowed together; without my team in Scottsdale, Arizona, and Jeremy Gabbert, who's my right-hand man, I could not have produced as good a book as I believe this to be. To Nick Savocchia, my CFO and friend, and to all the people who work with me on a daily basis to allow me to shine, to allow me to live in my unique ability, to allow me to practice the success habits that can make me rise to my full potential, I give thanks. I could never do it without them.

In one of my earlier books, I quoted the phrase, "It takes a village to raise a child." Well, it takes a village and a family to write a successful book and market it, promote it, and get it in the hands of the people who need it the most. Lastly, and most importantly, I acknowledge and appreciate the amazing family I have with my daughter, Breana, and my son, Brody. You are the light of my life. You are the reason I thrive, the reason I love, the reason I want to always evolve, to be a better man. No love could match what a father feels for his children. Thank you for the gift of being my kids.

ABOUT DEAN

If Dean Graziosi can make it, so can anyone. His story should give people hope as well as realistic expectations that they too can reach their full potential and live their own version of the American dream. Born in a little town in upstate New York, about 70 miles from New York City, Dean was raised in a family with financial hardships. At one point, he even lived in a bathroom with his father.

Struggling with minimal money, dealing with his parents' multiple marriages, and adjusting to over 20 moves by the time he was 19, Dean didn't have a chance to attend college nor did he feel he was smart enough to do so. But after years of ongoing inspirational messages from his grandmother Carmella Fanizzi Post, Dean adopted the belief that he could do anything, and that there were no limits. She implored him not to stress about the past, but rather invent his own future.

Dean took the one asset he did have, determination for a better life, and went on to become an extremely successful entrepreneur, real estate mogul, multiple *New York Times* best-selling author, success trainer, and world traveler, speaking on stages for up to 15,000 people. He is the author of the best-selling books *Totally Fulfilled, Be a Real Estate Millionaire, Thirty Days to Real Estate Cash, Your Town, Your Profits*, and *Profit from Real Estate Right Now*. Dean also has done a weekly wisdom video series on success every Monday for the last eight years inspiring millions of people around the world.

None of this would have happened without Dean's greatest gift: his past. From his dyslexia to his feelings of inferiority to growing up insecure because of financial struggles, Dean developed the unique ability to create easy-to-follow success recipes. It's been Dean's gift to share these techniques that can allow people to live life to their full potential.

Dean lives in Phoenix, Arizona, with his two children. He coaches Little League and softball and attends as many of his kids' events as humanly possible. He's also the creator of www.thebetterlife.com, a 30-day challenge that helps people make small shifts in their habits each day so that in 30 days, they can be on a path to wealth, abundance, and the life they deserve.

INDEX

NOTE: Page references in *italics* refer to figures.

C

D

E

F

WANT TO KEEP WORKING TOGETHER BY JOINING MY UNDERGROUND MILLIONAIRE MASTERMIND FOR JUST $7 A MONTH?

YEAH, $7 . . . CRAZY, RIGHT?

Here's why . . .

Hands down, being a part of masterminds and groups has been the biggest needle mover in my success and wealth.

I can directly correlate them in my own life to:

- Generating millions of dollars
- Becoming a multiple *New York Times* best-selling author
- Impacting millions of people around the world
- Becoming friends with my heroes
- And so much more . . .

I've also spent hundreds of thousands of dollars to be a part of them. Worth every dime.

And in case you're wondering, here's what a mastermind is:

It's the collective genius of like-minded people sharing their knowledge while simultaneously learning from the leader of the group.

Learning from your own trial and error is painful, costly, and simply outdated . . .

Masterminds are the answer and the new way to faster growth!!

I currently have masterminds ranging from $15,000 to $100,000 a year to be a member . . .

And the members come back year after year because of the value and results they receive.

But I wanted to create an entry-level mastermind group affordable for everyone while also delivering massive value.

And the result is Underground Millionaire Mastermind.

If you want more out of life . . . more income, wealth, freedom, abundance . . .

Then I want to make sure you know the value of being a part of a group where:

- Everybody is getting smarter
- Everybody has the same desires
- You don't feel like a dreamer
- And you're a part of something bigger than yourself . . .

So as a book buyer you can go to the link below and join UMM right now for just $7 a month.

Go watch the quick video sharing all the details and I can't wait to work with you month after month.

Just go to www.undergroundmillionaire.com to learn more!

NOTES

NOTES

NOTES

NOTES